The Ohio River Valley Series

Rita Kohn, Series Editor

FRONT LINE OF FREEDOM

African Americans and the Forging of the Underground Railroad in the Ohio Valley

Keith P. Griffler

THE UNIVERSITY PRESS OF KENTUCKY

Publication of this volume was made possible in part
by a grant from the National Endowment for the Humanities.

Scholarly publisher for the Commonwealth,
serving Bellarmine University, Berea College, Centre
College of Kentucky, Eastern Kentucky University,
The Filson Historical Society, Georgetown College,
Kentucky Historical Society, Kentucky State University,
Morehead State University, Murray State University,
Northern Kentucky University, Transylvania University,
University of Kentucky, University of Louisville,
and Western Kentucky University.
All rights reserved.

Editorial and Sales Offices: The University Press of Kentucky
663 South Limestone Street, Lexington, Kentucky 40508-4008
http://www.kentuckypress.com

08   07   06   05   04   5   4   3   2   1

Library of Congress Cataloging-in-Publication Data

Griffler, Keith P.
    Front line of freedom : African Americans and the forging of the
Underground Railroad in the Ohio Valley / Keith P. Griffler.
        p.   cm. — (Ohio River Valley series)
Includes bibliographical references (p.   ) and index.
    ISBN 0-8131-2298-8 (hardcover : alk. paper)
        1. Underground railroad—Ohio River Valley. 2. Fugitive slaves—Ohio
River Valley—History—19th century. 3. African Americans—Ohio River
Valley—History—19th century. 4. Antislavery movements—Ohio River
Valley—History—19th century. 5. Ohio River Valley—History—19th
century. I. Title. II. Series.
    E450.G82 2004
    973.7'115—dc22   2003024588

This book is printed on acid-free recycled paper meeting
the requirements of the American National Standard
for Permanence in Paper for Printed Library Materials.

Manufactured in the United States of America.

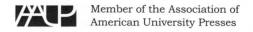

Member of the Association of
American University Presses

For Janina

Contents

Illustrations

Series Foreword

The Ohio River Valley Series, conceived and published by the University Press of Kentucky, is an ongoing series of books that examine and illuminate the Ohio River and its tributaries, the lands drained by these streams, and the peoples who made this fertile and desirable area their place of residence, of refuge, of commencement and industry, of cultural development, and, ultimately, of engagement with American democracy. In doing this, the series builds upon an earlier project, *Always a River: The Ohio River and the American Experience* (Robert L. Reid, ed.), which was sponsored by the National Endowment for the Humanities and the humanities councils of Illinois, Indiana, Kentucky, Ohio, Pennsylvania, and West Virginia, with a mix of private and public organizations.

Each book's story is told through men and women acting within their particular time and place. Each directs attention to the place of the Ohio River in the context of the larger American story and reveals the rich resources for the history of the Ohio River and of the nation afforded by records, papers, artifacts, works of art, and oral stories preserved by families and institutions. Each traces the impact the river and the land have had on individuals and cultures and, conversely, the changes these individuals and cultures have wrought on the valley with the passage of years.

Front Line of Freedom redeems a shamefully neglected part of our collective memory: that whites were the *conductors* and blacks were only the *passengers* on the Underground Railroad. The new and extant oral histories collected by Dr. Keith Griffler show that the relationship between races was actually far richer and far more textured than previously written accounts suggest.

By examining the events of eighteenth- and nineteenth-century America from the African American perspective as well as considering white sources and voices the expanse of the Underground Railroad widens. Griffler's episodic presentation spans six chapters, building portraits of individuals involved with the Underground Railroad and bringing forth many untold, uncelebrated stories of the time.

The interwoven narratives afford a deserved dignity to the African American population, a population that suffered the social indignities of invisibility and endured not only the burdens of enslavement but the stigma of the collective opinion that their station was determined by virtue of *scientific findings.* In truth, African Americans defined and acted in their own release from enslavement, in their subsequent education, and in the resettlement of freed persons.

In *Front Line of Freedom,* Griffler presents a significant body of work that attempts to correct errors in past judgments and scholarship. The book is a heartrending reminder of what happens to a nation torn asunder by racial inequality and is an equally heartwarming affirmation of what the present and the future hold for all races when we individually and collectively embrace our history.

Rita Kohn
Series Editor

Preface

The recent upsurge of interest in the Underground Railroad has spurred concerted efforts, including congressional legislation and the creation of the National Underground Railroad Freedom Center in Cincinnati, to officially commemorate this important American heritage. Among the readily apparent reasons for the rediscovery of the Underground Railroad's history is its inspiring story of interracial cooperation in the struggle against the institution of slavery. The greater attention to this freedom movement inevitably will change the way we understand both the Underground Railroad and the larger battle against American slavery.

This account of the Underground Railroad in the Ohio River Valley seeks to supplement a growing body of literature that examines the historical agency of oppressed peoples in their own liberation, thus addressing a question increasingly emphasized by scholars of African American history.[1] *Front Line of Freedom* demonstrates that African Americans were central to the development and operation of the Underground Railroad, a thesis that has been considered but not yet made the focus of a book-length study. In addition, rather than treating the struggles along the Ohio River as historical footnotes to emancipation, it argues that they played an important role in the combination of many complex factors that ended American slavery.

At the same time, the pivotal role of African Americans is examined without losing sight of the Underground Railroad as America's first successful interracial liberation movement. Evidence of the vibrancy of African American initiative in spiriting away fugitives has sometimes led to the conclusion of the existence of two separate, parallel institutions—one white, one black. Thus, Benjamin Quarles, in *Black Abolitionists*, has written of the existence of a "Black Underground," which, as Larry Gara aptly describes it, "supplemented and sometimes worked independently from the traditional underground railroad of white abolitionists." James Horton's *Free People of Color*, in adducing important empirical evidence of African American involvement, leans toward a more balanced approach, reinforced by the brief discussion in his and Lois Horton's *In Hope of Liberty*. There has remained the need for a detailed examination of the cooperation of African American and white activists on every aspect of the enterprise, accompanied by an analysis of the contours of that collaboration. Rather than arguing that there were two separate, albeit parallel, underground railroads or that the movement was an essentially African American institution, the present work throws into focus the often qualitatively different roles played by African American and white operatives.[2]

It does so by employing an explanatory framework that, for the first time, differentiates the Underground Railroad into its parts, distinguishing the more intensive *frontline struggles* from the *support operations* in the rear (areas farther north). Following the lead of mainly white participants themselves, Wilbur Siebert began the tendency of focusing on stations and routes in his book *The Underground Railroad*. Rather than thoroughly investigating the context in which the Underground Railroad existed, he chronicled personalities, often essentially providing a list of achievements in summary form. He linked participants and centers primarily geographically, as though the key to understanding the "mystery of the underground railroad" lay in charting the paths along which fugitives were led. That tradition largely has been preserved in the public history of the Underground Railroad as well, which abounds in the railroad imagery of "lines," "stations," "stationmasters," and "conductors." Thus, for example, the National Underground Railroad Act of 1990 emphasized the preservation and interpretation of the "approximate routes by slaves escaping to freedom before the conclusion of the Civil War."[3]

The analytical flaws of this traditional approach have yet to be systematically overcome even within the scholarly literature on the subject; the focus remains on an undifferentiated mass of "conductors," the routes they staffed, and the numbers of fugitives they

purportedly aided. Shunted into the background are far more essential issues: the importance of particular theatres of operation
and categories of work to the larger enterprise; the dangers individual operatives encountered; and the means by which the clandestine system of aiding fugitives was constructed. Transcending
the superficialities of the railroad metaphor requires analyzing the
structure of the underground movement. The vantage point of the
front lines, where African Americans composed a larger proportion—
and often the majority—of the participants, and where they rou-
tinely engaged in the most hazardous, intensive, and effective work,
produces a significantly different understanding of antislavery resistance in the antebellum Northwest.

So, too, does the interpretation of the Underground Railroad
change if the subject is approached chronologically. Gara calls attention to the imprecision of the "time setting" of the "popular legend" that "place[s] the underground railroad in a pre-Civil War setting
without regard for the actual years involved." Most studies, including Gara's pioneering work, pay even less attention to the movement's
historical development, and instead usually approach it themati-
cally and devote some attention to the origin of its name. Again, the
present volume constitutes the first chronologically organized, comprehensive study of the Underground Railroad over a large geographi-
cal area, thus revealing the institution's development and allowing
an examination of change over time. Such an investigation shows
that interracial cooperation developed slowly, with white abolitionists generally joining the activities that African Americans had pio-
neered early in the history of the Northwest.

Front Line of Freedom is the first book-length study to link the
Underground Railroad with the struggles to establish African American communities. This focus distinguishes the present work from
the pioneering work of Larry Gara, who successfully debunks the
mythological version. The approach of examining the development
of the institution against the backdrop of the formation and consoli-
dation of an African American presence in the Ohio Valley, particularly in the case of frontline communities, imparts new significance
to events that have been previously studied—restoring them to the
context of the advancement of the struggle against slavery. For example, the present account corrects existing historiography in dem-
onstrating that African Americans emerged victorious from the

Cincinnati Riot of 1829, a landmark triumph in the emergence of an effective underground.[4]

Finally, the study focuses on the Ohio Valley to allow a close reading of the extensive source material, which a consideration of the entire North would render impossible; yet, the coverage is sufficiently broad to show something more than peculiar local conditions of a given community. It makes careful use of the reminiscences of participants, indispensable to gaining needed insight into the enterprise's modus operandi, given its clandestine nature. At the same time, it balances those with contemporary, corroborative sources. In so doing, there has been an emphasis on the inclusion of African American voices and viewpoints. The volume therefore corrects numerous mistakes and omissions of the only existing comprehensive work on the subject, Siebert's *Underground Railroad*. For example, the most important African American operatives whose activities are chronicled here were omitted by Siebert's oral informants, and consequently do not appear in his list of conductors—despite their prominent presence in the historical record. At the same time, because Siebert did not consistently cross-check his sources, his account suffers from numerous inaccuracies, as when he misplaces so important a "conductor" as Elijah Anderson—locating his work in Cleveland rather than Madison, Indiana.

This book owes its genesis to two persons. Kevin Burke, a documentary filmmaker and professor at the University of Cincinnati, first approached me about a project he had been at work on for a considerable time on the Underground Railroad. Kevin had immersed himself in the history of the Underground Railroad, and the instincts that would make him a great historian convinced him that it was, at root, an African American story. He therefore wanted to bring onto the project a historian of the African American experience. From the first meeting, we found that we worked extremely well together and the unique collaboration proved fruitful. Kevin generously made me a coproducer on the project, although I had no previous experience with the medium. This book was originally conceived as a joint work. The practical considerations of carrying out the immense task of making a feature-length documentary ultimately compelled a change in that initial plan, but the finished product bears the indelible imprint of our collaboration over the last three years. It would be impossible to convey the extent of the debt I owe to Kevin as a collaborator, colleague, and friend.

Rita Kohn, who was a speaker at a conference on the Underground Railroad in Cincinnati where Kevin and I screened and discussed a short preliminary version of the documentary, first suggested the idea of a book for her series on the Ohio River Valley with the University Press of Kentucky. Throughout the process of conceiving and drafting this monograph, she has provided crucial support, advice, and a role model of a documentary maker and author. Working with her and John "zig" Ziegler, senior editor at the press, has been a wonderful experience, and I offer sincere thanks to both.

I have been fortunate to have been a faculty member in the Department of African American Studies at the University of Cincinnati while writing this book. Our two department heads over that time, Patricia Hill Collins and John Brackett, as well as the Dean of Arts and Sciences, Karen Gould, supported my efforts to combine the traditional role of a researcher with the more innovative one of documentary producer. I am particularly grateful to Pat Hill Collins for arranging time off from teaching duties to work on the book. I owe much to all of my colleagues in the department, Angelene Jamison-Hall, Joseph Takougang, and Patrice Dickerson, for providing the kind of collaborative working environment, in which ideas are freely exchanged, that makes the occupation of an academic both richly rewarding and congenial.

This book also reflects in profound ways hours of conversations and written exchanges with Stephanie Shaw over the years on African American and American history. In this, as in so many other things, I am greatly indebted to her. It similarly bears the mark of my other mentors in African American History, Marshall Stevenson, and at an earlier juncture, Nell Painter and Robin Kelley. I am inexpressibly grateful to all. William Luechtenburg and Warren Van Tine both imparted the kinds of lessons about the historian's craft that never leave you—and I am glad of the opportunity to acknowledge my debt to them in writing.

Like that of all historians, my research is built on the edifice of the expertise, generosity, and kindness of countless librarians. I would like to thank the staffs at the Ohio Historical Society, the Indiana Historical Society, the State Library of Indiana, the Rare Book Department at the Cincinnati Public Library, the Cincinnati

Historical Society, the Interlibrary Loan Department at the University of Cincinnati Library, the Jefferson County Historical Society in Indiana, and the Lawrence County Public Library. I would also like to thank Ben Jones for his hard and timely work in constructing the map of the Ohio Valley for this book.

There are also a number of individuals who deserve mention not for their contribution to my work, but for their dedication to keeping the history of African Americans' contributions to the Underground Railroad alive. Kevin Burke first introduced me to this remarkable network of women and men, many of whom, such as Henry Burke and Eugene Settles, were the descendants of fugitives and conductors. To all of them, I express my gratitude and, more essentially, my admiration. They have helped convince me that history is best told when not the exclusive province of the professional few but the embodiment of the lived experience of all of us.

My last and most personal debts are to my family. My parents, May Ellen and Carl Griffler, lent not only a lifetime of encouragement and support but also their editorial skills. Janina Brutt-Griffler endured far more to see this project completed than any spouse should ever have to. Most crucially, she shared with me the process of its composition, listening patiently to page after page, providing her characteristic rigorous criticism and invaluable suggestions. With heartfelt gratitude, I dedicate this book to her.

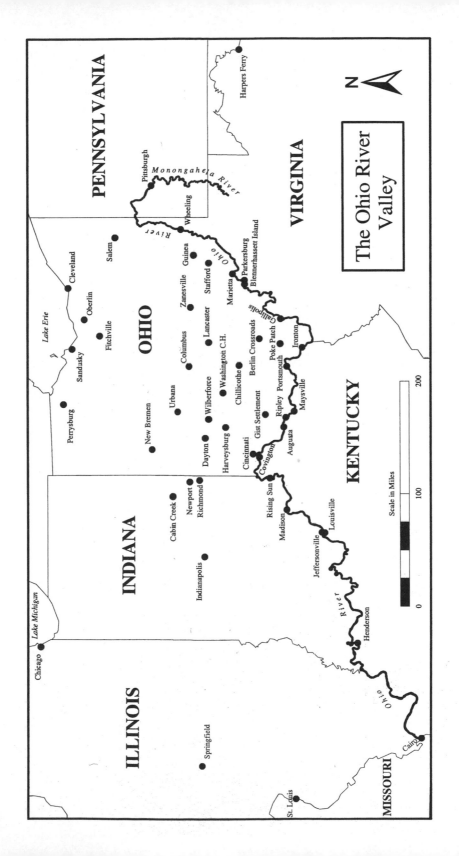

The Ohio River Valley

1

River of Slavery
River of Freedom

Wade in the water,
Wade in the water, children,
Wade in the water,
God's gonna trouble the water.
                    African American spiritual

The waters of the Ohio River reflected an accurate though troubling image of the young American nation for nearly a century after its founding. The last barrier across which thousands of fugitives from enslavement made good their escape, the river embodied the ideal proclaimed by the Revolutionary generation on the world stage: the young Republic as a beacon of liberty. Yet the Ohio also served as a means of transport for the internal trade in enslaved children, women, and men—tens of thousands of African Americans were shipped downriver to the Cotton Belt markets for human chattel. At once a river of freedom and of slavery, the Ohio embodied the stark contradictions of the existence of slavery in a free Republic.

The river both divided and connected a nation. With slavery legally confined to its southern bank, African Americans were on one side free and on the other in a condition of legal enslavement. The Ohio River was, however, at the same time more than the boundary between enslavement and free soil: it was the link between them, the tangible expression of their economic interdependence. The river constituted the longest commercial border along the Mason-Dixon Line in the antebellum period, a thriving trade route by which the farmers of the North provisioned the plantations of the South. The close interconnection of the commercial interests of Ohio's booming river ports and the South's "peculiar institution" created a region economically dependent on enslavement and the slave trade.[1]

The paradox that played out along the Ohio River presented a complex set of issues through which the United States would wade during the first century of its existence. A nation claiming to carry the torch of liberty in the world retained slavery in the decades following its abolition in the dominions of the motherland that seemed so tyrannical to a generation of revolutionaries. Founded in freedom, the United States had become the world's largest slave republic. A steady flow of escapees from slavery across the banks of the Ohio served as a constant reminder to North and South of the main issue—at once moral, political, and economic—that divided them and proved a harbinger of a full-blown civil war.

True to the words of the African American spiritual, the Ohio River was troubled water in the antebellum period. It was the site of a protracted, often violent, struggle between the forces of freedom and those of slavery that would continue to plague the nation until its system of bondage was permanently abolished. Whether the Ohio River carried African Americans on the Underground Railroad to the North's free soil or took them via the trade in human flesh to the living hell of the South's plantation slavery, it was always against stiff resistance. The strip of land along the northern bank of the Ohio River stretching from Pittsburgh, Pennsylvania, hundreds of miles west became the front line of African Americans' struggle to become free, remain free, and help others attain their freedom. For decades leading up to the Civil War a conflict raged over this terrain—one that came to be best known by the unlikely name of the Underground Railroad.

Wilbur Siebert, who did more than any other person to shape the nation's historical memory of the Underground Railroad, confessed what had originally set him on the subject. A professor of history at the Ohio State University in the early 1890s, he looked at the bored faces of his students in his American history survey sections and decided, as many instructors of history do, to enliven his class with some interesting anecdotes. He hit upon the idea of "a mysterious and romantic subject . . . rich in adventure"—the Underground Railroad. Discovering that it was a topic about which his students knew, or professed to know, much, he set about tracing the stories they related to him. As so often happens, he found exactly what he was looking for. He uncovered what he later gave the fitting title *The*

Mysteries of Ohio's Underground Railroads—a book-length explication of the romance he had used to coax his students to pay attention in class.[2]

It was clear to Siebert who had played the roles of the heroes of this romance: the parents and grandparents of his white students, members of the "antislavery denominations, Quakers, Scotch Covenanters and Wesleyan Methodists." In the words of the historian who penned the introduction to Siebert's first and purportedly authoritative opus on the subject, "In aiding fugitive slaves the abolitionist was making the most effective protest against the continuance of slavery; but he was also doing something more tangible; he was helping the oppressed, he was eluding the oppressor; and at the same time he was enjoying the most romantic and exciting amusement open to men who had high moral standards. He was taking risks, defying the laws, and making himself liable to punishment, and yet could glow with the healthful pleasure of duty done." Like many other war stories, this one had been converted into a romance.[3]

To be sure, it is unlikely that the African American participants, especially the fugitives from enslavement, would have regarded the story in a similar manner. A story focusing not on the heroic smuggler but on the illicit cargo would necessarily tell a far different tale. Runaways knew all too well what fate awaited them if their bold strike for freedom should fail. Told from their perspective, the inevitable unsuccessful attempts, while still providing the stuff of adventure stories, could not be passed over nearly so lightly.[4]

But then, to Siebert's mind, the African American fugitives who were whisked away to freedom with all the efficiency of the Protestant work ethic were no more than minor characters, providing merely the pretext for the heroic and wonderfully intricate operation on their behalf. Siebert even evinced a willingness to make light of the terror they commonly experienced in their flight. His preface to *Mysteries* dismisses their role with what purports to be a humorous anecdote—one in the racist tradition of Vaudeville (the Hollywood of its day) with its stock African American characters. Siebert relates a story of fugitive Asbury Parker, who on reaching the southern terminus of the Underground Railroad is provided with a new suit of clothing. The conductor taking him on to the next station tells him they can make the journey by day if the runaway plays the dignified part of a free person. En route, however, Parker happens to fall over a downed telegraph poll. Siebert quotes him as remarking, "Now what have I done! Dat wire will tell de white folks da's a nigger loose in the woods."[5]

For Siebert, the incident speaks for itself and requires no further commentary. In addition to signaling that, like any good adventure story, this one has its lighter side, he leaves his (white) reader of the Jim Crow era with the rather clear implication that this fugitive, at least, could not have made the journey on his own without the help of the organization known as the Underground Railroad. It is, in a sense, eminently fitting that Siebert, who first came to the subject in an attempt to entertain a white audience, reveals his underlying assumptions when he entices readers by highlighting his work's potential to amuse and divert.

The Underground Railroad, however, was no mere romance or adventure story. It was an epic, at once tragic and noble—tragic because a nation priding itself on liberty needed it at all; noble in that it represented the best in the human spirit of opposition to oppression. To those most directly concerned, those who are sometimes portrayed as playing a subordinate role in a drama ultimately revolving around their strike for freedom, the story of the Underground Railroad was a war experienced in the trenches.

The origins of the name "Underground Railroad" remain obscure. Starting a discussion of the subject by declaring that it was neither a railroad nor underground has even become something of a cliche, yet the traditional, almost legendary, name is perhaps more apt than any other potential substitute. The phrase captures the essential element of the Underground Railroad's modus operandi—one that has gained recognition over the century and a half subsequent to the close of its operations.[6]

Posterity has nevertheless had the unfortunate tendency to focus, as it were, on the wrong part of the name. The mythology of the Underground Railroad has laid emphasis on the second part of its sobriquet. The imagery with which it is associated is all derived from the terminology of the railroad—*stations* and *station keepers*, *conductors*, *lines*, and *passengers*. It has even been endowed with some of the clocklike efficiency with which railroads are supposed to operate. So much is that true that this myth, and the early historians who worked under its influence, virtually outfitted the historical personages they describe in the regulation uniforms for which railroads are known. The railroad metaphor has taken hold to such an extent that a great deal of attention is spent today reconstructing routes, documenting stations, and charting maps. It seems to be all but forgotten that even the notion of such an artifact as a map would have been alien to the participants in the clandestine movement—an important fact to bear in mind in the study of their history. Underground Railroad stalwart J.H. Tibbetts of Madison, Indiana, recalled, "[I]t was not safe at that time to put such thing[s] on paper for we did not know how soon our enemies would mob us and burn our houses, of course any such paper would be a good witness and caus[e] us to be perhaps put to death or whiped & driven from our" state.[7]

Aside from the persistent, popular myths of tunnels, the second part of the name is all but ignored. And yet it is solely this part that remains true to the nature of the institution described, perhaps the closest to an underground resistance movement that ever took root in American soil. While the metaphor of a railroad is singularly inapt to describe the methods of work, the mission, and the results of the Underground Railroad, the images of an underground movement do much to capture its drama, danger, and essential context.[8]

At first sight, such a characterization seems odd, even quixotic. We associate such "undergrounds" with resistance movements in occupied nations—those of World War II France and Poland, for instance. Those liberatory movements united large segments of the population in a life-and-death struggle for the right to walk freely and openly in the light of day, to enjoy the rights cherished by citizens of nations founded on liberty. Since its inception, the United States has never endured such a foreign occupation. And yet, for decades it nurtured in its heartland just such an underground—freedom fighters engaged in the desperate struggle to end the yoke of tyrannical oppression in the land of their birth.[9]

"The eyes of the world are upon you," the Executive Committee of the New York Anti-Slavery Society wrote to their counterparts of the Ohio Anti-Slavery Society in Cincinnati in 1836: "The fate of this nation—the destiny of posterity—the freedom of unborn millions—the fair flame of America—the hopes of a suffering world—are committed to your trust. The soil you occupy seems marked out by the

God of the oppressed, as the last, final Thermopylae of holy freedom upon the earth. The glorious Emancipator of his church and of the world, has seen fit to place you in the fore front of the battle."[10]

The Ohio River was known to enslaved African Americans as the River Jordan—across which lay the Promised Land. African Americans in the antebellum period often saw in their own struggle the reenactment of the Biblical story of the Exodus of the Jews from Egypt. Yet, as American liberty remained an unfulfilled promise, the American River Jordan constituted a conduit only to a contested freedom. Most African American fugitives who passed through this terrain did so en route to points farther north. For the thousands who remained, the territory immediately north of the Ohio was no Promised Land.[11]

The African American experience thus modified the Biblical story of the Exodus from slavery that led to the crossing of the River Jordan into the Promised Land. It was, rather, the saga of a determined struggle to create a Promised Land that would *convert* a river of slavery into a river of freedom. The constant stream of fugitives from the South was the prelude to the exodus that finally came only with the abolition of slavery.

The forces of slavery had great reason to loathe the presence of African Americans on free soil. The Underground Railroad relied on the ambiguity attached to any African American north of the Mason-Dixon Line. To be sure, an African American in the North might be a fugitive from legal bondage, or she might be a free person resident in the North. Far more often than African Americans were stowed in the false bottoms of wagons, they were given tickets on northbound trains and boats, where they openly "passed" for Northerners—not all of whom were white. This apparently small detail, all the more ignored since the false bottoms and secret hiding places fit the mood of the romance, actually conveys a tale far more worthy of telling, because it gets at the significance of the Underground Railroad that the adventure story ignores. For African Americans in the South to melt into the Northern black population, there had to be one. And that was not something to take for granted in the antebellum North, particularly in its western states.

From the first, the free African American population of the North suffered incessant persecution designed to disrupt and ultimately dislodge. The vast majority of the inhabitants on both sides of the river were staunchly proslavery—and willing to do virtually anything to prove it. If every "fugitive from service" (as the judicial system termed them) could be mistaken for a "legal" resident of the North, so could every Northern African American be taken for a runaway. African Americans were menaced by slaveholders and their paid agents on the southern shore of the Ohio, and by kidnappers, legal proscription, and systematic discrimination on the opposite bank. The region was converted into an armed camp. The port cities of the Ohio River's northern bank where free African Americans concentrated became flashpoints, the proslavery fervor periodically boiling over in particularly brutal fashion: mob violence unleashed on African Americans and white abolitionists.[12]

The Underground Railroad was significant not only for the individuals it helped to freedom, but perhaps even more for the struggle it represented against the complicity of free states in the trade in human flesh. It was at once an attack on the "Black Laws" that denied African Americans citizenship rights, the "Fugitive Slave" laws that menaced their liberty, and the spirit of slavery that sought their expulsion when not in Southern bondage. The results were measured most accurately not by the number of fugitives who arrived safely in Canada but in the populations remaining defiantly in states north of the Ohio, particularly those who settled along its banks. Not only the continuation of the enterprise known as the Underground Railroad, but the survival of the dream of freedom rested on the maintenance of the condition of African American freedom north of the Ohio River. In that simple condition—without which no clandestine network of conductors could have survived any protracted length of time—a complex history takes root to which attaches the significance that appears to be lacking in the romantic adventure of the Underground Railroad.

The history of the Underground Railroad in the Ohio Valley centers as much, perhaps ultimately more, on the making of the American River Jordan through the establishment of conditions of freedom for the African Americans on its north shore than it does on the means by which tens of thousands of fugitives were helped out of the clutches of American slavery. Restored to this context, the fact that leading centers of the Underground Railroad were also port cities of the Ohio where strong African American communities took root no longer appears to be accidental. Those communities were the fertile soil that "stations" of the Underground Railroad—that is, centers of aid to fugitives—required for a frontline struggle against slavery. The interracial movement that we call the Underground Railroad took the form of white activists acting not alone but in concert with African American communities. The received tradition of telling the story through the eyes of white activists has rendered the African American component of this struggle almost invisible, just as African Americans had traditionally been all but missing in the telling of American history.[13]

Today, the accuracy of the alleged facts that Wilbur Siebert records should not occasion as much concern as should the legacy of his passion for the history of the Underground Railroad. No doubt his diligence in preserving some of the available sources of his day—the oral traditions of white Ohioans that had survived in the many decades since the collapse of the institution from which the fugitives fled—has saved much that otherwise would have been lost, even if his sources also, as Larry Gara has forcefully argued, presented us with an Underground Railroad as much a legend as an actual institution. More important, Siebert transmitted with his collected materials the attitude that was current among white Americans that the Underground Railroad was essentially a white enterprise, albeit with some African American participation (certainly in the persons of the hapless victims smuggled to safety thanks to the ingenuity of the Quakers and fellow conspirators).[14] If Siebert chanced to stumble on a few African American conductors, he faithfully recorded the fact, noted its allegedly exceptional nature, and passed back to the white protagonists of the story who so fascinated him. Certainly their deeds were worthy of remembering. No one has yet done more to see that they were than Wilbur Siebert.[15]

White activists, with a few notable exceptions, thought of themselves as the "station keepers," as the motive forces of the line, and eventually as virtually synonymous with the institution itself. Levi Coffin, who rather too eagerly embraced the honorary title of "President of the Underground Railroad," was typical of this standpoint. Intensely proud of his own contributions, he tended to be more than a little too dismissive of those made by his African American coworkers. In describing his assumption of his Underground Railroad activities in Newport, Indiana, and later Cincinnati, he was less than generous in his assessment of the African Americans whose efforts preceded his: "[T]he fugitive slaves who took refuge with these people were often pursued and captured, the colored people not

Levi Coffin, "President of the Underground Railroad."
From the collection of the Cincinnati Historical Society.

being very skillful in concealing them, or shrewd in making arrangements to forward them to Canada." Coffin more than implies he
possessed greater aptitude for the work. He openly boasts of both
his unblemished record in sending runaways along and of the "various stratagems" he (and his fellow white conductors) devised to make
it possible. Siebert faithfully transmitted this view into his historical
accounts, an interpretation that, despite Gara's later rebuttal, remains widely diffused in the popular image of the Underground
Railroad.[16]

The white participants from whose perspective the narrative of
the Underground Railroad has been largely constructed were limited in their understanding of the context in which they operated.

Levi Coffin, for example, could disparage the effectiveness of African American operatives, explicitly criticizing their resourcefulness and implicitly praising his own, while writing the following: "I had many employes about my place of business, and much company about my house, and it seemed too public a place for fugitives to hide. These slave-hunters knew that if they committed any trespass, or went beyond the letter of the law, I would have them arrested, and they knew also that I had many friends who would stand at my back and aid me in prosecuting them. Thus, my business influence and large acquaintance afforded me protection in my labors for the oppressed fugitives." His Newport neighbor and fellow Underground Railroad activist Mayberry Lacey reported, "Our house had never been searched by one of these hunting parties."

African Americans enjoyed no such protections, whether legal, social, or economic. However ingeniously they laid their plans, it could not change the fact that their homes, places of employment, and persons were subject to unannounced searches that neither needed nor regarded legal formalities. They were effectively banned from proffering charges of any kind against whites, because they could not bear witness in cases involving white people. They were subject to any and all impositions; without a white person to testify on their behalf, they could not get the simplest forms of legal protection. Search, seizure, assault, murder: all could be and were perpetrated against African Americans without fear of legal repercussions.[17]

Coffin admitted to being shielded from his opponents by both class and racial privilege, advantages denied to African American combatants. On the contrary, they were hemmed in on all sides by economic, social, and political disabilities that made their very existence as residents of the North perilous and contested. No wonder that white conductors deemed themselves indispensable to an effective Underground Railroad.

And yet the very reverse emerges from an examination of the historical context of the development of the institution in the borderlands of the Ohio River. The principal towns and cities along the Ohio saw the emergence of African American communities with their anonymous cadre of abolitionists and Underground Railroad operatives who constituted the shock troops of the antislavery cause. These women and men made their home on slavery's doorstep, endured the innumerable bounties placed on their heads, and at times paid the ultimate price for their activities. Joined by a small but dedicated group of white and Native American activists, they founded a genuinely interracial freedom movement, a practical experiment in American democracy. The efforts of white activists like Levi Coffin were therefore situated within the process of the formation and preservation of free African American communities stretching from Pennsylvania to Indiana along the north shore of the Ohio River.

Telling that story requires a community-level focus, in which the workings of the clandestine operation can be carefully pieced together. The more the study of the subject is centered on the struggle on the front line of the battleground, the Ohio River, the more it emerges as an epic battle for freedom, the story of an underground resistance movement. What we have come to know as the Underground Railroad sprang from that struggle.

To recount the struggle that African Americans waged for freedom in the nation's Old Northwest, specifically in the cities and towns along the Ohio River, one must begin with the conditions that the first African Americans faced there upon their arrival. Perhaps even more than it has affected the imagined Underground Railroad, our national mythology has identified the North as the "Promised Land." On the contrary, the free soil north of the Ohio proved so inhospitable to Southern refugees of African descent that many of them concluded America could never be free to her black population.

2

No Promised Land

Ohio's not the place for me,
For I was much surprised
To see so many of her sons
In garments of disguise.
Her name has gone out through the land,
Free labor, soil, and men,
But slaves had better far be hurled
Into the lion's den.
Fare ye well, Ohio, I am not safe in thee;
I'll travel on to Canada, where colored men are free.
Antebellum African American song

June of 1818 witnessed an unprecedented scene along the Ohio River. The sight of a large group of immigrants making its way toward the young state of Ohio, with its cheap and abundant land, was not usual, but these newcomers were different. They had endured cruel usage during a lifetime of enslavement. They had known the sting of the lash, the pain of being separated from loved ones sold at auction in the Upper South's thriving traffic in human beings. For wanting to do nothing more than exercise their legal right to personal liberty, they had been "hunted down and shot like wild beasts." Having traveled some three hundred miles under military escort, the more than two hundred persons manumitted from the condition of legal enslavement by a recently deceased Virginia planter, Englishman Samuel Gist, finally came within sight of the river known to African Americans as the River Jordan. Freed from Virginia slavery, they were forced by that state's laws to relocate. Now, just across the river lay the free state to which they were bound.[1]

Like the others who made it across the Ohio River, the Gist settlers were coming to build a new life in a new land. Ohio, the first

state admitted to the Union without the stain of ever having permitted slavery in its territory, was a natural destination for persons
seeking escape from the cursed institution that had been imposed
on their ancestors. If there was a Promised Land within the borders
of the United States, this should have been it. Ohio gained a reputation as a refuge for enslaved African Americans freed by their repen-
tant legal owners, often only after their death, and not infrequently
involving at least some of their own children. The Gist settlers might
have been forgiven for believing that the ordeal that came with being of African descent in America was finally at an end. In truth, it
had just begun. Although lying across the river that divided freedom from enslavement in America, this was no promised land to
the African Americans who settled there.[2]

On Gist's death in 1815, the more than three hundred persons
he held in the condition of enslavement were to receive not only
their liberty but, according to the terms of his will, the greater part
of his considerable wealth in the form of a trust fund to provide for
their support. That intention was thwarted by his white relations,
who succeeded in defrauding the newly free persons of the greater
part of Gist's wealth and very nearly of their freedom. The remainder of the estate was used to purchase tracts of land lying near
Ripley, Ohio, which a longtime resident described as "so wet and
swampy . . . that it would be impossible for the greatest industry
and frugality to procure from it a good living." Public opinion was
set against them by a widely reprinted letter from a prominent Ohioan
with Virginia connections warning that a "most ignorant, degraded
and depraved set of slaves" was coming to settle in Brown County.
Left to fend for themselves on uncleared land, with neither agricul-
tural implements nor the resources to buy them, the new settlers
came very close to starving to death during the first year.[3]

Having been robbed of a significant portion of their freedom
dues in the slave commonwealth of Virginia, the group would find
its liberty severely constrained in the free state of Ohio. An elder in
the Presbyterian church reported, "The truth is, the blacks have
been most monstrously imposed on, cheated and wronged in a
multitude of ways." Given the impossibility of living off the land they
occupied, they were forced to seek employment in the surrounding
territory. When they did, they were rewarded with "offals hardly fit
for dogs or pigs." The money due them was often reduced to a pit-
tance, or not paid at all. Eking out a precarious, impoverished exist-

ence was not the worst. Female members of their community were subjected to rape at the hands of employers. And, from the first, the settlement was exposed to violent attacks by its white neighbors. Edward Abdy, an English visitor to their community, reported that "slave-traders and marauders . . . break open their doors, and subject them to outrage or insult, at all hours of the night, in violation of the law of the land as it affects the white, but in accordance with its spirit as it bears on the black man." Some weeks before his visit a man had been "cruelly beaten" to the point that he was bedridden for several days afterward. It was far from an isolated occurrence. Determined to put a stop to such attacks, the victim sought the advice of a lawyer, but he was told it was beyond the power of the law to intervene. There had been no white witnesses to the beating. As Abdy took leave of the Gist settlers, he learned from their white neighbors that the largest African American community in Ohio faced an uncertain future. White residents told him that they "had, in the first instance, endeavored to drive them away, declaring that they had no business there; had ever since insulted and threatened them; and were only waiting till they were themselves sufficiently numerous, to expel them by force."[4]

The name of Gist had already figured in the annals of Ohio history. The Ohio Company, formed to promote the territory's English settlement, employed Christopher Gist in the early 1750s as the original surveyor. Though of no known blood relation, Christopher had a connection to Samuel Gist: both were business associates of George Washington, himself a central figure in the history of Ohio. In 1754 the governor of Virginia dispatched Washington to negotiate with the French over control of the Ohio territory. Guided by Christopher Gist, the twenty-one-year-old Washington toured the area, concluding that only a war with France would ensure the supremacy of the English colonies. The French and Indian War, not long in coming, achieved the desired purpose, binding the Ohio territory firmly to the fate of the thirteen American colonies on the eve of their battle for independence. The American Revolution gave the impetus for the settlement of Ohio.[5]

If the Founding Fathers harbored antislavery sentiments, they revealed them in the form of the Northwest Ordinance of 1787. Prompted by a desire to expand the borders, promote the economic development of the fledgling nation, and generate revenue through the sale of federally controlled land, the act, predating the Constitution, forbade the extension of slavery into the territory that would give rise first to Ohio and then Indiana, Illinois, Michigan, and Wisconsin. In the words of Salmon P. Chase, the greatest legal mind in western abolitionism, future governor of Ohio, U.S. senator, and Supreme Court justice, the Northwest Ordinance "pronounced, for the first time in the history of the world, a solemn national censure on slavery, by interdicting forever, its existence in the only district, subject, in this respect, to the control of congress. So long as this ordinance endures, the people of the states, formed within this district, cannot introduce slavery." For Chase that guarantee constituted a declaration that the people of Ohio carried the torch of American liberty: "The provisions of the ordinance therefore, are the birthright of the people of Ohio. It is their glorious distinction, that the genuine principles of American liberty are imbedded, as it were, in their very soil, and mingled with their very atmosphere."[6]

Settlers arrived shortly thereafter, some brought by territorial land grants to veterans of the War for Independence. As waves of westward migrants poured across Ohio's border, many from across the Atlantic, its population grew spectacularly. By 1820, only seventeen years after Ohio became the fifteenth state in the union, it was the fifth largest state; by 1850 it was third.[7]

As the Gist settlers discovered, Ohio was not, however, equally welcoming to all comers. The revolutionary antislavery spirit that motivated the Northwest Ordinance received an unexpected check when Ohio's inaugural legislature passed the first in a series of measures that came to be known collectively as the "Black Laws." On January 5, 1804, the state's representative body put forward as one of its first laws "an act to regulate black and mulatto persons." Its initial clause required African Americans who settled in the state to prove their "actual freedom" with "a fair certificate from some court within the United States." In the absence of such evidence, they were not "permitted to settle or reside in this state." Another clause prohibited the employment of any African American who could not produce such a certificate of freedom. Revealing the motivation behind these liberty-abating provisions, the act made it a criminal offence to "harbor or secret any black or mulatto person" and granted slaveholders permission in no uncertain terms to trespass on the free state of Ohio to claim their human chattel. The presumption was to be that all African Americans who entered the state were fugitives from enslavement, unless they could prove otherwise. Property in human life was not to be permitted in the state of Ohio. It was to be returned to bondage whence it came.[8]

"The presence of the slave hunter, ranging at will, through the free states . . . above the control of state laws, and state constitutions, and state authorities . . . is a portentous anomaly," wrote Salmon Chase. "Every attempt to put this power into actual exercise leads, and must necessarily lead, to commotion and violence." In June 1842 Robert Thomas and a friend were passing through Davis County, Indiana, when they were seized by a group of armed white men. They fought desperately against their attackers, managing to break free. While his friend got away, Thomas was recaptured by what a newspaper correspondent termed a "gang of negro-hunters." He was immediately jailed on the charge of being a runaway slave. He had been apprehended without the issuance of any previous warrant, but the sheriff of the small town of Washington held him anyway, until Peter Stephenson, who evidently sympathized with the wrongfully incarcerated Thomas, succeeded in obtaining a writ of habeas corpus and threatened the officer of the law with legal process if he did not serve it. Absent the warrant needed for his arrest as a fugitive, the court released Thomas—into the waiting arms of two Kentuckians on horseback. As "no officer of the law offered to protect him," he was whisked away to Kentucky, and no further word of his fate was heard. In a similar case a few months later, a twenty-six-year-old African American from Cincinnati was pursued from Clark County to Jefferson County, Indiana, by "nineteen men with dogs," caught, and taken to Kentucky. Rather than selling him into slavery, the perpetrators turned him over to the state. Their reward was a payment of seventy-five dollars.[9]

   If the Revolutionary generation had shown at least some interest in limiting the territorial extent of the spread of slavery, it had manifested a positive zealousness with respect to the specter of the enslaved ending their own bondage by escaping from their masters. The Founding Fathers enshrined a clause in the Constitution designed to secure the return of "fugitives from service" who crossed state lines. They followed this up four years later with the Fugitive Slave Law of 1793, which both permitted slaveholders to reclaim their human property in any state—slave or free—and made criminal anyone who "knowingly and willingly" aided any fugitive. The terms of the law tended, said Salmon Chase, "to legalize assault and battery, and private imprisonment." He noted,

> The act of 1793 authorizes the claimant to seize the defendant, without process; to take him, by force, before any magistrate he may select; to hold him, by force, while the magistrate examines the evidences of claim; to remove him, by force, when the certificate is granted. The defendant, thus seized and held by force, has no rights, under the law. The act affords him no opportunity to adduce evidence, and imposes no duty on the magistrate to hear it, if adduced. On the other hand, the claimant is allowed to make out his claim by affidavits, which, taken by himself and without cross examination, will always be partial, and, often, false. And, upon such evidence, while the defendant is under such duress and without any right to be heard, the magistrate is to decide. To complete the atrocious business, and leave no semblance of justice whatever to the transaction, the magistrate is entitled to no compensation for his services, under any law, state or federal; but is left to make such bargain with the claimant as he may. What is this, but to make the claimant, judge, jury and sheriff in his own cause, and to establish his will as law?[10]

At best, Chase maintained, such a law was "liable to great abuse." All that was required was a certificate of justice issued by a magistrate, and the alleged fugitive, without the right to trial by jury or appeal to the state courts, could legally be removed to a condition of slavery. African Americans were thus denied all constitutional protections under the Bill of Rights. At worst, the Fugitive Slave Law amounted to legalized kidnapping; at best, the law encouraged it. "Can we wonder that these outrages against personal rights do not always terminate at the threshold of the magistrate? . . . Is not 'this inhuman and infamous act' [of kidnapping] the natural and inevitable consequence of this act?" To be sure, the Ohio legislature, for one, had been forced to acknowledge the increasing frequency of kidnapping, in passing a law forbidding it. As if the federal law were not draconian enough, Ohio's fugitive slave law, Chase insisted, "went far beyond even that" in suppressing African Americans' rights. The alleged fugitive was not required to be present at, or even be notified of, the hearing at which a magistrate would decide her or his fate. "The first intimation that a man would receive, under this section, that his liberty was questioned, would be from the arrest by the sheriff, to be delivered up as a slave!" Any African American living in the state of Ohio could be dragged into slavery at a moment's notice. Chase could only conclude, "Nothing could be more danger-ous or unconstitutional than this provision." Ohio law treated all African Americans as de facto fugitives—fugitives not from their own individual situation of enslavement but from the universal enslave-ment presumed to be the natural condition of all persons of color.[11]

This particular provision of state law would be repealed in 1807, but the amended "Black Laws" gave African Americans no comfort. Henceforth, they would be legally obliged to post five hundred dollars bond in order to enter the state. To make matters worse, they were forbidden "to be sworn or give evidence in any court of record" in a case involving a white person. While the former provision would be used periodically to stir up mob violence, the latter exposed African Americans to the daily tyranny of fraud, harassment, and abuse.[12]

For eighteen years, Vincent Wigglesworth had made his home just north of the Ohio River, in Clermont County, Ohio. Papers filed with the county clerk duly attested to the freedom to which he and his wife were legally entitled. They were not rich, but they had made the most of the opportunity afforded to them when they were manumit-ted from slavery. In the autumn of 1842 the Wigglesworths brought into the world their fourth child born in the free state of Ohio. Nine days later mother, newborn, and her three other children disap-peared without a trace. At midnight, their house was broken into by a band of more than half a dozen armed white men. While Vincent was tied up, his wife and four children were taken into Missouri slavery. After three years, more than three hundred dollars in ex-penses (money he did not have), and his family still in slavery, Wigglesworth faced the tragic reality that they would probably re-main enslaved for life.[13]

The kidnapping was far from being an isolated incident. In the fall of 1838, Alexander Johnson was offered a job on a steamboat on the Cincinnati riverfront. When he accepted, he found that he had walked into a trap. He disappeared into Southern slavery, his wife and several children left destitute. William S. Edwards was abducted as a young child from Springfield, Ohio, his birthplace, with his mother. The two were soon parted at the auction block, never to meet again. He remained enslaved until the age of twenty-seven. Two young Cincinnati boys were more fortunate. They were recov-ered from a steamboat before it departed for the South, where their captors intended to sell them. Eliza Jane Johnson, too, regained her freedom, though only after five months in a Mason County, Kentucky, jail. She had been stolen from her home in Ripley, Ohio, while her husband, Gabriel, was away. Her kidnapper, the son of the High Sheriff of Mason County, hid his crime behind the false contention that she had admitted to being a fugitive, upon which charge she found herself imprisoned before her eventual release. Few cases, however, had such a comparatively happy ending. And rarer still were the assailants brought to justice. The kidnappers of Eliza Johnson were tried but fled the state before conviction could be secured. The words of a correspondent for the *Philanthropist*, the only southern Ohio paper to bother to record the Wigglesworth abduction, seem fitting: "Such is the influence of the slave power over the action of the free people of our State. This woman and her children had the Slave-holders mark of property upon them—they were colored, and that seems sufficient to freeze all our sympathy. . . . The negro hunting tribe, like the hyena break open our dwellings, and steal our people."[14]

The illicit traffic in free residents of states north of the Ohio River went far back in the region's history and remained frighteningly common through the antebellum period. As early as 1819, the Ohio legislature felt compelled to pass a law against kidnapping of African Americans, commenting that "upon pretence of seizing fugitives from service" under the Fugitive Slave Law of 1793 "unprincipled persons have kidnapped free persons of color, within this state, and attempted to transport them out of the state, and sell them into slavery." In 1831, having failed to stamp out the practice, it stiffened the penalty for the offence. The African American population of Madison, Indiana, could identify the professional kidnappers in their region by sight. Southern Illinois, where Lucy Delaney's mother was abducted and taken across the river to St. Louis with four others, was said to be particularly rife with kidnappings. Eastern abolitionist Seth Conklin made a survey of the conditions there in 1854, reporting, "It is customary, when a strange negro is seen, for any white man to seize him, and convey him through and out of the State of Illinois to Paducah [Kentucky]." No Northern state was free from this scourge.[15]

Ohio's Black Laws emboldened the kidnappers: absent a white witness, no white could be tried for a crime committed against African Americans. Similar statutes existed throughout the Northwest.

As a result, African Americans received none of the legal protections enjoyed by freeborn (white) citizens. African Americans could be victimized with virtual impunity. For want of two white witnesses, the cold-blooded, premeditated murder of an African American man by a white man, who stalked him on the city streets and struck him down with a brick in front of eight eyewitnesses, went unpunished in Cincinnati. In a case heard before the same session of the court, another Cincinnati African American family appeared to be more fortunate. One of the two white men who took "a considerable amount" of their property turned "State's evidence and confessed the whole thing." The defense lawyer for the other perpetrator, seeing a loophole in this open and shut case, argued that there was no evidence that the property belonged to the African American family, their testimony being inadmissible. The jury promptly brought back a verdict of not guilty. A report of the Ohio Anti-Slavery Society in 1835 summarized the position of an African American living in the Ohio Valley: "His property may be taken away, his person assailed by the hand of violence, and his reputation blasted by the foul breath of calumny; and unless he can produce a white witness, provided his injurer is white, he can have no redress." During the Civil War, Norvel Blair, a new migrant to Illinois, discovered that little had changed, as two prominent whites robbed him of a year's worth of wages he had earned from them.[16]

A meeting of Clermont County citizens in December of 1842 denounced the abduction of their neighbor Vincent Wigglesworth's wife and children. However, showing equal concern in assuring Kentucky that they would do nothing to aid fugitives from that state, they declared flatly, "We, the citizens of Clermont county have been and ever will be ready to maintain and support the law provided for the redemption of fugitive slaves . . . nor do we in the least countenance the aiding, abetting or assisting the escape of slaves from legal servitude." They concluded, "[W]hen slaves so escaping are sought to be reclaimed in a lawful manner we have never interfered . . . the complaint sometimes made by the citizens of Kentucky, of our unwillingness to surrender up fugitive slaves when demanded by their owners, is utterly unfounded."[17]

"You must go to Africa," a ten-year-old resident of Madison, Indiana, told his neighbor, William Crosby. "There are so many of you; and you increase so much faster than we do, that you'll eat us out soon." Crosby and his wife heard this message from whites with increasing frequency in the early 1830s. Hints were dropped in casual conversation; less subtle were the "inducements" to sell their land and leave; worse still, the message was being preached to young African Americans in a Sunday school started by whites. *Go to Africa.* It had begun to wear on the Crosbies. It was taking an even heavier toll on their neighbors. Around the same time in Cincinnati, a respectable clergyman informed one of his parishioners that he would no longer be able to employ him as a laborer. He explained that doing so violated the Black Laws. With a wife and children to support, the now unemployed man set out to search for the means to feed his family. He could find none. In desperation, he returned to his pastor and former employer for advice. He was told: "I cannot help you, you must go to Liberia."[18]

The sentiment seemed to be common among white people in the Northwest. An 1835 report on African Americans in Ohio noted a "general desire among the white population that they should remove to Liberia, or elsewhere." English traveler Edward Abdy formed the same impression. "All the whites with whom I conversed upon the subject, admitted that they had been defrauded—but then their color! What right had they to remain where they were? They must go to Liberia—there were plenty of persons in Georgetown ready to make up a purse to pay their passage."[19]

The specific destination, if not the general feeling, was the work of one organization, the American Colonization Society. Founded in 1816, the society reached the apex of its support and influence in the decade of the 1820s. Its message was that white and black people could not, and should not, cohabit in the same nation—so long as the latter were not in bondage (it made no unequivocal objection to the presence of those who were enslaved). Its plan was simple: the removal, purportedly on a voluntary basis, to Africa of all black people no longer under the yoke of slavery. The society established a colony for that purpose in West Africa, which it named Liberia. For a time, the plan enjoyed significant support from the large number of prominent citizens who endorsed it and from the whites across the nation who embraced it. Among the supporters of the idea, if not the specific organization, were two men traditionally held up as embodying the principles of American freedom: Thomas Jefferson and Abraham Lincoln.[20]

This potentially threatening Northern movement targeting persons of African descent for eventual removal from American soil caused alarm. According to historian Joe Trotter, "Racism gained its most powerful expression in organized efforts to rid the region and nation of free people of color." To Presbyterian minister and Ripley, Ohio, resident John Rankin it was "evident that the Colonization Society owes its existence to prejudice." To make matters worse, he wrote, the group's effect was to "greatly increase" such prejudice. Its literature was filled with offensive references to African Americans, labeling them "notoriously ignorant, degraded and miserable, mentally diseased, brokenspirited, acted upon by no motive to honourable exertions, scarcely reached in their debasement by the heavenly light."[21]

The founding conference of the Ohio branch made clear its raison d'etre. As long as slavery existed, individual slaveholders would inevitably manumit their property: "This can only be done by sending the liberated slave out of the state, and thus it is done at the expense of *our* safety and happiness in this and other free states. These miserable beings, with all the ignorance and degraded habits of thinking and acting which pertain to slavery, are *flooded* upon us in Ohio and Indiana, in yearly accumulating multitudes, to live among us without any of either the qualifications or privileges of citizens and freemen." The tendency would be for the African American population to approach in size that of the white population. "Who would not then prefer a residence in a slave-holding state?" the convention declared. To accomplish its purposes, the society was not above raising a peculiar nineteenth-century specter: racial "amalgamation."[22]

One of the speakers at a meeting of the Cincinnati branch of the Colonization Society was Lyman Beecher, president of Lane Seminary and father of Harriet Beecher Stowe, who in 1851 published the most famous abolitionist work, the novel *Uncle Tom's Cabin.* Though Beecher was a proponent of immediate abolition, Edward Abdy found him "so far jaundiced, that he not only admitted the existence of the disease, under which he, in common with his countrymen, labor, but maintained that it was conducive to health, and in strict accordance with the order of nature. He called it a prejudice, yet he considered it a salutary preventive of that amalgamation, which would confound the two races and obliterate the traces of their distinction."[23]

The message resonated in states north of the Ohio River. Ac-

cording to Abdy, John Rankin was practically the only Northwest-
erner he could find who harbored "great good sense" on the subject
by subscribing to a principle of "perfect freedom of choice . . . to
regulate this like every other matter in which society can never have
such an interest as the parties directly concerned." Many others
disagreed with Rankin. One Quaker abolitionist in Indiana was so
obsessed with the idea that he came to oppose the Underground
Railroad on the grounds that it worked against the attempt to keep
the races separate in America. Even Levi Coffin, the self-proclaimed
"President of the Underground Railroad," professed that he was "not
in favor of amalgamation and did not encourage the intermarriage
or mixing of the races." He nevertheless refused to "criminate those
who had made the choice." He lived up to his words in the late
1820s by sheltering a young African American, newly free, who
married a white woman in Indianapolis and was consequently pursued by a mob that would in all probability have lynched the man if
it had caught him. "Not finding him, the mob dragged the bride out
of the house and rode her on a rail through the streets, as a demon-
stration of the popular indignation."[24]

Coffin later recalled, "The news of the marriage flew all over the
State. . . . The dreadful prospect of amalgamation loomed before the
people like an impending curse." Coffin's Quaker neighbors "regarded
[the groom] as a criminal": "many of the women in our town were
much afraid of him as if he were a murderer." For his part, Coffin
took considerable care in his memoirs to repeatedly highlight the
"near whiteness" of the young man (who, he insisted, "was really
almost white and possessed none of the negro features"), perhaps
in an attempt to emphasize the absurdity of racial categories, but
also leaving doubt as to whether he would have been so favorable to
the marriage had the bride been more than "a shade lighter" than
the groom. Coffin was roundly criticized for "harboring" the formerly
enslaved man, and the state legislature immediately passed a law
against interracial marriage. While the young man took refuge in an
African American settlement in the eastern part of the state, the
woman was intimidated into filing for divorce, which was granted
by the legislature. Later reunited, the couple went east to live as
man and wife, having passed through Cincinnati long enough to
ascertain that their cohabitation would no more be tolerated there.
Though some white men lived openly with African American women
in that city, this case was evidently deemed to be quite different.[25]

The government of Indiana did more than ban interracial marriages. As early as 1814, the territory's governor received a petition seeking a stop to African Americans' emigration. A few years later, the request of a Tennessee slaveholder to settle the forty enslaved persons he intended to free in the Hoosier state before his death was declined. John Randolph expressed his "deepest regret" that "the circumstances under which I inherited them, and the obstacles thrown in the way by the laws of the land" forced him to wait until his death to give them "their freedom, to which my conscience tells me they are justly entitled." In his case, the state to which he wished them transported did not create the legal obstacle; rather, his own heirs delayed the group's departure for fourteen years on the grounds that he must have been insane to claim religious conviction caused him to bestow liberty on those he had held in enslavement. Finally, in 1847, three decades after the group of persons formerly held in enslavement by Samuel Gist had trekked hundreds of miles from Virginia across the Ohio River to settle on free soil, another contingent of approximately three hundred made a similar journey. They were bound for New Bremen, Ohio, where a large tract of land had been purchased for them. White residents of Highland County had been vocal in their opposition to African Americans who moved into their county in the 1820s, but the Mercer County population would become the first to take action to prevent African American emigration. As the word of the imminent settlement spread, a meeting of the white citizens of the county declared that "we will not live among negroes." It added, ominously, "we pledge ourselves *to remove them, peaceably if we can, forcibly if we must.*" When the would-be settlers arrived, they found the armed white citizenry blocking their attempt to take possession of their land. Forced to leave at gunpoint, they moved farther south, only to have the same scene repeated in Shelby County. They were never compensated for the land thus taken from them. Fifteen years later a member of the Ohio State Senate from the Cincinnati area vividly recalled his outrage—at seeing "negroes coming in droves." Having been chased out of Massachusetts by his "disgust" at seeing African Americans exercising their right to vote, he found John Randolph's manumitted bondspersons' Cincinnati arrival, which coincided with his own, "repugnant to my feelings": "is this the population that is to cover the rich bottoms, the fertile hills, the pleasant valleys, and at some future day, by the aid and under the misguided philanthropy of the negro wor-shippers, sway the political destinies of this great commonwealth[?]"[26]

Given the state's size and location, the attempt to ban in-migra-tion of African Americans was geographically important. However, given that Ohio was the first state admitted to the Union from the Northwest Territory and the first to enter without ever having had slavery on its soil, the attempt was perhaps even more symbolically significant. In the words of John Rankin, "Still this relentless preju-dice, dark fiend of hell, cried they shall not be free among us! They shall not be free among us!!" If African Americans could not live freely in Ohio, where in the United States could they?[27]

The warnings to the African American population of Cincinnati to leave that city took on a threatening tone in the summer months of 1829. Black residents were given thirty days to comply with the law requiring them to post five hundred dollars bond as surety against their menacing the community by their unsecured presence. As the tension grew, a meeting of African American community leaders looked into the prospects of leaving the ostensibly free state—and the country. The hundreds of black Cincinnatians who left, forming the first large-scale migration to Canada of free African Americans, had every reason to feel justified in giving up on the prospects of African American freedom in an American nation so evidently com-mitted to their bondage.[28]

Contrary to the popular notion today, not all African Americans who went to Canada were fugitives from enslavement, and not all were escaping the Fugitive Slave Law. Many left because, as Rev. David Smith put it, they were "devoured on every side by the wolves of slavery, prejudice and ostracism." John Malvin advocated leaving the American Republic because, he said, "I found every door closed against the colored man in a free State, excepting the jails and peni-tentiaries, the doors of which were thrown wide open to receive him." Eli Artis left Ohio, the place of his birth, in the early 1840s to escape its "mean, oppressive laws." Henry Johnson, a native of Pennsylva-nia, left Massillon, Ohio, after a residence of twenty-three years be-cause his daughter was expelled with all the other African American children from school, by a vote of its trustees in compliance with state law, after complaints from wealthy locals. He refused to change his mind even in the face of an offer from the teacher to keep his daughter in school in opposition to the exclusionary law, a position supported by her white classmates, who took a symbolic vote in school to repeal the state legislation. "One *must* know how I would feel about it," he explained, from Canada. Ephraim Waterford, of free birth in Virginia, went to Canada "on account of oppression in Indiana," where he had resided for two years in the mid-1840s. The last straw for him was a new addition to the Black Laws that sought to prevent him from leaving his forty acres to his family on his death. "I told them, 'if that was a republican government, I would try a monarchical one.'" He led an emigration to Canada of some three dozen African Americans.[29]

By the late 1820s, a definite note of discouragement set in among African Americans in the North, especially the Northwest. The first African American newspaper, *Freedom's Journal*, editorialized in early 1829, "[S]hould each of us live to the age of Methusalah, at the end of the thousand years, we should be exactly in our present situation: a proscribed race . . . a degraded people, deprived of all the rights of freemen." It reasoned, "[T]he present prejudices in the way of the man of colour . . . are not of our creating, and they are not in our power to remove."[30]

The proposed solution of the proprietors of *Freedom's Journal*, emigration to Africa, was not a distinctly popular one among African Americans; but there was a nearer and more attractive option. While the abolition of slavery in the United States remained a distant dream, the English abolitionist movement was on the verge of success, adding to the attraction of the British dominion to the North. Better still, Canada had no discriminatory legislation aimed at persons of African descent. Moreover, while Northwestern states had done all they could to discourage African American settlers, the Canadian government, contacted by potential in-migrants of color, expressed itself happy to give them refuge. Interested African Americans received word that "so long as we remained true and loyal subjects, we should have every privilege extended to us that was enjoyed by any of her majesty's subjects, no distinction being made on account of color." In contrast to the continual threats of fraud, disfranchisement, abuse, assault, and kidnapping, this written assurance presented an inviting alternative.[31]

African Americans in Cincinnati were not alone in their interest in leaving the country for a more veritable land of liberty. Still, they certainly had the most immediate incentive to undertake the journey. Never particularly friendly to African American newcomers, the atmosphere in Cincinnati was rapidly becoming openly hostile. The immediate impetus for the city authorities' attempt to evict African Americans stemmed from a petition presented by a group of white citizens in the fall of 1828 that asked the authorities to "take measures to prevent the increase of the negro population within the city." The proponents of the action of the Cincinnati authorities could point to no other reason for it being taken than the increase of the African American population of Cincinnati. The black population had grown dramatically in the second half of the 1820s, increasing more than fourfold within four years of the movement to enforce the Black Laws, and reaching perhaps as many as two thousand persons, or 10 percent of the city's total. While the provisions barring African Americans from bearing witness in court were rigorously enforced (a point often forgotten for those who argue that the laws were completely ignored), the portions of the Black Laws aimed at limiting African American settlement had effectively fallen into disuse. Indeed, the editor of the *Cincinnati Gazette* claimed, with considerable exaggeration, that they had been "almost forgotten even by the learned in the law."[32]

A more likely explanation is that in the early days after the laws' passage, the paucity of African Americans made enforcement unnecessary, and now that there were sufficient African Americans in residence there was no precedent for doing so. An opinion of the chief justice of the Ohio Supreme Court provided the pretext city leaders were seeking. In a case relating to the right of habeas corpus, he affirmed his belief that the Black Laws of Ohio were fully constitutional and enforceable, a point that had previously occasioned some debate. A Cincinnati proponent of the enforcement of the Black Laws summarized the justice's argument as being that the state's constitution and laws were "framed and adopted by white people, and for their own benefit." As a consequence, he asserted: "We have a right to legislate for our own protection in regard to them. If we had not this right, our condition would be deplorable indeed, surrounded, in part, as we are, by states filled to overflowing with this class of people. Besides, they are relatively increasing in numbers, and if we open our doors to them, we shall be overwhelmed by an emigration at once wretched in its character and destructive in its consequences."[33]

On June 29, 1829, the "trustees and overseers of the poor of the township of Cincinnati" issued a proclamation that "hereafter" the

Black Laws would be "rigidly enforced." They gave African Americans thirty days from that date to "enter into bond, as the said act directs" or "they may expect, at the expiration of that time, the law to be rigidly enforced." The notice warned any white person who might "employ, harbor, or conceal any such negro" that they were subject to heavy fine. Finally, and rather ominously, the officials called for the "co-operation of the public" in carrying out enforcement.[34]

Although some African Americans sold out at a great loss and left town, a newcomer to the city, John Malvin, called together African Americans to confer on what course to take. The thirty-four-year-old Malvin was quite familiar with the injustice meted out to free African Americans in both the North and the South. Although he was born free in Virginia, his impoverished mother was forced to give him in apprenticeship to the master of his enslaved father. For the first quarter century of his life, he experienced the worst slavery had to offer. He even once attempted to run away. Chance had placed him on an oasis of enslavement in the middle of the River Jordan, the Blennerhasset Island plantation. He developed a deep longing to cross the Ohio River to the free soil side. When he finally did, he was deeply disappointed: "I thought upon coming to a free State like Ohio, that I would find every door thrown open to receive me, but from the treatment I received generally, I found it little better than in Virginia."[35]

Malvin later wrote of that community meeting of Cincinnati African Americans: "None but those who have experienced the misery of servitude, or the pangs which result from the consciousness of being despised as a caste, from being shut out from the benefit of enjoying the pure atmosphere of heaven in common with all mankind, and not only being personally despised, but not even having the protection of the laws themselves, can fully appreciate the patriotic ardor which animated that little assembly." Among the leaders who emerged was J.C. Brown, also born into bondage in Virginia. After buying his freedom from his father's sister, who was also his master, he eventually removed from Kentucky to Ohio with his wife and two children. He found its conditions little more to his liking than did Malvin. When Malvin "suggested to the meeting the propriety of appointing a committee to go to some country with power to make arrangements for the purchase of some place to live free from the trammels of unsocial and unequal laws," Brown embraced the idea. He assumed the position of president in the resultant colonization society charged with finding a suitable destination in Canada for these refugees from the Queen City of the West. They named the town in Canada they obtained for the purpose Wilberforce, after the distinguished English abolitionist. Calling itself the "Board of colored people in the city of Cincinnati," the organization issued a call over Brown's signature not only to Cincinnati African Americans, but "our brother Africans throughout the United States" to follow them. At least three hundred Cincinnatians opted to do so. Many of them were no doubt recent arrivals, at a time when Cincinnati's African American population was dramatically increasing. But others, like the colonization society's agent, Thomas Cressup, were long-time residents with deep community roots.[36]

On July 29 Brown issued another appeal—this time to white Cincinnatians to offer financial assistance to those African Americans who could not pay their own way to the new African American settlement. The city authorities were only too happy to oblige. A town meeting voted to appropriate municipal funds for the purpose of "defraying the expenses of the coloured population of [Cincinnati] in their voluntary removal from the state." One of the leaders of the effort to expel African Americans chortled, "I am as kindly affected towards the unfortunate blacks as any one: and rejoice to learn that they have the prospect of finding a pleasant retreat in Canada." He would find that he had declared victory too soon.[37]

3

Home Over Jordan

Deep river,
My home is over Jordan.
Deep river, Lord,
I want to cross over into campground.
                                    Traditional spiritual

Frances Jane Scroggins, Major James Wilkerson, John Parker, and
John Mercer Langston were among America's forgotten children of
the revolution. Their fathers and grandfathers, Virginia aristocrats,
had been officers in the American forces in the Revolutionary War.
Those such as Scroggins, Wilkerson, Parker, and Langston would
have to join with a group of Americans fighting a decades-long war
for their freedom. In another place and time, they might have lived
lives of ease and luxury. Instead, they were relegated to the ranks of
America's dispossessed. In the United States of the day, it did not
matter that their fathers and grandfathers were men of means and
social standing: it only mattered that their mothers had been enslaved. Residents of Cincinnati in the 1830s and 1840s, they found
themselves in the front line of the struggle against American slavery. Like that of their African American sisters and brothers all
along the Ohio to the east and the west of Cincinnati, their presence
on the river's north bank constituted a beachhead of freedom. They
would not relinquish what they had gained without a fight, and
they were willing to lay down their lives to prove it.[1]

Hemmed in on all sides, the African American community not
only survived but initiated and sustained a protracted struggle
against slavery. Viewed against this backdrop, the historical significance of the Underground Railroad lies not in its success in spiriting
away of thousands of fugitives to Canada. Rather, its importance

centers on those who remained in the United States, and most especially those who settled in the river port cities and communities that constituted the front lines of the struggle against slavery, carving out the political and social space to wage a war for their own liberation. The Black Laws were designed above all to sustain slavery by making the existence of free African Americans north of slavery as precarious as possible. The community's survival, growth, political activity, and participation in the Underground Railroad gave the measure of the laws' failure.

Most people seemed to know what precipitated the mob that descended on the African American part of Cincinnati in August 1829, but few were willing to talk about it. The one paper that covered the event blamed it on the white working class, "two or three hundred of the lowest *canaille* of our city" lured by the prospect of eliminating the competition for working class jobs and raising their own wages in the process. British visitor Edward Abdy heard differently from his sources when he visited Cincinnati a few years later—that the instigators included many prominent white citizens, which, he maintained, explained the silence of the press. Whoever started it, and for whatever reason, its result was clear, albeit unexpected. The mob had its way for several days, making "the most violent assaults, in great numbers upon the blacks, . . . throwing stones, demolishing houses, [and] doing every other act of riotous violence." On Saturday night, three hundred whites prepared to descend on Cincinnati African Americans once again. This time, the latter changed their tactics. Having hunkered down in their homes the previous night, a group of some two or three dozen armed themselves, determined to fight back. As the rioters approached, the residents took up strategic positions in the windows of a number of houses. Greatly outnumbered, they had to take advantage of the element of surprise. Their lives, and the survival of the community they were defending, were on the line. If they failed, no one could forecast the result. They took careful aim and fired. Three of the attackers fell, one never to rise again. Shocked and disorganized by this response, the mob was put into full retreat. The African Americans pursued, "sallying out as the enemy fled, and shooting them down with a spirit, as much superior to that on the other side, as the cause they fought in."[2]

The tide had turned. The lone newspaper to cover the event

noted that the concerted efforts of African Americans on their own behalf "operated as a *quietus*." A number of black persons were arrested, "but nothing criminal being proved against them, they were discharged." City authorities conceded that African Americans had acted in self-defense. In contrast, eight of the instigators of the mob were convicted and fined. The mob attacks were not renewed. The events of the night of Saturday, August 22, 1829, were given as little publicity as possible. The crisis in the African American community in Cincinnati brought on by the attempt to enforce the Black Laws was brought to an end. "Since that period," Abdy noted four years later, "the victors have been suffered to reside in the place unmolested."[3]

The defense of their right to reside freely in Cincinnati on a summer night in 1829 marked a turning point in the history of African Americans in the Ohio Valley. The resolve of the community to maintain a beachhead of freedom on slavery's doorstep had been tried. Its numbers would be somewhat reduced for a time. It had nevertheless survived. The presence of African Americans along the northern banks of the Ohio River became a tangible threat to the slavery on the opposite side by serving as a beacon for others to follow across what was being transformed into a veritable River Jordan.

Though born into Virginia slavery, Jemima and Thomas Woodson had built a home over Jordan for themselves and their descendants. It was now time to help others. Having moved their family to a strip of land outside the reach of the harassment and segregation they faced in Ohio's first state capital in Chillicothe, they founded the comfortable community of Berlin Crossroads in 1830. According to Byron Woodson, "[O]ur family's oral history . . . identifie[s] Thomas Woodson as the oldest son of Thomas Jefferson and Sally Hemings, Jefferson's enslaved concubine"—a claim disputed by the Monticello Association, the Jefferson family foundation, which denies that Sally Hemings's first son, approximately the same age as Thomas Woodson, lived past infancy. By 1820 Thomas Woodson had obtained his freedom and was living in Greenbriar County, Virginia.[4]

The Woodson family moved to Ohio from their native Virginia to escape the untenable existence of free African Americans in a slave state. Perhaps to their surprise, certainly to their disappointment, life for African Americans north of slavery, though better, was still far from adequate. The Woodsons, therefore, began to contemplate the idea of founding African American communities. In the words of Jemima and Thomas's eldest son, Lewis, "Such a settlement would entirely alter our conditions, there we should be on perfect equality—we should be free from the looks of scorn and contempt—free from fraud—and, in time, free from all the evils attendant on partial and unequal laws." In the face of these oppressive social conditions, a sizeable proportion of Ohio's population decided to undertake voluntarily what the Black Laws had forced on the Gist settlers. Pooling their resources to buy good land, they founded the African American settlement movement. Throughout the states of Ohio, Indiana, and Illinois, communities of African Americans put down deep roots—though the majority continued to reside in the southernmost counties along the Ohio River for the entire antebellum period.[5]

Establishing a community was a more inviting alternative to permanent deportation. "To aid or encourage such exile," Woodson declared, "is a high crime and outrage upon innocent and unoffending humanity." But, then, neither would African Americans submit to the prejudice "the extinction of [which] is to be attained [only] with great difficulty." The settlement movement provided an interim solution rooted in resistance to both options. "Separate settlements" in the Northwest were the only efficacious response to a "condition in the towns and cities" that found African Americans "degraded to the last extreme."[6]

The Woodsons were among the pioneers. Whatever the reason the Woodsons left Chillicothe, the cause does not appear to have been economic. They had done well economically in Virginia; they would do even better in Chillicothe. In 1830 they purchased land in rural Jackson County on which they founded an African American farming community, which they named Berlin Crossroads. One of many in Ohio, the settlement grew to encompass about thirty families, with the older generation consisting mainly of formerly enslaved Virginians. "Most of them were the children, as well as the slaves of their masters," noted Augustus Wattles, a white abolitionist devoted to African American education. In total, residents owned more than 2,000 acres of prime Ohio farmland—with the Woodson's 372 "acknowledged to be the best cultivated farm in Jackson county." Wattles declared, "I have never found a more intelligent, enterprising, farming family in the State of Ohio." The residents of Berlin Crossroads founded a church and a school that provided their children quality education. The Woodsons' eleven children all went on to distinguished careers in the church or in education. Woodsons were instrumental in the educational efforts of African Americans in Ohio, playing a prominent role in the creation of institutions of higher learning such as Wilberforce University.[7]

Berlin Crossroads became a model that other African Americans followed. In the mid-1830s, a colony comprising mainly persons who purchased themselves out of slavery left Cincinnati and located in an unsettled portion of Mercer County, Ohio. When they first moved to their new homes, they were remote from any white settlers—the nearest market town being some forty miles distant. Within a decade, however, the pressure of new white migrants began to tell, and the settlement experienced its first trouble, the prospect of the kind of racial violence black Cincinnatians had experienced. The local authorities, being the "ringleaders and major instigators of the mob," offered the harassed African Americans no help. But the governor-elect of Ohio put an end to the unrest before it assumed a more threatening shape. By that time, the success of the experiment was assured. The inhabitants had cleared nearly forty thousand acres and were said to be living in "comfortable circumstances, comparatively independent." A similar farming community, known as Cabin Creek, sprang up just across the Indiana border in Randolph County. By 1838 a memorial to the state legislature from the Ohio Anti-Slavery Society seeking repeal of the Black Laws identified no fewer than thirteen thriving, full-fledged African American farming settlements in that state alone, composed mainly of formerly enslaved persons who had purchased their freedom; a similar number probably existed in Indiana.[8]

Still, wherever African Americans resided north of the Ohio River, racial antipathy surrounded them. From the South, there was the threat of enslavement, with visible reminders close at hand. African Americans in the Northwest did not have to look across the Ohio River to see the evidence of slavery. It was enough to look at the river itself. When John Parker first saw the Ohio River during his enslavement, he was struck most by the number of Ohio and Indiana farmers who floated their produce down it to feed the plantations of the Deep South. Even more galling was the trade in enslaved persons that thrived up and down the river. With auctions held at frequent intervals along the southern shore, the sight of the enslaved being transported to the Cotton Belt was common. Such persons did not always passively accept their fate; mutinies aboard slave trading vessels were not confined to the high seas. While making his way down the Ohio with 175 enslaved African Americans, wealthy Kentucky slave trader Ned Stone met his end with his four white assistants in such an uprising. Under cover of darkness, the human cargo revolted, killed their captors, attached their chains to the corpses, and sank them to the bottom of the river. They navigated to the Indiana shore and made a break for it. Only a few got away cleanly, however. The rest were retaken; subsequently, five were hanged and the remainder sold into the Deep South.[9]

The African American communities of the Northwest could not remain aloof from this conflict that raged around them and, in large part, centered on their presence. An observer familiar with the African American community in Cincinnati estimated that one-third of its African American population was working to earn the money to liberate family and friends still enslaved. He reported, "It is literally true, that they stint themselves in food and clothing, and go bareheaded and bare-footed, so that they may appropriate their earnings to the purchase of relatives in bondage. Noble spirits! An emancipated slave said to me to-day, '*Even freedom is bitter to us, while our friends are in slavery!*'" Like others in the settlement movement, the Woodsons of Berlin Crossroads were deeply involved in the African American freedom struggle. The prominence they gained as some of its most visible leaders was to cost them dearly. In September 1846 Thomas Woodson Jr. was found on the side of the road, beaten to death, for refusing to divulge the location of the fugitives he had aided. The Woodson household continued to receive runaways as long as slavery existed.[10]

Perhaps the most difficult choice faced by enslaved African Americans was deciding whether or not to attempt escape. To imagine the plight of an enslaved person, according to Kentucky fugitive Andrew Jackson, meant conceiving the "hardships and cruelties of such toil as slaves only know, with none but fellow sufferers to sympathise with him, and they unable to afford relief—with no prospect of a better state, for life—deprived of the blessings of knowledge and the sweets of intellectual pursuit." Still, successful flight meant leaving loved ones behind, most likely forever. Failure meant, Jackson related, "severe punishment, and almost unendurable torture"—even death. And the chances of success were not great. An enslaved

Alabama man shot four times as he headed north to freedom spent four days recovering, unable to move and without the slightest medical attention; during his subsequent travails, he went as long as a week without food. As he approached the Ohio River, he was finally caught, put in jail, and sold back into the slavery he had endured so much to leave. Everyone in the South had heard such tales. Yet every enslaved African American probably at least thought of attempting escape, so all-consuming was the desire for liberty.[11]

For many would-be runaways, nothing could hurt more than cutting the ties between themselves and their fellow bondspersons. Frederick Douglass had been separated from his family, yet for him "the thought of leaving my friends, was among the strongest obstacles to my running away." It was even more difficult to contemplate voluntary separation from parents, children, and siblings. The decision was made more painful by the knowledge that vengeance might be sought against those very persons. As he prepared to leave, Francis Fedric was nearly overcome by the specter of the treatment his mother would receive: "I could foresee how my master would stand over her with the lash to extort from her my hiding-place. . . . How she would suffer torture on my account, and be distressed that I had left her for ever until we should meet hereafter in heaven I hoped." The trauma of losing loved ones, however, also worked as a motivating force for escape attempts, which were often precipitated by the imminent threat of separation of families through the ever-present slave trade.[12]

However strong, emotional impediments to flight paled in comparison to the physical. "Everything was organized against the slaves' getaway," remembered John Parker, a former fugitive. "The woods were patrolled nightly by constables. . . . Every ford was watched. . . . Once word came from further south that runaways were on the way, the whole countryside turned out . . . to stop the fugitives." Perhaps the most feared obstacle to escape were the dogs kept for tracking down runaways. They were known to eat a person alive before they could be called off. If the dogs did not stake their claim, hunger or the elements often did. Louis Hughes stowed away aboard a Cincinnati packet in Memphis, but hunger and thirst overcame his resolve several days out and led to his recapture before he reached free soil.[13]

When John Parker ran, he knew that to his pursuers "I was only a beast of labor in revolt." Getting caught, however, meant treatment of a brutal nature that was reserved for human property. John Warren remembered a returned runaway being greeted back into slavery on his Mississippi plantation with "two hundred lashes every morning for seven mornings." After Peter Bruner was caught, he suffered a whipping that nearly killed him. His master "cowhided and cowhided me until the blood stood in pools on the floor . . . I guess he whipped me for about three hours." Bruner kept running off. He was not alone.[14]

The yearning to be free was so irrepressible that it was enough to conquer fear and induce persons young and old to endure the severe hardship that was the lot of the fugitive from enslavement. The total number of African Americans who escaped Southern slavery will never be known with precision, but estimates put it in the tens of thousands. That does not include the much larger group that never made it as far as freedom—or those who ran off temporarily, a practice known as "lying out," to gain a respite from a life of incessant labor, to visit loved ones, or to seek concessions in exchange for their return. The prevalence of attempted flight attests to the perpetual desire of enslaved African Americans to be free, a desire expressed no more eloquently than in the words of Martin Jackson: "Even with my good treatment, I spent most of my time planning and thinking of running away." The many hundreds of thousands of attempted escapes from bondage embodied the unbroken spirit of resistance running through the three centuries that slavery lasted on American soil. As Henry Bibb put it, "I first entered my protest against the bloody institution of slavery, by running away from it." That fighting ethos was nourished by the actions of free African Americans who dedicated their lives to helping their brethren in slavery. As Thomas Cole made his way north in his personal exodus from slavery, he was inspired to persevere partly by the fervent hope that he would encounter Harriet Tubman on his way to Canada. His case demonstrates how much the efforts of African American freedom fighters served to inspire others to risk it all. So, too, did the existence of a free African American population north of slavery. Israel Campbell was numbered among the privileged few enslaved African Americans who had set foot on free territory. When he related this fact to fourteen fellow bondsmen who had been imprisoned for running off, he was amazed by the result. "As soon as I had told them about my visits almost to the country where there was no slavery, they were highly pleased, and seemed to take new life, and commenced sawing the iron bars out of the windows, and broke my hand-cuffs off, and said they would all be out soon, and they wanted me to lead them to the Free States."[15]

By the mid-1820s, considerable alarm about fugitives emanated from Virginia and, in particular, Kentucky, where the legislature promulgated a series of resolutions calling on the federal government to take action. Their congressional delegation succeeded in having a resolution passed that called on the State Department to undertake negotiations—ultimately unsuccessful—with the British authorities on a treaty for securing the return of fugitives from Canada. Instructions to the U.S. envoy charged with the task called attention to "a growing evil which has produced some and, if it be not shortly checked, is likely to produce much more irritation. . . . In proportion as they are successful in their retreat to Canada, will the number of fugitives increase."[16]

In the context of the constant efforts in the South to break the yoke of slavery, the presence of free African Americans in such close proximity to slavery menaced the institution's existence on the southern bank of the Ohio River. At the same time, the black Ohioans' active participation in and encouragement of the stream of fugitives from slavery threatened the security of their own lives on the river's north side. When English traveler Abdy looked into the causes of the attempt to dislodge African Americans from Cincinnati by proclamation and violence, he found that the motivation had included the intention to "break up an asylum, which the fugitives from Kentucky, amounting to the number of two or three hundred every year, are sure to find [in the black community] on crossing the river." Rev. David Smith recalled that the 1829 riot was just a continuation of the violence that had been aimed at African Americans by the "white companions of blood hounds and negro hunters. In search of fleeing slaves, they would come in our houses at night and maltreat our wives and daughters." The Cincinnati press began to take note of African Americans' involvement in the runaways' cause as early as 1815—activities that included rescuing enslaved persons who passed through the city's port, one of the fugitives a white woman sold into slavery by her husband with their eight children. Josiah Henson found on passing through the Queen City of the West in 1825 that "the colored people gathered round us, and urged us with much importunity to remain with them; told us it was folly to go on;

Cincinnati waterfront, 1848. From the collection of the Public Library of Cincinnati and Hamilton County.

and in short used all the arguments now so familiar to induce slaves to quit their masters." Fugitive Henry Bibb was helped twice by the same Cincinnati-based African American steamboat steward during escapes in the late 1830s along the Ohio River. John Lindsey also used that route to liberty in 1834.[17]

John Malvin, an initiator of the Canada exodus, took part in one such rescue during his brief residence in Cincinnati. Gazing at the river steamers on one occasion, he saw a contingent of thirty enslaved persons being shipped downriver. One of them, Susan Hall, chanced to speak to him. He was amazed to find that they came from the same Virginia county. She knew Malvin's mother well. The thought that this woman should be condemned to a life of bondage in the Deep South was too much for him. "So great was my abhorrence of slavery, that I was willing to run any risk to accomplish the liberation of a slave." He offered to help her and her two young children escape. He surreptitiously boarded the river craft that night, enacting a daring plan. With the freedom of both himself and the fugitives at stake, he decoyed the armed guards who always ac-

companied slave vessels on the Ohio River, diverting their attention
to a nearby boat. "We could see the barrels of their guns glisten in
the moonlight." At any moment, they could have commenced firing
at him. His ruse worked. He also helped three other persons to
safety. The night's work was not a total success, however. Susan
Hall's daughter had to be left behind to the fate that awaited African
Americans sold to the Cotton Belt. Even then Malvin's interest in
the woman he had liberated from bondage did not end. He provided
her with the means to live in Cincinnati while she awaited the birth
of her third child. Malvin helped them reach Canada.[18]

Malvin's fellow colonizationist, J.C. Brown, had his own experience to relate. Before Brown left for Canada, he had an unexpected
taste of how any African American living in the frontline zone could
be drawn inexorably into this work. In the mid-1820s, a white Quaker
named Hethers resided in Louisville, where he established a school
for free African American children. Indignant local slaveholders laid
a trap for him, paying an enslaved African American to ask Hethers
to forge free papers for him and help him escape to Canada. Hethers
said he would do so. Evidently knowing no one else to help secure
safe passage for the man, he advised the purported fugitive to go
through Cincinnati and look up an African American there named
J.C. Brown, who had recently purchased his freedom and settled in
the city. Hethers was jailed and Brown sent for on the pretext of a
business transaction. As a mob descended on the house where he
was staying, Brown calmly walked out through their midst. As the
son of his former white owner and the latter's biracial enslaved
woman, Brown could not be distinguished from his pursuers, and
none of them knew him by sight. A sympathetic white man hid him
on a river steamer bound for Cincinnati. Ten miles out of port, the
fugitive freeman was discovered by the steamship's captain, who knew
of Brown's predicament—and the reward offered for his capture. The
captain had Brown seized and bound. Like thousands of other African Americans, Brown arrived in the Cincinnati harbor in chains.
After his release, he had a warrant issued against the captain on
charges of false imprisonment, but it was never served. Brown later
recalled bitterly, "I got no recompense nor justice for that treatment."[19]

In 1845 John Parker found himself conscripted into the clandestine forces that conducted the struggle against slavery along the
banks of the Ohio. Parker had recently purchased his freedom in
Alabama, settling in Cincinnati. An African American neighbor talked

John Parker House, Ripley, Ohio. From the collection of the Ohio Historical Society.

him into participating in the rescue from slavery of two young girls just south of Maysville, Kentucky. The friend soon turned back, but Parker was determined to see the mission through. For the first of many times, Parker stole secretly into Kentucky by himself, and located the people he was to assist. They did not make his task any easier: "They had on not only their mistress' tilter hoops, one had on four dresses, the other confessed to three and much underwear. . . . In addition to this extra clothing each had brought a bundle almost as large as herself filled with trinkets and satin slippers, and other truck down to a frying pan, with which they proposed to fry their bacon on the road." Parker surreptitiously divested them of their excess baggage as he loaded them on a boat to cross to safety.[20]

As he guided the boat, he became aware that they had not stolen away without notice. "Just before I reached a low pass through the high hills, I heard the rhythmical beat of oars back of us. Then I knew the bundles left behind had told their deadly story." Parker managed to reach the shore before the slave catchers, and the three made their escape into the hills. Even then they were far from being out of danger. Ripley, Ohio, was full of the news of the escape and of officers charged with retrieving the fugitives. The nearby African American settlement to which Parker had been instructed to head had been thoroughly searched and was under surveillance. "The man I wanted would not leave his house in our company but told me to take the girls and hide under the Third Street bridge and wait." It was then that Parker was initiated into the secret network of activists banded together to make successful escapes possible. He became one of its most active, daring, and successful operatives, settling defiantly in Ripley, his house right on the Ohio River's northern bank.[21]

With the climate of hostility toward African Americans that existed in the Northwest, fugitives were more likely to look to a source that provided significant hope of receiving support: the black communities along the border dividing free soil from slave. This trust was all the more natural as, in the words of William Wells Brown, "The slave is brought up to look upon every white man as an enemy to him and his race." John Little concurred: "I supposed a white man would be my enemy, let me see him where I would." Everyone who took an interest in the fate of fugitives from slavery seemed to agree that during the first few decades of the nineteenth century the business of helping refugees on the front lines was a virtual African American monopoly along most of the Ohio River—and often for a considerable distance north. No one had yet thought of calling the clandestine facilities for aiding fugitives on their journey out of slavery the Underground Railroad.[22]

The chances of success were far better if operatives in the underground could rely on nearby help. For that reason, the early centers of activity consisted of communities that could band together for self-defense when necessary. During his escape, Henry Bibb found shelter for the winter with the residents of the African American settlement at Perrysburgh, Ohio, "many of whom were fugitive slaves," he reported. The African American community in Cabin Creek, Indiana, along the Ohio border, had become expert at handling the alarms that resulted from its active underground work. Slave hunters bent on applying force were frequent visitors in their midst. Given the legal constraints that hemmed African Americans in on all sides, such open conflicts required a combination of boldness and ingenuity. When a slave catcher appeared with a constable, a writ, and a posse of local "roughs," the situation appeared hopeless for the two young girls being chased. The house they were staying in was surrounded—the only other person at home their elderly grandmother. She was determined, however, to sacrifice her own life if necessary to save them from a return to slavery. While a neighbor gave the prearranged signal to rouse the populace, the old woman "seized a corn-cutter and placed herself in the only door of the cabin, defying the crowd and declaring that she would cut the first man in two who undertook to cross the threshold." Her stead-fast resolve stopped them just long enough for help to arrive. The young girls' uncle, with some other men, joined the woman barring the door—the small cabin's only egress. But the danger was by no means over. The law was on the side of the bounty hunters, who would have to end the standoff by claiming the "fugitives from ser-vice," as the Fugitive Slave Law deemed the girls. The uncle bought extra time by demanding to see the writ and disputing its fitness and legality. The posse, growing angrier and more violent, demanded entry, which finally was granted to avoid a bloodbath that would end the existence of the community. The slave catchers ransacked the premises, but could find no trace of the young girls. During the commotion, they had dressed as boys, slipped out, and were taken to safety on horseback.[23]

The Chillicothe, Ohio, African American community found itself in a similar position when a white Methodist minister betrayed a fugitive from enslavement in his congregation for the one hundred dollar reward. The husband and father of three was seized by three armed men, who tied a rope around his neck and bodily dragged him along the road leading south. As the posse attempted to rapidly remove him from town, word of the kidnapping circulated among the town's African American population. A large group of two hun-dred, by one count, caught up with the slave catchers a few miles from town. The latter, hopelessly outnumbered, cut loose their prey and fled. The man was never again molested, though he remained resident in Chillicothe, only some forty miles from the Ohio River.[24]

Given the principle of safety in numbers, communal institu-tions became important centers of underground activities, none more so than churches. The oldest in the Northwest lay within a short distance of the Ohio River. The Macedonia Missionary Baptist Church had been founded by African Americans in Lawrence County, Ohio, in 1813, its underground work probably commencing soon after its religious. The Cincinnati African American community had two churches that served both functions: Zion Baptist and Union Bap-

Susan Gordon (holding her infant grandson), manumitted from Virginia slavery in 1849 with thirty-six others, all of whom became members of the Macedonia Missionary Baptist Church, Lawrence County, Ohio. From the collection of Owen Pleasant.

tist. Cincinnati boasted other societies as well that served directly or indirectly in aiding the steady stream of fugitives that passed through. When David Smith, a self-purchased freeman, arrived in Cincinnati in 1831, he found the community desperately in need of basic services, including a place to bury its dead. He organized a benevolent society that soon began operations, working to strengthen community ties that certainly facilitated the ongoing underground work. The Iron Chest Company, a mutual aid society to which belonged such notables as John Woodson and Gideon Mercer Langston, worked more directly to aid fugitives.[25]

No Cincinnatian had a more distinguished record of community service than Henry Boyd, who probably had a longer tenure in the city's underground than anyone, having settled in the city in the late 1820s—some two decades prior to Levi Coffin—and remaining active until the end of the Civil War. Boyd was born at the beginning of the nineteenth century and spent the first two decades of his life

Susan Gordon with descendants of members of the Macedonia Missionary Baptist Church, Lawrence County, Ohio, circa 1909. From the collection of Owen Pleasant.

in slavery. Having at least once attempted to escape, he eventually succeeded in buying his way out by working literally day and night. Arriving in Cincinnati with nothing but his considerable skill as a carpenter, he found all avenues of employment shut off to him. He was forced to hire himself out to slaveholders—who alone in the vicinity were willing to employ African Americans. By the mid-1830s he had amassed the tidy sum of $3,000 and employed several white journeymen and one African American. A decade and a half later he had accumulated the enormous fortune of $420,000 as a successful bedstead manufacturer. He amassed such wealth despite devoting large portions of his resources to helping others out of slavery—not only his brother and sister, but others to whom he bore no relation. His house became a refuge to the destitute, including an elderly man reputedly over age one hundred who had been dumped on the Cincinnati docks to die. The *Anti-Slavery Record* wrote of Boyd, "Without having received a day's schooling in his life, Henry Boyd is well read in history, has an extensive and accurate knowledge of geography, is an excellent arithmetician, and is remarkable for his morality, generosity, and all those traits which mark a noble character." When Martin Delany traveled to the city in the late 1840s, he wrote that Boyd's "name is widely known among abolitionists." Much later, abolitionist Huntington Lyman, a Cincinnati resident who allowed the "Underground men" use of his horse, was under the impression that Boyd's residence, not Coffin's, was "Station A" on the clandestine network. He maintained that Boyd even had a secret room where up to five fugitives at a time could be hidden. Joining Boyd as one of the "Old Guard" of Cincinnati's underground "directors" (as antislavery minister Calvin Fairbank identified them) was William Watson, whose participation also dated to this early period of activity.[26]

Cincinnati was certainly one of the early Underground Railroad's most vibrant river port centers. But it was far from alone. Madison, Indiana, some forty miles downriver, was a close second. By the mid-1830s, the African American farming community located just a few miles from the center of town boasted more than 130 persons. Underground operations dated to at least 1830, according to local sources, though Levi Coffin reported receiving fugitives who passed through African American hands even earlier. Whatever its exact start date, there was a functioning "secret road" by the early 1830s in the hands of the African Americans of Madison and its surrounding communities. When Edward Abdy passed through in 1834, he got to see it in action. A female fugitive had been concealed at the house of Fountain Thurman, a self-purchased, formerly enslaved man who had become a prosperous farmer. Having made her way to Madison, the runaway, as seemed safest, tried her luck among its African American residents, finding her way to the home of Thurman, who hailed from the same part of the Bluegrass state. The African American community in the vicinity contributed money to aid her in making her way out of slavery.[27]

William Anderson, later described by the *Louisville Courier* as "the Chief of the Abolitionists of Madison," became one of Madison's central operatives from the time he moved there in 1836. Anderson had been born in Virginia to a free mother and an enslaved father but was first apprenticed to a slaveholder and later stolen into slavery. Enduring a two-month forced march in chains hundreds of miles into Tennessee at the age of fifteen, he spent the next decade in bondage. During that time, he made two escape attempts. The first one ended with his betrayal by "Northern men with southern principles" in Indiana. On his return, he received five hundred lashes and a salt bath. On his third try, this time from New Orleans, he succeeded in getting aboard a steamship headed north up the Mississippi—assisted by an African American steward on board. Reaching the Ohio, he contrived to make his way to the Indiana side, settling in Madison. Anderson became a minister and "preached and lectured" against slavery. In the course of his twenty-year residence, he also aided more than one hundred African Americans who had fled enslavement, involving "many instances of narrow risks of life and limb."

> My two wagons, and carriage, and five horses were always at the command of the liberty-seeking fugitive. Many times have my teams conveyed loads of fugitive slaves away while the hunters were close upon their track. I have carried them away in broad daylight, and in the grim shades of night. I have scouted through the woods with the fleeing slave while the barbarous hunters pursued as if chasing wolves, panthers or bears. . . . I had learned by sad experience how the poor hound-driven slave pants for freedom from such inhuman bondage— how the heart is made to leap with joy when a friend indeed offers the protection sought. No, my whole duty must include this kindness to my unfortunate fellow beings.[28]

Like the majority of frontline outposts, the Madison underground had considerable ties on the slave side of the Ohio River. Many of the fugitives they received were forwarded to them by African Americans, both free and enslaved, in Kentucky. A woman named Rachel, born in Kentucky but sold into Mississippi, made it all the way back to Kentucky on her journey out of slavery, where she was helped by her African American friends. An enslaved man rowed her across the river and directed her to Madison's African American community. She remained there some time before the recapture of a fugitive nearby convinced her and her hosts that it would be better for her to move on. John White took advantage of connections in Rising Sun, Indiana—virtually the only African American community between Madison and Cincinnati—to make good his escape.[29]

Others, however, including the few that received help from sympathetic whites, simply sought comfort where they felt most likely to find it. Henry Bibb crossed into Madison, but only long enough to board a steamboat for Cincinnati, where he felt surer of meeting with friends. A group of seventeen fugitives from Kentucky, men and women, paid a sympathetic poor white man to take them across the Ohio. Landing near Madison, they took to the woods before a chance encounter with an African American Madisonian connected them to the underground. A group of twelve led by fugitive Louis Talbert was less fortunate. Eight were recaptured near Madison before the rest found friends and made it through. Talbert subsequently took up residence in the Cabin Creek community, joining the select group of operatives who crossed deep into enemy lines to rescue others.[30]

It was dangerous work on the front lines. Louis Talbert was recaptured in one of his forays into Kentucky in search of his sisters, put on public display as a warning to others, and finally sold back into slavery in the Deep South. Henry Bibb, too, was recaptured on his return for his wife and child. It was not even necessary to operate in slave territory to face the worst. Levi Coffin noted, "In the counties of Indiana bordering the Ohio River, fugitives were in as much danger of being captured as on the other side of the river, for there were many persons on the look-out for them who hoped to get the rewards offered by the slaveholders in such cases." Milton Clarke's public assistance of fugitives in Oberlin, Ohio, led to his arrest as a fugitive himself. Remaining in the frontline zone became too dangerous for one of Madison's principal operatives in the underground movement, George De Baptiste. He was forced to relocate to Detroit, where he could seek refuge across the river in Canada in case of extreme peril. The brutal murder of Thomas Woodson Jr. illustrated how slave hunters treated African Americans who were known to aid fugitives.[31]

By the late 1830s, underground operations along the Ohio River had intensified. Kentucky dispatched two emissaries to the Ohio Legislature to attempt to convince its northern neighbor to do something to stem the tide. The owner of Moses Roper preferred to sell him rather than risk his escape when the slaveholder found himself compelled to transport his possessions through part of Ohio. *Philanthropist* editor James Birney wrote to New York abolitionist Lewis Tappan, "The Slaves are escaping in great numbers through Ohio to Canada." He added, "Such matters are almost uniformly managed by the colored people." When Adam Rankin, the oldest son of Ripley's famous Rev. John Rankin, arrived in Cincinnati in 1836, his contacts in the underground missions he undertook were uniformly African American. Henry Bibb, passing through Cincinnati in 1838, was assisted by African Americans, including Jemima and Thomas Woodson's son John, who piloted him out of town and gave him money. Edward Moxley's 1837 escape from Kentucky slavery was also made possible by African Americans in Ohio. His father had bought his freedom and moved to Cincinnati, where he arranged the escape of several members of his family. They made a midnight crossing of the Ohio River, and by daylight were miles north of the city, passing through a network of African American contacts in and around Dayton, Urbana, and Sandusky, Ohio, and on to Canada. Their journey was not without incident. Of the original nine, only six made it through, though the remaining three were successful in a later escape.[32]

The Ohio River brought a steadily growing supply of fugitives like Edward Moxley and his family. Charles B. Ray found on investigating Wheeling, Virginia (later West Virginia): "This species of property, they cannot keep here; as soon as they are sufficiently old, to be of any service to their masters . . . they are off to provide for themselves. . . . The best of all was that none have recently been overtaken who have exercised this inalienable right. Our informant told us, he had known slaves to be missing, and in fifteen minutes a strict search set on foot, to no possible purpose, and they [were] never heard of unless by intelligence from Canada." An Ohio newspaper gathered information from African American contacts who reported over a thousand such fugitives that they could account for through the 1830s. The editor noted the considerable irony of how much more effective this Canadian "colonization" scheme was than the African variant favored by the American Colonization Society: "The secrecy of the society in its operations, is another strong recommendation in its favor. It is also cheap and voluntary." From Cincinnati, Birney reported, "Six weeks ago, a young married woman escaped from N[ew] Orleans by Steamboat and was successfully concealed by her colored friends. Yesterday, her husband arrived, and at 5 o'clock in the afternoon they were both in the Stage on their way from this place to Canada."[33]

Around the same time, Frances Jane Scroggins chanced to become part of just such an escape. Like many other African American Cincinnatians, she had been born into Virginia slavery in 1819. Her grandfather, an officer for the American forces in the War of the Revolution, emancipated his child, Scroggins's mother, and her four young daughters. No longer enslaved, they were nevertheless left

Frances Scroggins Brown, Cincinnati underground
operative. From the collection of the National Afro-
American Museum and Cultural Center.

without means. Frances Scroggins had to be put into apprenticeship that so often led to re-enslavement. Though she suffered frequent beatings, she was fortunate. Her mother remarried a freeman,
and Scroggins was reclaimed from bondage. The family migrated to
Ohio, and around the age of twenty Scroggins went to Cincinnati,
where she boarded at the home of Major James Wilkerson.[34]

Wilkerson had much in common with his young lodger. He, too,
had been born into slavery in Virginia—and his grandfather had
also been an officer in the Revolutionary army, a colonel under Gen.
Horatio Gates at the Battle of Saratoga, where the Americans val-
iantly held off the British. In 1835 at the age of twenty-two, Wilkerson
bought his freedom and that of his mother, both by then in New
Orleans. He also was a newcomer to Cincinnati, brought by David
Smith from New Orleans in 1838 to take a ministry in the African
Methodist Episcopal Church. Finally, Wilkerson and Scroggins

shared a hatred for the bondage they had been born into and in which languished the majority of people of African descent in the United States. Frances Scroggins became an active member of a Wilkerson household devoted to the cause of abolitionism and the assistance of runaways.[35]

When a young African American woman asked her for assistance, therefore, she did not hesitate. Caroline had stepped off a steamboat in the Cincinnati harbor, her master in hot pursuit. Though a newcomer to the city and the excitement of its escape dramas, Frances Scroggins knew just what to do. She took the woman's hand and ran with her through Cincinnati's streets to the nearest place of safety. The master, who saw them enter that abode, forcefully demanded the return of his enslaved woman. While he was briefly detained at the front door, Caroline was rushed out the back. Within seconds she was hidden at a neighbor's house—a process that was repeated until she was safely out of Cincinnati and on her way to Canada. James Birney observed to a fellow abolitionist back east that this work by the African American community was starting to create the prospect that Cincinnati could take on an "abolition character." So frightened of such a development were the slaveholders to the immediate south and their allies on both sides of the river that they opted for an open frontal assault in the guerilla war.[36]

The increased activity of the underground along the river was not lost on those whose property was thus threatened. Supporters of American slavery were particularly appalled by the declaration by an Ohio judge in 1841 that any enslaved person transported into that state was thereby rendered legally free. From as far away as Louisiana came calls for Ohio to desist from its role in encouraging escapes, or to "prepare for non-intercourse" with the South. But the real threat to the antislavery underground arose much closer to home, in the form of the slavery forces dominating the southern bank of the Ohio, as well as their allies living on the northern side.[37]

In the summer of 1841 the tension in Cincinnati was palpable. At issue was the growing threat the antislavery underground posed to the coexistence of Cincinnati with the slavery just across the river. The *Cincinnati Enquirer* editorialized, "[A]bolition influence had so far prevailed, that a citizen of the slave States could not come to Cincinnati to trade—to spend the warm months, or pass the night in course of traveling, without having his negro servants decoyed or

John Mercer Langston, Cincinnati resident during
the 1841 riot. From the collection of the Ohio Historical Society.

stolen away." The word began to spread: Keep your slaves as far
from Cincinnati as possible. Slaveholders willing to summer in Cincinnati—once a commonplace occurrence—were becoming something of a rarity. They took their business to other locales, or so the
Cincinnati proslavery press attempted to convince the population
of the Ohio Valley. The illicit traffic in stolen (human) property was
bad for business. Abolitionism was "ruining the city." The editor of
the *Western Christian Advocate* (an organ of the Methodist Episcopal Church) opined, "The effect of abolition on the temper and ex-
pectations of the colored people of the North has been bad; and we
dread serious results from the lessons they have received, or de-
duced from abolition doctrines and measures." What they would

learn from a movement aimed at securing their liberty was that they were entitled to live freely in America, South and North.[38]

One of these freedom-seeking African Americans in Cincinnati was John Mercer Langston, the young son of Lucy Jane Langston, born into Virginia slavery, and Ralph Quarles, a wealthy Virginia plantation owner and an officer in the Revolutionary army. Though Lucy Langston was acquired as Quarles's property, she ended as his common-law wife. The two openly cohabited in the large residence attached to Quarles's Louisa County plantation, managed by Quarles and made profitable by slave labor. Since Quarles had freed Langston, her later children were free from birth, including the youngest, John, born in 1829. He would later recall his childhood fondly, remembering the attention lavished on him by both parents. It did not last long. In 1834 Lucy Langston and Ralph Quarles died within a short time of one another. Though well provided for in their father's will, John and his brothers were forced by Virginia law to leave their home. Ohio became their adopted home, as it did for most refugees from the cradle of American independence. After spending some years in other parts of the state, Langston arrived in Cincinnati in 1840 to join two of his brothers. One of them, Gideon, had established himself as a leader in the Cincinnati black community. John Langston boarded with the family of John Woodson, the eighth of Jemima and Thomas's eleven children. At age twenty-two, John Woodson had already begun to make his mark in Cincinnati's African American society as a successful craftsman who was beginning a career as an educator and clergyman.[39]

From the time young Langston arrived, he sensed the coming of a racial storm. The first forays in the looming battle occurred in late June of 1841, when an escapee from northern Kentucky was tracked to the house of Cornelius Burnett, a man described as a "swaggering Englishman," whose ties to the underground extended back more than a decade. The fugitive was recovered on the basis of a warrant served by Cincinnati constable Robert Black. This happened, however, only after a brawl between Burnett, his three sons, three neighbors, and the Kentuckians who had come to claim their bondsman resulted in serious injury to two of those involved and slight harm to Black. Burnett and his associates were immediately arrested and asked to post three thousand dollars bond, which they refused. That night, a mob numbering "several hundred persons" gathered at the Burnett residence, broke a few windows, began "an attack . . . upon the door," and exhibited "very decided manifestations of a determination to break into the house, for the purpose of destroying whatever might be therein," before the authorities finally succeeded in breaking up the violent assemblage. The editor of the *Daily Gazette* could not forbear remarking with prescience, "This is peace-loving and law-abiding Cincinnati!"[40]

Once again, the spirit of the mob was about to be unleashed on the African American community. Langston later wrote, "For several weeks feeling against the Abolitionists, so-called, friends of the colored people, and against the colored people themselves, had been showing itself in high and open threats, conveyed in vulgar, base expressions, which indicated the possibility and probability of an early attack upon both the classes mentioned." The antiblack sentiment among proslavery Cincinnatians reached its highest pitch since the riot of 1829. Once again, calls for enforcing the Black Laws began to be heard. The *Enquirer* commented, "We heard an impudent negro . . . boasting that [the Black Laws] could not be enforced." African Americans, it insisted, were enjoying "pretensions and privileges that they neither deserved nor could appreciate." The editors of Cincinnati's Democratic newspaper wrote, "To this we invoke every good citizen—we entreat, we enjoin upon every man . . . to array himself on the side of the whites—on the side of justice to our own citizens—justice to our own interests."[41]

On Friday, September 3, 1841, a full-scale racial riot broke out. "About nine o'clock, a large ruffianly company, coming over from the adjacent towns of Kentucky, called together a large number of the baser sort of the people of Cincinnati, and opened, without the least delay, an outrageous, barbarous and deadly attack upon the entire class of the colored people," John Mercer Langston wrote. Major Wilkerson took charge of trying to hold off the white mob that threatened Cincinnati's African American community. "Never did man exhibit on the field of danger greater coolness, skill and bravery, than this champion of his people's cause," Langston declared. Cincinnati's African Americans took up defensive positions protecting their property, armed with rifles and muskets. "They were ready to follow Major Wilkerson even to death," Langston noted. With Wilkerson leading the charge, the African American fighters drove the mob back with a well-executed counterattack. Rumors were spread that the African Americans' fire had killed a number of whites; it was later admitted that a Kentucky man had been the only one to die. The *Daily Times* reported, "[T]he coroner assures us that the reports in circulation that many have been killed are without foundation."[42]

The mob responded by taking deadly aim at the African American defenders with a cannon. Three times they fired it at the house where the African Americans made their stand. The black combatants were finally compelled to retreat. "The diabolism of this mob reached its highest pitch, when thousands of infuriated, ungovernable ruffians, made mad by their hatred of the Negro and his friends, came down Main Street with howls, and yells, and screams, and oaths, and vulgarities, dragging the press of Dr. Bailey, the great Abolition editor, which they threw, in malignant, Satanic triumph, into the river," Langston wrote.[43]

Cincinnati's largest circulation newspaper, the *Daily Times*, noted that the riot represented, in no small part, an attack by the forces of slavery just across the river. "It is generally believed that many of the most forward and efficient leaders of the rioters were volunteers from Kentucky, urged on by a feeling of revenge, created by the action of the abolitionists in relation to the runaway slaves who take refuge in this city." The response of the Cincinnati authorities to this incursion was as revealing as it was draconian: they gave into vigilantism by not just threatening but actually *enforcing* for the first time in its history the provision of the Black Laws that had occasioned the 1829 riot. In the aftermath of the most intense skirmishes, no fewer than 330 African American men were rounded up by forces that the *Daily Times* characterized as "unauthorized persons." African Americans "were hunted up with indefatigable industry, all over the city, and some were found secreted in the culverts, and various other out of the way places."[44]

The invasion force from Kentucky—with those from the Ohio side who aided and abetted it—seemed to work hand in glove with city, county, and state authorities in Cincinnati. The prisoners were "placed within the line of sentinels around the district under Martial Law," then promptly jailed under the pretext of protecting them from the mob. On the contrary, the men's incarceration left African American women and children, as well as the property belonging to the black community, open to assault. That day "the Sheriff, City Marshal, and other officers of the city examined thoroughly the premises of the blacks"—ostensibly to enact a decision of a white "citizens' meeting" to enforce the Fugitive Slave Law of 1793. As a result,

"several runaway slaves" were taken into custody. (It was later reported that "Claimants have appeared, we learn, for all of them.")
After nightfall, with the men behind bars, the mob descended once
again on the African American sections of town. Despite an order by
the sheriff to disperse the rioters, the occupying troops refused to
intervene, falsely contending that they lacked authority to do so. In
the ensuing violence "the mob attacked their property, destroyed it,
drove out the women and children from their houses, and some
ruffians went as far as to ravish the person of a young black girl."[45]

Subsequent events revealed that the African American men had
been detained not for their own protection, but because authorities
suspected them of violating the Act of 1807, which required persons
of color to post bond before entering the state. The illegality of the
procedure led the *Daily Times* to label the judicial process by which
they were tried "semi official." The majority were either required to
post bond, or were released upon providing a "certificate of nativ-
ity." At least one hundred, however, were either required to leave
town or held "for further disposition under the laws."[46]

In the aftermath of the violence, anti-African American sentiment
continued to simmer. An outraged resident reported that he had witnessed the transporting of two more fugitives through "the negro boarding house on Gano street." Increasing his wrath, he observed that
"[t]he house was full of negroes, and one of them insolently boasted
that the woman with whom he was staying, was a slave." He noted
that such activities had been the "first cause of the late riots." Three
weeks after the riot, sentiments like these led to a public meeting to
form an "Anti-Abolitionist Society" that proclaimed, "Experience shows
that the two races cannot live on terms of equality. And while we will
protect the black man from inhumanity, we shall firmly and steadily
endeavor to fix him in his proper place." It renewed the call for the
enforcement of the Black Laws and proceeded to appoint a "vigi-
lante committee to investigate whether the city and township authorities have put in force the law of 1807, respecting negroes residing
amongst us." The Cincinnati Colonization Society redoubled efforts
to convince African Americans that removal to Africa constituted
the only solution—and again met with an unequivocal rebuff. Mob
violence had as its goal the intimidation of African Americans into
quitting their Ohio homes and communities and ceasing their frontline struggle. Their refusal to be harassed into emigration—and even

more so their continuation of underground activities—signaled how little the mob had succeeded.[47]

Cincinnati was not the only location to experience a race riot that year. Dayton, Cleveland, and African Americans across the border in Indiana were targeted by similar violence. There was, however, a difference in the quality of the attacks on the antislavery forces in the aftermath of the 1841 riot as compared to that of 1829. This time, some of the most potent vitriol was aimed at white persons. The Anti-Abolitionist Society declared, "We speak plainly in order to prevent misunderstanding, we war against Abolitionists— white men—who, disregarding the misery of the whites, make a parade of their kindly feelings towards the blacks." This new target of the wrath of the "mobocrats" showed that an important change had taken place in the period between Cincinnati's two antebellum racial riots. Kentucky supplied Cincinnati with more than just fugitives from enslavement and revenge-minded representatives of the forces of slavery. It also provided, together with its neighboring slaveholding states, the impetus for the emergence of a strong white presence in the Northwest's antislavery underground.[48]

4

Band of Angels

I looked over Jordan and what did I see,
Coming for to carry me home?
A band of angels coming after me,
Coming for to carry me home.
                                        African American spiritual

Virginia natives John Fairfield and John Parker had much in common. Frontline operatives in the struggle against slavery, both willingly crossed into the South in pursuing their objectives. Both were said to have liberated hundreds of enslaved African Americans. Parker's efforts on behalf of the enslaved meant that his life was in constant danger. He later wrote, "I never thought of going uptown without a pistol in my pocket, a knife in my belt, and a blackjack handy. Day or night I dared not walk on the sidewalks, for fear that someone might leap out of a narrow alley at me." So deeply ingrained did this habit become that it never left him, though he lived until 1900. Commencing his operations in the early 1830s, Fairfield was among the most daring conductors on the Underground Railroad for a period of two decades, operating throughout the South in the course of his career. He made the fugitives he guided pledge to fight to the death rather than submit and told them he would shoot them down if they displayed cowardice. "Slaveholders are all devils, and it is no harm to kill the devil. I do not intend to hurt people if they keep out of the way, but if they step in between me and liberty, they must take the consequences."[1]

Fairfield and Parker had more than their position as frontline operatives in common. The fathers of both were wealthy slaveholders, probably from Virginia. While Parker derived from his mother the status of an enslaved person, Fairfield inherited from his father a fortune founded on the proceeds of slavery. Unlike Parker, he had never himself tasted that form of human bondage and would never face a threat to himself or his liberty on account of his race. Instead, he risked his freedom and his life by his actions. He renounced the privileged existence that he could have had as the *acknowledged* son of a wealthy father, casting his lot instead with the dispossessed in the struggle for the liberty that their nation denied them. There is no Fairfield in any Virginia census from 1810 to 1850, so it would appear that either the name Fairfield was a *nom de guerre*, as is most probable, or that Fairfield was not really from Virginia—or both. In any case, a number of independent and corroborating accounts attest to his prominence in the underground; four alone confirm his most famous trip with twenty-eight fugitives. Marven Butler is the only one who identifies Fairfield's home as Camden, Virginia (present-day West Virginia), and gives his approximate date of birth. Other corroborating accounts include periodic reports from Virginia and Kentucky telling of mysterious strangers who showed up in small towns under assumed names and left some time later with a group of fugitives. In early 1844 such a "slave stealer" carried off six fugitives from Winchester, Virginia, and later wrote to a free African American there that "they were well and on their way to Canada." The man was never caught. Given his mode of life and the evident cause of his death, it is not at all surprising that little trace should remain of Fairfield. The few accounts of his life and work serve as a useful reminder of the nature of an underground movement.[2]

The bravery, skill, and resourcefulness of African American operatives on the front line were unquestionable. Their ability to strike deep into Southern territory and make it back out was nothing short of remarkable. More than one even returned to freedom after capture. Taken on an expedition into Kentucky, Louis Talbert was sold down the river, but with timely help by an African American woman working on board the boat, he slipped off along the Mississippi and disappeared into a network of enslaved African Americans who got him back to Indiana. His case is not unique.[3]

Still, an underground movement, however organized the African American community, however intrepid its operatives, could not succeed without a network of supporters, like John Fairfield, whose position in society gave them the room to maneuver. Beneficiaries of the privileges of full citizenship in the North, able to travel

in the South without exciting suspicion, social position made them
a powerful motive force both in organizing frontline operations and
in securing support in the rear—the territory into which fugitives
had to disappear. Building such a support base, however, would
take considerable time in the climate of the early Northwest.[4]

The first offers of help came from what might have seemed an
unlikely source. Led by the Ohio Valley's two most famous white
operatives, John Rankin and Levi Coffin, a handful of white migrants from the South appeared on the scene to fill key positions as
an interracial underground began to take shape in the Ohio Valley.
Not everyone was surprised by their origins. Marven Butler, himself
a committed activist, was very familiar with the white participants
in the antislavery movement in Indiana and surrounding states.
John Fairfield, however, impressed him as no other he had met. He
remembered, "No Abolitionist raised and living in the north could
equal him in his hatred and denunciation of slavery."[5]

Fairfield was not alone in such feelings. The movement that
came to be called the Underground Railroad would never have gotten off the ground without the dedicated group of whites who hailed
from the South, providing the African Americans engaged in the
life-and-death struggle with American slavery indispensable allies
in their frontline struggle. If the South had bequeathed to the Ohio
Valley much of its proslavery animus, it also ironically supplied it
with some of its most ardent and militant antislavery white activists—willing to risk their reputations, their fortunes, their freedom,
and even their lives. It might not be too much to say that the Underground Railroad in the region would have taken much longer to
initiate without the zeal they brought to the cause they espoused.
Their fervor was equal to that with which the love of slavery inspired
in leaders of the South. Having witnessed—and learned to hate—
slavery at close quarters, they brought not only a passion but also
the willingness and desire to work closely with the African American communities whose existence on the northern bank of the
Ohio defied both Northern and Southern public opinion.

Stanley Harrold, in *The Abolitionists and the South*, has revived interest in the question of the interconnectedness of the
struggle against slavery and activities below the Mason-Dixon Line
and also in "the cooperative spirit of blacks and whites in support
of southern antislavery action." The influence of refugees from the
South also played a strong role in the organization of the Under-

Rankin House, Ripley, Ohio. From the collection of the Ohio Historical Society.

ground Railroad in the Ohio Valley, with the relocation of antislavery groups, such as a large contingent of North Carolina Quakers who moved to eastern Indiana and were already experienced in assisting in escapes from enslavement. Their contribution to the underground movement can hardly be overstated.[6]

Once introduced to the underground struggle along the Ohio River, John Parker decided immediately that therein lay his life's calling. He chose, however, to make Ripley, Ohio, not Cincinnati, his base of operations. Drawing him irresistibly to Ripley was the presence of one extraordinary man—John Rankin. The house belonging to Rankin and his large family, atop a hill overlooking the town, became the single most famous landmark on the Underground Railroad, one said to be immortalized in the African American spiritual *Swing, Low, Sweet Chariot*. The Rankin house always had a light in its window to guide fugitives to its door, which was ever open to them. Frederick Douglass, as always disdaining to divulge details of a war far from over, paid tribute to Rankin's work in his paper,

John Rankin, Ripley underground operative. From the
collection of the Ohio Historical Society.

saying that the latter had "quitted [himself] bravely in the anti-slavery warfare." His literary collaborator, Martin Delany, was far less
reticent: "John Rankin [has been] long and favorably known to the
friends of humanity in this country as a firm friend of the panting
fugitive. His house has been made the resting place for the way-
worn and weary for years, to the great chagrin of the slaveocrats of
his neighborhood, and the slaveholders of Kentucky.—One friend
informs me, and it certainly appears like an over-estimate, that he
has known as many as forty to be there at a time! 'packed away' in
the underground depot." The joint work of John Rankin and John
Parker made Ripley, which probably rivaled Cincinnati in the numbers of fugitives passing through, as important an escape route as
any in the nation.[7]

Born in 1793 in Tennessee, Rankin derived his passionate hatred for the institution of slavery from his mother. Resident in the

South throughout her eighty-two years, she never made a secret of her antislavery views, which she passed along to all of her children. Adam Rankin, the oldest of John Rankin's thirteen children, recalled, "[G]randmother not only persistently presented her anti-slavery and temperance views upon the attention of her children, but also upon the attention of her neighbors and church members." Only one of her progeny, Thomas, ever bought an enslaved person—and in doing so ironically launched one of the most impressive public careers in antebellum America. Upon hearing that his brother had become a slaveholder, John Rankin sent Thomas a series of letters so forceful in nature, so straightforward yet elegantly argued, that the recipient of the letters immediately emancipated those he had held in bondage, brought them to Ohio, saw to their education, and lived out his life a confirmed opponent of the institution. Upon publication, those letters found their way into the hands of a young New Englander, William Lloyd Garrison, and possibly helped convert him to the abolitionist cause, of which he became the best-known proponent.[8]

Having already gained a reputation as a powerful speaker and organizer in the antislavery cause, Rankin was chased out of his native Tennessee and then Kentucky. On January 1, 1822, he and his family crossed the Ohio River in a skiff—as would so many of the fugitives whose first contact with the Underground Railroad would be Rankin's home. He settled in the Ohio river port of Ripley, where he would remain for more than four decades of active service in the frontline struggle. Rankin and his large family took part in the escape of certainly hundreds and perhaps even thousands of fugitives. Though a minister of the gospel, Rankin was as militant a defender of the fugitive from enslavement as any person in America. Threatened, harassed, and occasionally attacked, he never wavered from his commitment to the cause to which he devoted his life.[9]

Rankin not only threw himself into the antislavery struggle but also became a key ally of African Americans in the region. Almost alone among Brown County's residents, he extended the hand of fellowship to the beleaguered residents of the Gist settlements, offering his home for their use when they passed through town, a gesture that incurred the disapproval of his white neighbors. He alone fought to ensure the ordination of a Brown County African American within the Presbyterian Church. His family adopted and raised a young African American girl, who remained with them un-

til she married at age twenty-five. He insisted that white abolitionists pay as much attention to their own comportment and attitudes
toward their African American comrades in arms in the North as to
the cause of abolition.

John Stauffer's description of Gerrit Smith and John Brown as
white men who "embraced the ethic of a black heart" might also be
said to apply to Rankin, who, like his more famous Underground
Railroad contemporaries, came to something of what would today be
called a social constructionist view of race. He argued, "The skin is
but the dress which God has thrown over the human frame. As a
kind father dresses out his daughters in white, red, olive, brown and
black, while he esteems them all alike his children, so the good Father of the Universe has dressed out his children in colors according
to the various climates in which they dwell. All are beautiful; why
should they despise one other?" That "[d]ifference of color, peculiarity
of hair and features are made the occasions of prejudicing men against
their fellow-beings" he deemed "most unreasonable, and highly criminal"—nothing less than a "reproach [of] our Maker." He made clear
that to his mind "such prejudice is one of the blackest crimes of the
human heart. It ought to be, and it can be abolished."

Martin Delany expressed skepticism about the belief in equality
of most abolitionists, particularly in the West. But Rankin's un-
swerving views on that account "I believe to be beyond a controversy," Delany told the readers of Douglass's *North Star*. Though
Rankin's views were to some extent a function of his religious be-
liefs, his crusade against slavery and racism reflected tenets as deeply
held as his Christianity. An Indiana Quaker abolitionist attending
an antislavery meeting at which Rankin spoke was "surprised" to
hear the Presbyterian minister declare, "[I]f you convince me that
the bible sustains such an institution as American slavery, then I
will trample the bible under my feet."[10]

Few exceeded John Fairfield's zeal for the antislavery cause or his
accomplishment as a frontline operative. When he was once put in
jail, he vowed to liberate one enslaved person for every day he was
incarcerated in the Bracken County, Kentucky, prison. He kept his
word. A short time later he arrived in Cincinnati with a group of
twenty-eight fugitives from Kentucky slavery—heading straight for
the home of his good friend John Hatfield. As bands of slave catchers descended on the city, the escapees from slavery marched out of

it in the guise of a funeral procession, made tragically real by the death of an infant carried out of Kentucky slavery in her mother's arms.[11]

The author of that bold stroke was native North Carolinian Levi Coffin, known to friend and foe as the "President of the Underground Railroad"—a title by which he even introduced himself to a visiting minister, a formerly enslaved man from Kentucky. The Coffins' Cincinnati home came to be known to many as "Command Central" of the Underground Railroad. In time, Levi and Catherine Coffin and their two daughters were in constant contact with a network of activists who operated from various points along the route to Canada in the states of Ohio, Indiana, and Michigan. By then, Coffin could arrange safe passage for fugitives at a moment's notice.[12]

It had not always been so. The popular image of the Underground Railroad is one of a smoothly functioning organization—one so much a part of the nation's Northern terrain that it would almost seem to have been laid together with the roads and later railroad tracks that crisscrossed its territory. And yet that was far from the picture presented to John Rankin and Levi Coffin when they moved into the Ohio Valley region in the 1820s. On leaving his home state of North Carolina to settle in Indiana in 1826, Coffin was surprised to find that no one in the Quaker settlement of Newport, Indiana, to which he relocated was willing to associate with runaways. Rather, those fugitives who passed in the vicinity stopped in the African American community nearby. Henry Bibb, traveling north in Ohio, was a case in point. Helped by African Americans in Cincinnati, he stayed in public houses during his subsequent flight northward while his money held out. Josiah Henson and his family were also assisted by "good samaritans" in Cincinnati, evidently white in his case, and then left to find their way to the shores of Lake Erie on their own. The only friendly faces they encountered belonged to a village of Native Americans. William Wells Brown, equally distrustful of all persons, was compelled by the threat of freezing to death as he made his escape in the winter of 1834 to seek shelter from a white Quaker family. Significantly, however, these sympathizers with the oppressed did not forward him on to friends. Lone humanitarians in southern Ohio, they evidently had no contacts with persons farther north. Brown resumed his journey as he had commenced it, alone and left to his own devices, stopping at inns when he could. On joining Buffalo's vigilance committee, he found it to consist solely of African Americans. Milton and Lewis Clarke's 1840 and 1841 flights through Cincinnati followed very similar scripts. Milton's journey northward, like so many others, was prompted by the African Americans in Cincinnati as he passed through on a steamboat, and he, too, fell in with a group of African American operatives in northern Ohio upon arrival. Lewis also went through Cincinnati, found shelter in its black community, and proceded on to Canada, getting only the kind of hospitality that money procured at guest houses. Even earlier, in 1824, James Adams and a comrade found white friends near the Ohio River but again were left to fend for themselves as they journeyed through the state of Ohio happening occasionally upon an isolated ally but no organized network of stations.[13]

After Coffin put out the word among African Americans in his vicinity that his home would be open to those seeking refuge from slavery, his fellow Quakers expressed disapproval of him that was hardly consonant with the antislavery reputation the Society of Friends has since gained. The issue of slavery caused a deep split in the Quaker church. Quaker pioneers like Levi Coffin, his cousin Addison Coffin, Isaac Beeson, Valentine Nicholson, and Laura Haviland found themselves compelled to break off from their meetings into minority splinter groups dedicated to the abolitionist cause. Haviland was even forced to leave the Society of Friends and convert to a different denomination to pursue the cause that consumed a considerable portion of her life. The hostility directed at abolitionists like Coffin and Haviland by their coreligionists contrasts with their reputation for pacifism and mildness—let alone staunch abolitionism. Whatever their antipathy to slavery as an institution, their hostility to African Americans appears to have been even stronger. Despite the opposition of their brethren in England, American Quakers threw the support of their national body behind the colonizationist movement, in the words of Coffin, bringing "the weight of their influence against the few true abolitionists who advocated immediate and unconditional emancipation."[14]

Contrary to the image often portrayed of them, the white population of the Northwest, including such religious groups as the Quakers, did not immediately embrace the cause of the fugitive. Even in the mid-1850s, an Indianapolis newspaper called the operators of the Underground Railroad "a disgrace to our country, men who, in a revolution, would become second Arnolds, with the treason in their hearts which marked the betrayer of Washington, but with none of his bravery." When Jefferson County, Indiana, resident J.H. Tibbetts, a son of one of John Rankin's old friends, first helped a fugitive in 1838 at the age of nineteen, he was sobered by the knowledge that "nine out of every ten men I would meete would condem me for such conduct." Another early participant, Valentine Nicholson, agreed: "[T]here were not many persons in those days who would take the risk of offending popular sentiment, which seemed to be in more sympathy with slaveholders than with slaves who committed the unpopular act of trying to secure their own natural right and Liberty." Like Coffin, the network Tibbetts linked up with was, according to his testimony, largely African American.[15]

Coffin also found allies among fellow antislavery refugees from the South like John Rankin. Though Rankin and Coffin found themselves isolated at first, a strong antislavery movement eventually took root in the Ohio Valley. One of its triggers came in the form of a remarkable series of debates at an upstart Presbyterian theological seminary near Cincinnati that helped shape the course of a region—and a nation.[16]

The odyssey that put James Bradley at the epicenter of the formation of western abolitionism began as it had for so many Africans caught up in the slave trade before him—with his kidnapping from his native land. At the age of "two or three," he later wrote, "the soul-destroyers tore me from my mother's arms, somewhere in Africa, far back from the sea." He was raised on a South Carolina plantation, "always obliged to be in the field by sunrise, and . . . labor[ing] till dark." When his master died after relocating him to the Arkansas territory, Bradley's life changed. His mistress, for whom he managed a plantation, allowed him to hire out his time: "After toiling all day for mistress, I used to sleep three or four hours, and then get up and work for myself the remainder of the night." Nearly a decade later, in 1833, he succeeded in buying his freedom. "As soon as I was free, I started for a free State." He landed in Cincinnati, enrolling in Lane Seminary a year later. "I had for years been praying to God that my dark mind might see the light of knowledge." He planned to spend several years preparing "to preach the gospel." Instead, his principled opposition to the institution of slavery embroiled him in a controversy that led him to resign his position barely a year later.[17]

Bradley's matriculation at the school coincided with the arrival of one of the most talented and important leaders of the abolitionist movement in America, Theodore Weld, a noted reformer from the East who thought he could forward the antislavery cause by enrolling a number of Southern slaveholders' sons at Lane. With Weld's prodding, and perhaps partly inspired by the presence in their midst of the once enslaved Bradley—who was treated, he reported, "as much like a brother by the students, as if my skin were as white, and my education as good as their own"—the focus of these would-be devotees of the cloth soon turned to the issue of slavery. It was fitting that they should have settled on that subject. As one of them observed, "The [Ohio] Valley was our expected field; and we assembled here, that we might the more accurately learn its character, catch the spirit of its gigantic enterprise, grow up in its genius, appreciate its particular wants, and thus be qualified by practical skill, no less than by theological erudition, to wield the weapons of truth." The future of the region would remain, as it had begun, tied to the politics of and the warfare over slavery. Despite the objections of the faculty, which included Calvin Stowe, future husband of Harriet Beecher Stowe, and Lane president Lyman Beecher, Harriet's father, the students determined to examine thoroughly the questions of slavery and the doctrines of colonizationism and abolitionism, an examination that would culminate in ninety hours of debate over seventeen evenings.[18]

Nearly all of the participants were intimately acquainted with slavery. Eleven of the eighteen were from the South—most of them from slaveholding families—and a number of others had lived for a period in the South, or had at least traveled there "making inquiries and searching after truth." Of course, no one knew the conditions of the enslaved better than James Bradley, who assumed a central place in the debate. One of the student leaders, Henry B. Stanton, wrote soon after the conclusion of the discussion that Bradley had "addressed us nearly two hours; and I wish his speech could have been heard by every opponent of immediate emancipation." He met head on the objection most often raised against abolition, that free African Americans, incapable of supporting themselves, would constitute a menace to white society:

> This shrewd and intelligent black, cut up these *white objections* by the roots, and withered and scorched them under the sun of sarcastic argumentation, for nearly an hour, to which the assembly re-

sponded in repeated and spontaneous roars of laughter, which were heartily joined in by both Colonizationists and Abolitionists. Do not understand me as saying, that his speech was devoid of *argument*. No. It contained sound logic, enforced by apt illustrations.

Bradley disposed of the myth of African American dependence on white people simply and efficiently: African Americans "have to take care of, and support themselves *now, and their master, and his family into the bargain*; and this being so, it would be strange if they could not provide for themselves, *when disencumbered from this load.*" Bradley's eloquence and skill, joined with that of likeminded classmates carried the day. When put to a vote, the debaters almost unanimously endorsed the principles of immediate abolitionism without expatriation. The lone slaveholder among them emancipated his bondspersons, and as his classmate expressed it, "now, instead of their working to educate *him*, he is working and studying, and educating *them*." The students formed an abolitionist society—among the first in the West—and a number embarked on decades of service in the antislavery cause.[19]

Perhaps most remarkably, the students reached out to Cincinnati's African American community, which had been recently harassed and brutalized by the events of 1829. The students, probably highly influenced by Bradley's presence and participation in their search for answers, informed the western public so inimical to the presence of African Americans: "We threw ourselves into the neglected mass of colored population in the city of Cincinnati, and that we might heave it up to the light of the sun, established Sabbath, day and evening schools, lyceums, a circulating library, &c.; choosing rather to employ our *leisure hours* in offices of brotherhood to 'the lame, the halt, and the blind,' than to devote them to fashionable calls and ceremonial salutations."

One student in particular, Augustus Wattles, devoted special attention to this work. A native of Oneida, New York, he had recently been elected to head the local chapter there of the Colonization Society. Described by a colleague as "a sincere friend of the negro" (an opinion shared by Lewis Woodson), "and what is quite as rare . . . a consistent and practical man," he did what no other white colonizationist would likely have considered—he canvassed the opinions of dozens of African Americans on the subject. To his surprise and consternation, all, with one exception, spoke against the project.

His discovery threw his thinking into disarray—a confusion that gave way only to enlightenment in the course of the Lane debates. Not waiting for their conclusion, he abandoned his studies "for the purpose of commencing a school for the education of the people of colour in Cincinnati, and . . . devoted himself to the elevation of the free blacks on our own soil, and to the making up of a public sentiment favourable to the abolition of slavery without expatriation." Joined for a short time by his classmate who had liberated his human property, he took up lodgings in the African American community, breaking a social barrier that otherwise almost completely separated the races in the Northwest. In fact, it was reported that he "lived almost exclusively among this part of the population, as it was pretty plainly intimated to him, that his visits would not be acceptable elsewhere." Weld, too, maintained that "while I was at Lane Seminary my intercourse was with the Colored people of Cincinnati I think I may say exclusively."

Other former Lane students took this work to other African American communities elsewhere in Ohio and beyond. That association undoubtedly led to the initiation of at least a few of the Lane students into the work of aiding fugitives. Wattles himself was later named by a fugitive as being centrally involved with the Mercer County African American underground operations. Lane student Huntington Lyman believed that Theodore Weld, Henry Stanton, and a classmate were also involved. James Thome's father, having emancipated his human chattel, was said to be active in forwarding fugitives across the river to nearby Ripley. John Rankin Jr. recalled that when visiting his oldest brother, Adam, at the student dormitories in 1838, he found that a fugitive had been given shelter there for more than a week. Adam Rankin's autobiography, however, conveys exactly the opposite impression—that the Underground Railroad activities he engaged in were the source of considerable friction between himself and other students, faculty, and administrators. He does report one exceptional occasion on which Calvin Stowe aided him in forwarding a fugitive. He nevertheless makes it clear that his contacts in this work were all outside of Lane, among African Americans in the vicinity. Adam Rankin's account corroborates available contemporary source materials but contradicts assumptions that Lane's antislavery reputation implied participation in the underground work of harboring fugitives; further, the account reminds us that the wish to appear to have been in advance of the reality of the times may color post–Civil War claims about decades-long involvement with the Underground Railroad. Overwhelming evidence from the period attests to the Rankin family's participation in the Underground Railroad; much less attests to that of persons associated with Lane Theological Seminary after the time of the student rebels.[20]

One thing is certain: the Lane abolitionist students' intimate involvement with the outcast African American community drew down upon them the wrath of a large portion of white Cincinnati. The students were charged with furthering the ends of amalgamation. As would be the case elsewhere in the West as abolitionists spread the word, unfounded rumors circulated that alleged various sexual improprieties on the part of the seminarians with young African American women of the vicinity. The storm of abuse heaped upon them drew the attention of the trustees of Lane, and the students were ordered to disband their society and desist from antislavery work. Refusing to be silenced or to place their career ambitions above their principled opposition to slavery, forty-nine students, including James Bradley, preferred to withdraw from Lane to a chorus of approval from religious journals throughout the North.[21]

Among the most laudatory voices raised in their defense and in criticism of Lane was that of John Rankin, who as an influential Presbyterian minister became a powerful ally. He wrote a stirring justification of their actions, reminding Lane authorities that "[t]he society was right in itself; it was founded in the noblest feelings of the human heart, and in opposition to one of the blackest sins that ever stained human character. It was brought into existence by the call of degraded, weeping, bleeding, tortured and perishing humanity. How could the humane heart resist such a call?" He charged that the steps taken to destroy it were "of unusual severity." As a champion of the students' cause, Rankin helped introduce Theodore Weld to a larger audience in Ohio, inviting him to speak in and around Ripley on the subject of abolitionism.[22]

Weld, though himself an Easterner, would be instrumental in bringing another renegade Southerner, James Gillespie Birney, to the Ohio Valley. Birney, a former slaveholder and a prominent colonizationist residing in Kentucky, was to become an important founder of the organized western abolitionist movement. Though so recent a convert to the cause of immediate emancipation, he would be among its most energetic exponents. Of particular importance would be his help in pushing the abolitionist movement away from its roots in moral suasion toward tactics of political struggle, a movement in which westerners would be somewhat in advance of many of their Eastern brethren. Birney, too, found himself pulled into underground work, despite his assertion as late as 1837 that he had little or nothing to do with what was an essentially African American enterprise in Cincinnati. In fact, later that year, he was convicted and fined for participation in an escape, pronouncing himself "determined to advocate what I believed to be the truth, to take a high stand on the ground of humanity in assisting the oppressed." Defending him was the West's most famous antislavery attorney, Cincinnati's Salmon P. Chase, veteran representative of fugitives from slavery and those charged with abetting their escapes. Chase's legal work on their behalf led Cincinnati's African American community to present him with a testimonial of their "grateful respect." In bestowing the recognition, A.J. Gordon of the Union Baptist Church praised him for his "remembrance of our brethren in bonds as bound with them" and for his "zealous and disinterested advocacy of the rights and privileges of all classes of [his] fellow-citizens, irrespective of clime, color or condition."[23]

The rush of antislavery activity in Cincinnati and its environs culminated in the founding of the Ohio Anti-Slavery Society in 1835 and the 1836 establishment of its journal, the *Philanthropist*, under Birney's editorship. At the organizing convention, John Rankin delivered the opening address, and he represented the fledgling organization in the field in embarking on a yearlong lecture tour. From the first, Ohio abolitionists would have to contend with the same violence that plagued the existence of African Americans, violence that Rankin had been dealing with for a decade. The formative convention of the antislavery association was moved from the church in which it was supposed to be held to "a barn outside the town amid scenes of mob violence." A year later, an anti-abolitionist riot broke out in Cincinnati, resulting in the destruction of the *Philanthropist*'s printing press.[24]

Western abolitionism picked up steam in succeeding years, the movement spilling over into Indiana, where a state antislavery society was founded in 1838. Indiana's organization was even more closely tied to the Underground Railroad, with its leading figures having gotten their start in antislavery politics through that means. As one Indiana Quaker abolitionist put it, "Our house was always a welcome stopping place for Antislavery speakers as well as for fugitive slaves." Levi Coffin hosted John Rankin and other traveling antislavery orators who canvassed the state in the name of the cause, and Adam Rankin was among the founders of the Indiana Anti-Slavery Society. As with Rankin and Coffin, a large proportion of the founders hailed from the South and had gained their introduction to antislavery politics via participation in the Underground Railroad. The large group of Quakers who had recently migrated to Richmond, Indiana—known as "the Jerusalem of Quakerism for all the northwest"—from North Carolina played a particularly important role, which included spearheading formation of the state antislavery society, whose founding convention was held in the Quakers' Wayne County stronghold. It was in his native North Carolina, according to his cousin, that Levi Coffin first became initiated into the Underground Railroad work he took with him to Indiana. Addison Coffin, too, got his start there. When he moved to Indiana and attended an antislavery convention in Wayne County, he found "two hundred people assembled from the neighboring counties . . . four-fifths of them Carolinians and of Carolina descent." He recalled, "To my surprise the subjects discussed were almost identical with those of the manumissionists in North Carolina twenty years before, and some of the speakers when young men had discussed them in the south."[25]

Given its roots, the more the abolitionist movement emerged as an organized force, the more it advanced the underground work of receiving fugitives forwarded from the frontline communities. Prior to that period, as the experiences of fugitives who went through the Ohio Valley in the 1820s and 1830s attest, there was little more than a scattering of activists, who evidently maintained only the most rudimentary, if any, contact with one another. Only after western abolitionism emerged as a consolidated movement did anything approaching the customary picture of the Underground Railroad begin to coalesce—the more-or-less connected network of operatives filling the terrain from the Ohio River to the Great Lakes. The work advanced slowly. Coffin observed, "Friends in the neighborhood, who had formerly stood aloof from the work, fearful of the penalty of the law, were encouraged to engage in it. . . ." At first they limited their involvement, Coffin said, to contributions of clothing or "aid in forwarding [runaways] on their way." They shied away from "sheltering them under their roof. . . . Some seemed really glad to see the work go on, if someone else would do it. A considerable amount of time would pass before the rear lines of the physical war against slavery were as battle ready as the front lines. That task's completion meant bringing to an end the second phase in building a powerful underground movement against slavery.[26]

African Americans had given the struggle against slavery in the Ohio Valley its initial impetus. The integral connection between the roots of the Underground Railroad and western abolitionism have not hitherto been fully appreciated, and, as a consequence, neither has the centrality of African Americans in creating and sustaining the antislavery movement in the region. The movement took root in the first place on the determined efforts of African Americans to escape bondage. Even at its height the Underground Railroad did not entice African Americans to escape; rather, the loosely organized support operation was formed in response to the constant stream of fugitives. Along the front lines, the precursor to the fully formed movement involved first and foremost the African American communities that sprang up and gained a foothold on the northern bank, a view not traditionally held by scholars. Nevertheless, the integral connection of these beachheads of freedom, the flow of refugees from slavery they drew strength from and in turn nurtured, and the antislavery movement that emerged in the Northwest is so strong that reinterpretation of western abolitionism along these lines is warranted.[27]

This seminal role of African American communities north of the Ohio River has been partly obscured by the barriers to black political participation in the Northwest, conditions that left that form of abolitionism in white hands. Possessed of few rights, disfranchised, and more or less excluded from the polity, they had recourse to few legal forms of struggle. They certainly took what opportunities they could. As early as the 1820s, African Americans in Cincinnati and Chillicothe began concerted campaigns to have the Black Laws repealed. Ohio's general assembly, however, refused to so much as give their petitions a reading throughout most of the antebellum years. A legal, political movement—a necessary complement to a formidable underground movement—was effectively impossible absent white participation. The broader that involvement the better, even if largely confined to the operations supporting the frontline campaign waged by African Americans, as in the efforts of people like Levi Coffin, who received fugitives from points farther South.[28]

This expansion of the movement nevertheless constituted something of a double-edged sword. As the ranks of the antislavery movement swelled with white participants, it was inevitable that not all who joined would match the qualities that made pioneers like John Rankin, John Fairfield, and Augustus Wattles trusted allies and coworkers. Some made an effort to include African Americans— Quaker Valentine Nicholson invited Cincinnati's William Yancy and Cleveland's Julianne Tillman to share the antislavery podium in Harveysburg, Ohio, beside white abolitionists such as Salmon P. Chase—and insisted on integrated schools. But there were those made of different stuff. African American Charles B. Ray thought the difference between the East and the West in its treatment of African Americans spilled over into the abolitionist movement: "Our people in Ohio, in general, Cincinnati not excepted, are too much cut off from intercourse with the white people, and the whites are not enough inclined to bring them into contact, and intercourse with them, abolitionists by no means excepted." Lewis Woodson, who had lived in Ohio and Pennsylvania, thought that such a charge could be brought against virtually all white abolitionists. Isaac Beeson could have served as a case in point, although he was something of an extremist in this respect. A leading member of the antislavery Quaker meeting and willing to brave the ire of his brethren, he was, to be sure, a staunch opponent of slavery and a mainstay of Indiana's antislavery movement. At the same time, he was also a confirmed opponent of social contact between the races. As such, he believed that the long-term solution to the "threat of amalgamation" would require Northern states to takes steps to confine African Americans to the South and whites to the North. His notions were certainly not in the majority among western abolitionists—but neither were the consistent stands that Rankin, Fairfield, and Wattles took against manifestations of racism.[29]

As a result, when the Anti-Slavery Society was formed in Ohio, it eschewed African Americans' participation in their own cause, and, despite being largely acceptable to African Americans, its program was not without its flaws from their standpoint. Insistent that the abolitionist cause was intimately tied to the fate of free African Americans in the North, the founding convention vehemently protested against the restrictive conditions of the North. It pledged, "We shall earnestly seek the emancipation of our free colored citizens from the bondage of oppressive laws and the tyranny of a relentless public sentiment, and extend to them our hearty encouragement and aid in the improvement of their condition and the elevation of their character." That last clause—which fell considerably short of breaking with the prevalent attitude among white Americans toward their fellow nationals of African descent as a "degraded" people—might have given pause to African Americans in the struggle. Moreover, Ohio's white abolitionists seemed to indicate their unwillingness to remove all civil rights' deprivations specific to African Americans, at least not at once: "We do not mean that they shall be immediately put in possession of all political privileges any more than foreigners before naturalization or native citizens not qualified to vote. . . ."[30]

Worse still, the tone of the all-white conferees implied that the participation of African Americans was not important. Further unsettling to African Americans was that while white women were issued a special invitation to membership, no such call was made for African American participation. The *we* in which the conference resolutions were phrased clearly and unambiguously referred to white Ohioans. Nor were appeals made directly to African Americans, who were represented always in the third person, the *they* about which white people, both pro- and antislavery, engaged in political controversy. Quick to assure white public opinion of their opposition to "amalgamation between the white and colored people," most members of Ohio's antislavery society apparently did not frame the struggle in interracial terms. If this was a political struggle, what role were African Americans to play? They did not vote, had no social standing in the North, and held no power over public opinion. Consistent with its mission as the legal, political arm of an underground resistance movement, the Anti-Slavery Society distanced itself from violent struggle. It pronounced itself opposed to liberation by any means enslaved African Americans themselves could effect, and repudiated any attempt at "exciting discontent in the minds of the slaves." On the contrary, in the only direct address to African Americans among its resolutions, African Americans both enslaved and free were advised that "patience, submission, and good conduct on the part of the slaves, not only to such masters as are 'good and gentle' but also to the 'froward' are highly important to the successful inculcation of its principles, and to the ultimate, entire, and peaceful acquisition of those inalienable rights that are now withheld from them."[31]

Conventions in succeeding years stiffened their opposition to the Black Laws and became more encouraging of African American involvement in the antislavery movement. The second anniversary session voted to "approve of the exertions of the colored people in their own behalf, and cordially recommend to the friends of equal rights, throughout the state, to encourage them in their endeavors to elevate themselves." The succeeding year it fulsomely praised "[t]he earnest devotion of the spirit of abolition to the free people of color" as "one of its most striking and beautiful characteristics. In the face of a corrupt public sentiment, which would doom the colored man to perpetual degradation or exile from his native land, and brands with odium every attempt to ameliorate his condition, it comes forth in his behalf, and taking him by the hand, lifts him out of the depths of abasement into which the cruel spirit of caste has plunged him; and proclaims to him that even here his rights shall be acknowledged, and his interests protected."[32]

Such proclamations notwithstanding, an undercurrent of criticism ran within the ranks of white abolitionism in the Northwest with respect to how effectively such words were put into practice. Milton Sutliffe of Warren, Ohio, wrote to the founding convention of the Ohio Anti-Slavery Society with unusual candor: "There are many ashamed to advocate the degradation of our colored brethren to the lowest rank of being, who would join the advocates of his manhood in urging the importance of his elevation, provided it might be to a privileged rank or a higher order of brutes, rather than to a level with human beings. These profess to kindle with sympathy for the sufferings of the poor slave, but really kindle with anger when the appellation *man* is given to the negro."[33]

John Rankin used the occasion of Ohio's antislavery conference's first anniversary meeting to read before that body a stirring denunciation of racial prejudice. He called it "highly criminal" as a "palpable violation of the law of love" and of "Divine Law": "Surely such prejudice is one of the blackest crimes of the human heart. . . . Millions have indulged it without reproof, and few seem to have thought it criminal. . . . Let all be made to feel that they cannot inherit the kingdom of God while they entertain a prejudice ruinous to their fellow men, and soon the rights of the poor colored people will be restored to them, and they will be owned and cherished as brethren."[34]

Years later editor Gamaliel Bailey of the *Philanthropist*, the Cincinnati-based state abolitionist newspaper, remained greatly vexed by how few white abolitionists seemed to have gotten the message.

> The Anti-Slavery people are far from giving that countenance and substantial encouragement to their colored neighbors, which a generous sympathy demands. Let us imagine ourselves in their condition—aliens in the community where we live—borne down by a horrible weight of prejudice—unprotected by the laws—excluded from the privilege of educating our children—shut out from honorable employment, and doomed to see our offspring growing up under the curse of caste, listless, hopeless and idle, because unable to obtain situations with tradesmen or artisans. . . . What should we think of the conduct of those, who, professing to be our friends, behaved towards us like enemies? With what gratitude should we greet him who, too courageous to fear the scorn of the proud, or violence of the rabble, would dare treat us as MEN, seeking to do us favors, vindicating our rights, patronizing our industry, and encouraging in every way our efforts at self-improvement.[35]

By the early 1840s this campaign against prejudice within the ranks of the western movement began to pay dividends. The 1842 Ohio state antislavery convention passed a strong censure of the recalcitrant in its ranks: "[A]bolitionists who refuse to crucify prejudice against color by treating all men as equals, are unfaithful to the principles they profess—and deserve severe rebuke."[36]

Despite the progress made against racism in its own ranks, the legal, political arm of the underground struggle in the Northwest continued to do its organizational work in isolation from the African Americans who carried the main burden of the frontline struggle. In an arrogant tone heavily tinged with condescension toward its African American comrades-in-arms, the organization proclaimed itself the leading force in the fight against slavery. At conventions and in the press, white abolitionists patronizingly passed judgment on the "progress" of the efforts of African American to "elevate" themselves. White activists showed a propensity to monopolize the credit for any concrete steps forward the African American community made. Ohio's white abolitionists magnified their own impact, insisting, "It is hardly too much to say, that for the last few years almost every project of successful benevolence in [African Americans'] behalf, has originated with abolitionists." To them, the very word *abolitionist* denoted a white person. Whites had done more than step forward to join the movement for African American liberation. They had asserted their dominance within it and their leadership over it.[37]

The same attitude held sway among combatants in the physical battle against slavery. Having emerged as providers of support to the frontline struggle, white participants in what began to fashion itself as the Underground Railroad asserted their own importance in the liberation of enslaved individuals. They emphasized the part of the freedom struggle they knew best—their own place within it. With the adoption of the flawed railroad analogy, evidently begun as a makeshift descriptor, attention shifted from the frontline operations—the main theatre of the war, the epicenter of the underground movement—to the support services rendered in the rear. At best, the two components of the underground were confused, and the distinction between them lost. At worst, the Underground Railroad came to be viewed as encompassing only the support portion of the underground resistance to slavery. Activists focused on the conditions of their own involvement as "conductors." Their locales, far removed from the environs of slavery, became "stations," and they "stationkeepers." Their links to their coworkers were designated "lines"—and fugitives "passengers."

And yet, both organizationally and historically, the better-known rear component, the network of "stations" and "lines," was the subordinate, dependent part. It arose out of, and came into operation as a result of, a struggle waged to the South, on the front lines and within the territory of the slave states. The Underground Railroad did not organize the flight from slavery but was organized by it. It did not create the frontline struggle for which it served as support operations but was its creation. It did not start the struggle against slavery but took root in it. African Americans, numerically dominant among the operatives on the front lines, but an increasingly smaller proportion as the ranks swelled in the rear, found their own efforts going unrecognized. Given how the clandestine operation was necessarily organized, few removed from the front knew much about its modus operandi, let alone its personnel. Despite their limited knowledge, they became the conduit for ideas about it, with profound implications for both its contemporaneous reputation and its later legacy. By the time the "President of the Underground Railroad" relocated to Cincinnati in 1847, it was natural to conclude that Levi Coffin and the white women and men who joined him were behind the whole project—and always had been. Memory of the origins of the "institution" had been all but obliterated, the centrality of African American communities along the banks of the Ohio River at best dimly perceived.[38]

If African Americans were willing to overlook these flaws in western abolitionism—and for the most part they were—it was because the aggressiveness and fearlessness of its modus operandi appealed to those engaged in a furious struggle against forces that should have been more than their match. Advanced neither in its program nor relations to African Americans, western abolitionism was out in front in methods of struggle. While Garrisonian moral suasion continued to hold sway in the East, political abolitionism took much stronger hold and sank much deeper roots in the West, roots that would pay dividends twenty years hence. As the nation teetered toward a war over the politics of slavery that would have profound implications for America's enslaved, the battle along the front lines raged on, growing in intensity with the passage of each decade.[39]

5

Egypt's Border

Go down, Moses
Way down in Egypt land
Tell ole Pharaoh to let my people go.
                    African American spiritual

No operative in the thriving underground along the Ohio River of
the 1840s took greater risks than John Mason. On what was to be
his last mission, he had no fewer than four fugitives. Although he
had safely delivered larger parties before, Mason encountered a problem that taxed even his considerable abilities as a "slave stealer."
Daylight was rapidly approaching, and it would no longer be safe to
venture onto the Ohio River. He and his party would have to find a
hiding place and await nightfall. Long before the sun set, however,
the five African Americans were discovered. There was no choice
but to fight for their freedom.[1]

John Mason had been doing nothing else since the age of twelve,
when he effected his own escape from Kentucky slavery in the 1830s.
Waiting tables, he worked his way through Oberlin College, the only
institution of higher learning in Ohio open to African Americans.
When he graduated in the early 1840s, he decided to dedicate himself to underground work, making the Ohio Valley his base of
operations. William Mitchell reported receiving and promptly dis-
patching North 265 fugitives brought by the intrepid Mason, who
was "determined to devote his life to the vital interest of his brethren, by redeeming, as many as possible from the undying grasp of
the greedy monster, the Slaveholder." By Mitchell's estimate, Mason liberated at least another 1,100 via other routes, which included
the Rankins upriver.[2]

Mason's charges lost their nerve when confronted by their masters. The longtime operative never lost his. Though severely wounded in the ensuing struggle, his quick wits and coolness under pressure spared his life. He identified his former master, knowing that his captors would be less likely to kill him if it meant a loss to someone they knew. That man was only too glad to reclaim the value of his lost bondsman but not the troublesome property itself. Following the usual practice, he sold him down the river to the New Orleans market. Bought by another plantation owner, Mason managed yet another successful escape, with one more liberated African American in tow. The two made their way up the Mississippi River by steamboat, disembarking, like so many others, at Cincinnati.[3]

As Arnold Buffum traversed Ohio in the early 1840s as a speaker for the American Anti-Slavery Society, he could not help but take note of the freedom struggle of a more material nature that was waged all along the Ohio River. Stopping for a time in the river town of Marietta, Ohio, Buffum was met by the sad spectacle of "a young man from Virginia on horse back, accompanied by a boy . . who had fled from oppression . . . but had been overhauled by this man-hunter . . . with his loaded pistol." He investigated further and learned of the case of Jesse, who two decades earlier had lost his legs below the knees in an escape attempt. Thinking little of his own chances, Jesse had aided his wife and three children to make off with another woman. Afterwards, faced with a severe flogging, he decided to try his own luck once again, succeeding in crossing the Ohio in a boat, and heading after his family "being occasionally concealed from his pursuers, and occasionally helped on his way, by the friends of humanity." According to Buffum, the man "was hotly pursued by the bloodhounds of the *peculiar institution*" since "they concluded, that when a man without legs, could successfully make good his escape, it was about time to relinquish the idea of *holding* property in man." While Jesse's case was particularly remarkable, it was far from unusual for Marietta to witness the formerly enslaved making their way to freedom. Buffum reported, "Escapes from Virginia through this part of Ohio are frequent, and the disposition to help the flying fugitive on his way, to a land of safety, a city of refuge, is rapidly increasing among the people generally." So, too, was the opposition mounted from the other side of the river. In 1845 three Washington County, Ohio, men were seized in their home state and dragged across the river to Virginia, where they were jailed for aiding fugitives from service, the alleged crime having taken place in Ohio. The antislavery underground fought back. When word reached Richard Rankin that slavehunters were making the rounds of Ripley, he confronted them and advised them to leave town immediately. As one reached for his pistol, the son of Rev. John Rankin clapped a revolver to his head and warned, "[I]f you raise your arm I will put a bullet through your brain." Just then, John Parker entered with his double-barreled shotgun. The slave catchers were arrested and fined.[4]

For those engaged in the work of aiding fugitives, it was not even necessary to get out of bed to find danger. On a Sunday night a few weeks after the Cincinnati riot of 1841, Calvin Rankin heard a whistle emanating from the dark outside. He instantly sprang for his gun. Rev. John Rankin was one of the many underground operatives with a price on his head. His house, a frequent target, was under surveillance, with men lying outside hoping for him to emerge so they could get a shot at him. One had entered the abode and made straight for Rankin's bed, only to find it unoccupied. Calvin, with a cousin, went out to investigate. Not wishing to shoot an innocent man, Calvin loudly inquired what was wanted at the Rankin home. The reply came in the form of a series of gunshots, at least one of which found the young Rankin's shoulder. He and his cousin shot back and sent the six assailants into flight. The men had intended to set the Rankins' barn on fire, lying in ambush to pick off the family as it responded to the blaze. Following the incident, Reverend Rankin put out the word through the newspapers that nighttime prowlers on his property would be shot on sight.[5]

William Parker, a fugitive living in the North, described "[t]he insolent and overbearing conduct of the Southerners, when on such errands. . . . They did not hesitate to break open doors, and to enter, without ceremony, the houses of colored men; and when refused admission, or when a manly and determined spirit was shown, they would present pistols, and strike and knock down men and women indiscriminately." Amanda Smith, whose family was well known for harboring runaways, could testify to that. She watched in horror as a group of slave catchers, having savagely beaten her father, came within inches of fatally stabbing her mother, who was holding her infant daughter in her arms. Of course, such raids were particularly dangerous for African Americans, as they could—and did—result in kidnappings. After two Virginians lost a hearing under

Ohio's Black Laws to reclaim a local Marion County resident alleged to be a fugitive, they drew guns in the courthouse and abducted the African American they claimed as their human property. A melee ensued in the streets in which "the citizens interfered, and commenced operations upon the kidnappers with brick-bats, stones, and every missile that could be commanded." When that did not work, they raided an armory to equip themselves with stronger firepower. In the confusion, the African American man succeeded in escaping. Interestingly, although nine townspeople were arrested, the Virginians were not charged with any offense.[6]

The battles that took place could be fierce. William Parker recalled that on one occasion a group of African Americans inflicted such a beating on a party attempting to kidnap a young girl they said was a fugitive that two later died of their wounds. As Jacob Green was being transported by steamboat to Sandusky, Ohio, he found, to his surprise, "the Black people, in large numbers, made an attempt to rescue me, and so desperate was the attack, that several officers were wounded." Though these direct means failed, his allies later conspired with the captain to effect his escape.

Nowhere on the Ohio River was the contest between the forces of freedom and those of slavery more heated—or more violent—than in Madison, Indiana. Once, on charges of conspiring to help enslaved persons escape, an underground operative was turned over to his enemies by order of Indiana's governor at the instigation of his Kentucky counterpart. When the prisoner's comrades-in-arms obtained a writ of habeas corpus to bring the case to an Indiana court, the Kentucky official transporting the man refused to hand him over, threatening to shoot the three sheriff's deputies charged with serving it. They did not press the matter further, and one of Madison's African American operatives was carried off to a Kentucky jail.[7]

According to a report of a select committee of the Ohio Senate in 1849, "Such instances are growing numerous. The free States are reduced to a common hunting ground for slave catchers, through means now said to be reduced to a system." The slave catchers did not always win, however. When a group of seven bounty hunters overtook two fugitives under the escort of three underground operatives just north of Madison, the latter gathered an even larger party and "re-captured them," as the *Madison Courier* account expressed it. In pursuing their ill-gotten gains, the hunters of human flesh incurred significant risks themselves. A Kentuckian was beaten unconscious by one of Madison's most intrepid conductors, Henry Harris—but the latter lost his charges anyway, defeated by the superior firepower the slave hunters wielded on this occasion. Sometimes, however, the force of arms lay on the other side. One of the most notorious slave catchers who patrolled the Ohio Valley region, Madison's Wright Ray, was left for dead after a beating by a desperate fugitive who made good his escape. A few months passed before Ray was back in the chase. Fellow Madisonian Caleb McQuithey was "dangerously wounded" by a fugitive he attempted to apprehend. It was not unusual for fugitives to travel armed. Andrew Jackson had only his "trusty hickory," but he made the blows count when accosted by a bounty hunter. He no doubt spoke for many in declaring, "[I]f it was right for the revolutionary patriots to fight for liberty, it was right for me."[8]

Many conductors traveled armed as well, especially along the front lines. As Francis Fedric was transported through Ripley, he was "well guarded by eight or ten young men with revolvers . . . . A dozen such men would have defied a hundred slaveholders . . . and I verily believe they would willingly lay down their lives rather than allow one fugitive slave to be taken from them." Farther north, such protection was not always forthcoming. Henry Parker was told by a Quaker involved in the work, "I'll take thee in, I'll feed thee, and I'll travel with thee, but thee must do thy own fighting, as we Quakers never fight." A slave hunting party of thirteen that had ventured into the terrain along the Ohio/Pennsylvania border almost caught two of the fugitives working there until a party of seven African Americans and two whites arrived on the scene with shotguns and chased them away. According to Charles Garlick, "Squire Marshall inserted a notice in the papers warning them that, if they came again, they would meet with a warm reception and hospitable graves. This ended the last raid of the slave holding, slave-catching cohorts to that station of the underground railroad."[9]

Like every underground movement, this one had its traitors. Madison's work in aiding fugitives had long been meeting with too many obstacles of the kind conductor Henry Harris encountered. It became increasingly clear that a double agent was feeding information to area slave catchers for the substantial rewards offered. Finally, the perfidy was brought home to one who had seemed above reproach. An African American man, John Simmons, whose "reputation as a philanthropist pervaded the whole country for miles," had been selling out fugitives over a long period, in return for the monetary rewards always offered in such cases. Having finally smoked him out, Madison's African American underground, approximately thirty strong, "inflicted upon him such a drubbing as he will long remember, accompanied by the wholesome warning, that if he should ever repeat his heartless villany upon another fugitive, his life would be the forfeit"—a response not unlike that of Cincinnati African Americans on finding a similar person in their midst. Simmons, however, was not so readily dispatched. Taking advantage of the vulnerable position of any illegal movement, he successfully sued two of Madison's leading combatants, Elijah Anderson and Chapman Harris; Anderson apparently bore the brunt of the verdict.[10]

This event combined with another to seriously damage the antislavery forces in Madison. Even as the city became home to an impressive array of operatives with extensive connections on both sides of the river, proslavery Southerners made their presence felt in the Madison population. They determined to stop at its point of entry the flow of fugitives moving northward through Indiana. Descending on the African American community without warning, a mob of more than one hundred proslavery whites ransacked houses looking for fugitives and arms. A longtime stalwart, Griffith Booth, was taken to the river and "ducked"—held under water repeatedly to the point of drowning—in an effort to get him to reveal the whereabouts of a group of fugitives, which he refused to do. Saved by the valiant intervention of two white antislavery activists, the former fugitive fled once more and spent the remainder of the antebellum period in Canada to escape assassination. A founder of Madison's African American underground, George Evans, faced a public lynching from the same mob, and was saved from that fate only by the timely intervention of a prominent white businessman, who held off the vigilantes at gunpoint. The mob then repaired to the house of an elderly veteran of the underground, who kept his attackers at bay for hours, until his ammunition ran out. Rendered defenseless, he suffered a life-threatening beating. Violence was endemic to the chosen calling of the underground operative. Three decades after the end of the Civil War, a leading figure in the Madison underground, John Carr, still feared retribution from his proslavery enemies if he talked about his role in the movement. In addition to the havoc wreaked by physical force and treachery from within, no underground was subjected to more arrests than that in Indiana's largest river town.[11]

Through the periodic waves of violence and repression the work of aiding runaways continued uninterrupted and even gained momentum. With the intensification of the frontline struggle, operatives in Cincinnati organized themselves into a Vigilance Committee as early as 1838. So confident, so emboldened, were its leaders that within a few years they were advertising in the press—just two years after the 1841 riot—their intention "To extend to our fellow beings, attempting peacefully to escape from a galling bondage, that charity and aid which the God of nature and revelation has commanded us to bestow." They boasted, "[I]n Cincinnati, owing to its peculiar locality and circumstances, there will be continual and exhausting demands upon our aid and charity."[12]

As a result of the stepped-up activities of the frontline underground, the clandestine enterprise began to reach the attention of the public farther north. A Mansfield, Ohio, newspaper informed its readers in 1840 that there existed "chains of depots for the reception and concealment of runaway slaves, extending from various points of the Ohio and Mississippi rivers to the lake shores."[13]

Rial Cheadle, a white "slave stealer" who operated on both sides of the Ohio River, left a detailed description of one of his missions along the network fast taking shape. Having left the front lines, he moved through central Ohio with the fugitives he was conducting: "A few miles travel brought us to a colored man's dwelling, Mr. Marlowe's. We tarried until night and then we went to Putnam. From the summit of the hill they (the slaves) gaze in wonder at seeing so many gas lights in the city of Zanesville. The next day I went to a Wesleyan preacher's dwelling. . . . He took me to a colored man's house where we were kindly entertained." At that point, one of the fugitives saw the son of his owner, resulting in their removal "to another part of the town." Cheadle's description reveals that like any underground movement, the antislavery movement relied on flexibility in responding to the conditions it encountered. When slave catchers were known to be in the vicinity, the use of African Americans' homes as stopping points was considered too risky, since their domiciles were subject to search without warrants. Cheadle's description of the transfer reveals much about the inner dynamics of the Underground Railroad: "The Baptist preacher of Putnam saw the colored brother, greeting him with cordial friendship."[14]

J.H. Tibbetts was among a group of white abolitionists who joined the Madison, Indiana, underground in the early 1840s. Working closely with the African American veterans who had aided the fugitives Levi Coffin received in his Newport, Indiana, home, Tibbetts received as many as ten fugitives at a time to pilot further inland in his wagon. He knew firsthand that the notion of a railway operating with clockwork efficiency was more myth than reality, as his missions—always north of the river—kept him away from home for up to five days at a time and occasioned considerable danger: "If I was ever taken there would be trouble as I was determined never to give up." In his frontline locale, he usually received the fugitives that he helped north from their initial African American contacts: George De Baptiste, Elijah Anderson, and Chapman Harris. Tibbetts helped recruit other whites into the operation, including a young man named Alexander Brandon who "had ben raised to look on the collard man not better than the brute, but when he once consented to go & did actuly engage in the buisness . . . became as warm a friend to the collard man as he well could be."[15]

The closeness of the relationships that developed between the interracial group of operatives is attested to by many. When not engaged in his chosen life's work of helping liberate the enslaved, John Fairfield made his home in African American communities. Upon his release from prison after more than a decade, the first person Calvin Fairbank visited was Henry Boyd, the former slave who had become a bedstead manufacturer and underground activist in Cincinnati. He felt happier to see no one than Kittie Doram, who led the efforts to raise the money to get him back on his feet.[16]

Even after Coffin's removal to Cincinnati, much of the fugitive traffic passing through the city continued to be handled by African Americans. Often, they turned to their white comrades only when trouble appeared imminent, the African American community being perpetually vulnerable to forced entry. Such was the case with a group of fourteen runaways housed at the African American Zion Baptist Church. One of them, an ailing two-month-old baby, did not make it through the first night, despite the best efforts of the entire abolitionist community. The same was true when Mary French turned up in Cincinnati at the head of a contingent of nine—and a slave posse on her heels.[17]

Mary French's master permitted her to work as a domestic in Cincinnati, believing the family she left behind across the Ohio River effectively bound her to him. She had other ideas. She approached Laura Haviland for help. The latter provided encouragement and suggested a plan, but ventured no further concrete aid. The advice she proffered does much to expose the legend of the Underground Railroad that assigns centrality of place to conductors like Levi Coffin and John Rankin. Haviland, not only a stalwart and consummate insider of Cincinnati's Underground Railroad, but a close family friend and frequent boarder at the Coffin residence, recommended that the fugitive seek out one of three safe houses. Two of these were the homes of African Americans, those of John Hatfield and a man she identifies only as Hall (probably Baptist minister John Hall, a native of Kentucky). The third was that of the Coffins. Of the three alternatives, she asserted: "At either of these places you are as sure of going through safe as if you were already in Canada."[18]

Following her daring escape, and with a reward of one thousand dollars for their return serving as incentive for her betrayal, French chose to bring the eight children she had rescued from Kentucky slavery to Hall's residence. Some of Hall's African American coworkers in the underground quickly alerted him that slave hunters were hot on the trail, and the contingent dispersed throughout the Queen City's extensive interracial network of activists. Mary French herself was lodged with the Coffins. Cincinnati's African American brain trust ensured their safe passage north with an audacity and flair that revealed the increasing boldness of the black population along the front lines. As the nine fugitives were spirited out of the city, a large carriage was rushed to a location known to be under surveillance, where nine African American residents of roughly the same description "were hustled in with haste, and driven off with speed." The slave catchers immediately hailed the police and descended on the vehicle. Recalled Haviland, "[T]he [African American] man beside the driver demanded the reason why he and his ladies should receive this insult to hinder their pleasure ride. By throwing a light from their dark lantern in the faces of their pursuers, the hunters they had suspected were recognized, to their great annoyance. There were those among them who would not have been exposed, perhaps, for half the amount of the reward."[19]

The multitude of incidents such as this one formed the fabric of the frontline struggle. As the basis for his portrait of the Underground Railroad, Wilbur Siebert relied on the testimony of the white participants' children, many of whom recreated the networks as they remembered them, concentrating on the white "stationmasters" with whom they were most familiar. The recollections of the participants themselves tend to provide a different picture. W.B. Campbell, a Ripley abolitionist, said that John Parker "was often a leader of the whites in perilous rescue work" in addition to "always carrying on an independent campaign for his race." Calvin Fairbank, one of the Coffin's close associates and a special friend of Laura Haviland's, fondly recalled just before his death Cincinnati's large, well-coordinated vigilance committee, with its interracial group of "directors." These included not only famous white abolitionists like Levi Coffin, Salmon P. Chase, and Gamaliel Bailey, but African Americans who have not achieved the same recognition, including Henry Boyd, Kittie Doram, William Watson, and William Casey. When Fairbank was employed to cross the Ohio River into Kentucky to rescue an enslaved woman, he in turn called in Casey, whom he considered an "expert" in this category of work.[20]

With the exception of John Fairfield, Calvin Fairbank, Rial Cheadle, and a very few others, this specialized group of slave rescuers consisted mainly of African Americans. It was not simply a case of Northern white Underground Railroad operatives not being cognizant of opportunities. On the contrary, in a surprisingly large number of cases they received advance notice of the intention of an enslaved person or persons to escape. Levi Coffin, perhaps somewhat inconsistently, considered such aid immoral. For pragmatic reasons, John Rankin, too, was skeptical of the practice, though at least a couple of his sons engaged in it, possibly without his knowledge. Laura Haviland most often deemed it beyond her limited means of rendering assistance to the cause.[21]

Long before Levi Coffin took up residence in 1847, Cincinnati was well stocked with more than its share of combatants in the struggle with slavery. From that most active center of the western underground, operatives initiated into its modus operandi fanned out along the Ohio River and to points farther north. Frances Scroggins married coworker Thomas Brown, taking up residence and Underground Railroad work in Pittsburgh. John Parker relocated just upriver to Ripley; Gabriel Johnson took Cincinnati's organizational methods to another frontline river town, Ironton, Ohio. William Mitchell left for Washington Court House, a little distance north of the river.

Frances and Thomas Brown helped convert the Monongahela House in Pittsburgh into a resource for helping liberate and forward fugitives, before moving into their own home that they dedicated to the same purpose. Associates of such prominent African Americans as Lewis Woodson and Martin Delany, they joined forces in the boarding house in which they first lived and worked with other African American employees and its white proprietors, the abolitionist Crossan family. As with other Ohio River towns, Pittsburgh saw its share of slaveholders bring their species of property with them into its environs during their stopovers. One of them from Maryland had the misfortune of choosing to stay in the Monongahela House with his half-sister, who, in an example of the strange workings of the trade in human beings, was also his property. She had attempted escape once too often for his patience, and he had determined to sell her down the river to the Deep South.[22]

Thomas Brown could well identify with the woman's plight. He had himself been held in bondage in Maryland by close relatives before he succeeded in buying his freedom and that of his family through determination, skill, and hard work. In an instant, he activated the network for assisting escapes. While others arranged the woman's safe passage north aboard a carriage, Brown was given the daunting task of sneaking her out of her room—under lock and key and the watchful eye of the slaveholder. Strategically stationing a sentry to keep a lookout for the temporarily occupied master, Brown frantically sought the means to quietly release the captive from behind the deadbolted door, for which he had no key. In the last few desperate moments before the scheduled departure of slaveholder and bondswoman, Brown lifted her through the transom on top of the door by means of an improvised pulley. In a matter of moments she disappeared, leaving her irate brother to vent his spleen on the Crossans, the African Americans they employed, the city of Pittsburgh, and the entire North.[23]

Thomas Brown also worked on the Ohio River, from which strategic locale, he, like many others, helped enslaved persons escape. Once, while en route from Pittsburgh to Cincinnati on the *Diana*, he encountered a young girl. Discovering her condition of enslavement, he set to work at once to free her. Dressed up in the disguise of an

Thomas Brown, Pittsburgh underground operative.
From the collection of the National Afro-American
Museum and Cultural Center.

old woman in black, replete with veil, Brown first managed to slip
her onto a neighboring boat while the *Diana* put up at Portsmouth,
Ohio. He then carried her ashore and passed her to friends who
arranged her journey to Canada.[24]

Thanks to the efforts of people like the Browns, the nationally
prominent African American leader Martin Delany could report from
Pittsburgh that by the late 1840s, despite public sentiment far from
congenial to abolitionism, "The Underground Railroad is in high
flight, and doing a fair business here." He added, "[W]hile I write, a
panting fugitive enters my room, in company with a brother, seeking aid and advice. Of course I immediately sent the brother out for
aid. He returns—a ticket is obtained—and another moment, and he

is on his way rejoicing! 'He, the car Emancipation/Rides majestic through our nation!'" When Charles Garlick passed through, he was aided by another prominent Pittsburgh African American, John B. Vashon.[25]

Gabriel Johnson knew the slavery the fugitives were escaping from, having been born into it in Spotsylvania, Virginia. His knowledge of the ways of the South may have been helpful in establishing the connections on the southern side of the river that the Ironton Underground Railroad station put to use. While Johnson handled the organizational end, the chief conductor was James Ditcher. In Johnson's experience in both Cincinnati and Ironton, he never saw a more zealous worker than James Ditcher: "He would take more chances for his life than any man I ever saw. I've known him to have a pistol in each ear." In a period of five years, Ditcher personally piloted almost three hundred fugitives from the Ohio River to inland agents. Members of a secret African American organization called the "Order of Twelve" that worked in tandem with wealthy white furnace operator John Campbell, Johnson and Ditcher established Ironton as an active center of the frontline struggle.[26]

Ditcher found himself in a desperate situation when he received a woman and her baby rowed across the river in a skiff by some free African Americans from Virginia. He recalled, "The slave catchers were close onto them when they got here." Ditcher rushed to Campbell's stable and got a horse, obtaining another from a local minister. Riding hard, they reached Olive Furnace, where they stayed with an African American named Harris. The pursuers might have caught them had the slave catchers not stopped at a whiskey shop and gotten drunk. Ditcher got his charges safely to another African American settlement, Poke Patch, where they were conducted north. But Ditcher was not out of the woods himself: "On my way back, I met the fellows who were after the slaves. I knew them—one was the owner of the slaves. I was riding Mr. Campbell's horse and leading preacher Chester's, with the sidesaddle on it. They asked me what I had been doing with that horse and sidesaddle. I told them I had been to Gallipolis to a dance and had had my girl with me. They called me a damn liar, threatened to shoot me and swore they would shave Chester's horse's tail. I sidled away from them and they did not disturb me." Ditcher's coolness under fire earned him the sobriquet of the "Red Fox of the Underground."[27]

William Mitchell, who had been first aroused to action on behalf of a fugitive in Chillicothe, Ohio, began his underground work in earnest in Cincinnati in the mid-1840s before leaving to establish an active center at Washington Court House eighty miles to the East. Mitchell was a dedicated combatant. Joining the ranks of those who made forays into slave territory, his residence also became a main refuge for runaways.[28]

Jane's owner did not like the religious ideas she had begun to espouse. The Covington, Kentucky, gentleman decided to sell both the woman he had forced into sexual relations and their three-year-old daughter to the first slave trader who came along. He refused an offer from an English neighbor to buy Jane's freedom, preferring to see her transported to the Deep South. The Englishman appealed to freedom-loving Cincinnatians across the river. Levi Coffin did not believe in "stealing" African Americans out of slavery. William Casey did. With his extensive experience in arranging escapes, Casey, a stalwart of Cincinnati's underground, was the perfect person to conceive and execute a plan to rescue Jane and her daughter. Casey piloted her across the Ohio River in the dead of night. A few weeks later Jane was attending an African American school in Randolph County, Indiana— in the Cabin Creek settlement that experience had proven would protect her freedom with the lives of its members.[29]

Those willing to cross into slave territory like William Casey constituted the special forces of the underground. This elite interracial group of men and women operatives took the struggle to liberate the enslaved into the belly of the beast. Some of these specialists— like John Mason and John Fairfield—were shadowy figures, claiming no place as home, following their trade where it took them, impossible to track down for both friend and foe. Others—including Ripley's John Parker and Madison's Chapman Harris—were prosperous, respected members of their communities, always available on need. Between the two was a group of operatives, like George White and William Phelps, whose missions across the river to arrange the details of assisted escapes necessitated a base but also required frequent changes of locale. The two relocated from Cincinnati to Madison in 1845, departing for parts unknown three years later.[30]

For all of them, the dangers were considerable, and the price to be paid for failure high. Cincinnati operatives suspended cross-border operations for a time in the late 1840s after the arrest of one of their number—almost certainly John Fairfield—near the river. When underground veteran Thomas Smallwood, who once served the cause in the slave states after escaping slavery, appealed to African American contacts in Cincinnati about arranging the escape of a friend's family, he was told that "so great an excitement and vigilance [reigned] on the Kentucky side of the Ohio river, that . . . we were advised to return and wait for a more favorable time." Around the same time, another Cincinnati veteran, Calvin Fairbank, with a Kentucky school-teacher from New England, Delia Webster, was imprisoned for the first of two long terms he would serve.[31]

Yet as a whole the special forces of the antislavery underground were remarkably successful. The most famous operative of all was Harriet Tubman, who seems to have preferred to work in the East. However, other women in the Ohio Valley underground also undertook this most dangerous work. One of them, remembered by respected abolitionist and former Lane Seminary student-rebel Huntington Lyman as Mrs. Annis, was a Cincinnati resident. According to Lyman, she rowed a skiff over to the Kentucky side early one morning to arrange the details of an escape. Unfortunately for her, she ran straight into the slaveholder, who threatened to turn the dogs on her. Lyman recalled, "Affrightened, she retreated to her skiff. But without turning her head, she contrived to tell the slaves that at 10 1/2 o'clock a way of escape would open to them, and so it turned out. The old man, who was a slave holder when he went to bed, was a non-slave holder when he awoke."[32]

Not all conductors on the Underground Railroad did their work on the north shore of the Ohio River or availed themselves of the promise of freedom it offered. Across from Marietta, in Parkersburg, Virginia (now West Virginia), a mysterious elderly enslaved woman known only as Jinney helped fugitives cross the Ohio River. A little upriver lived and worked a man named Josephus, nicknamed "The Ferryman," who was said to have taken hundreds of fugitives across the Ohio River in his boat for more than two decades. A number of enslaved African Americans worked the Kentucky side of the Madison operations, including Richard Daly and a man his colleagues in Indiana knew simply as Jack. Both worked many years before effecting their own escapes, in Jack's case, only after being caught the first time, despite his long experience. Harry Smith helped a large group of runaways get across the river from Louisville but did not attempt to go with them, not wanting to leave his family.[33]

Enslaved Arnold Gragston began to pilot fugitives when he was a teenager. Born on a plantation just across the river from Ripley, Gragston, like many others, became involved in the underground by chance. He was asked by an elderly woman to take a young girl across and found himself unable to refuse, despite his terror of being caught and punished. Conquering his fears, he navigated the small craft to the Ohio side, though he "couldn't see a thing there in the dark." Following the instructions of the woman who recruited him for the task, he rowed toward the "tall light." "When I got up to it, two men reached down and grabbed her." One asked him, "You hungry, boy? . . . [I]f he hadn't been holdin' me I think I would have fell backward into the river." That was his first introduction to the Rankin family. It would not be his last. "I soon found myself goin' back across the river with two or three people, and sometimes a whole boatload. I got so I used to make three and four trips a month." All told, he piloted more than a hundred fugitives across to the Rankin House. "It always meant freedom for a slave if he could get to this light," Gragston recalled.

> After that first girl—I never did see her again—I never saw my passengers. It would have to be the "black nights" of the moon when I would carry them, and I would meet them out in the open or in a house without a single light. The only way I knew who they were was to ask them, "What you say?" And they would answer, "Menare." I don't know what that word meant—it came from the Bible. I only know that was the password I used, and all of them I took over told it to me before I took them.

Gragston worked with a white abolitionist named John Fee, who hid fugitives until the enslaved pilot took charge of them. Only after four years of service did Arnold Gragston finally avail himself of the freedom that could have been his at any time, taking his new bride with him.[34]

The lives of Jinney, Josephus, Richard Daly, Jack, and Gragston expose some of the persistent myths about the experience of the runaway. The image of fugitives from enslavement is often closely tied to that of the Underground Railroad, which is usually portrayed as a well-organized conspiracy of sympathetic Northern whites. The examples of these five of the many thousand operatives within the institution of slavery show that the enslaved themselves were the clandestine network's most crucial component, both in giving impulse via their flight and in aiding others to freedom. Gragston spent four years as a frontline operative, Jinney and Josephus far longer in the struggle against slavery—willingly sacrificing their own opportunity for freedom in order to help others attain that goal.[35]

As Gragston's cooperation with John Fee suggests, not all of the operatives on the Kentucky side were enslaved, or even African American. Before Gragston took up his post ferrying fugitives across to Ripley, an Augusta, Kentucky, abolitionist, the father of James Thome (one of the Lane Seminary student rebellion leaders) was known to aid runaways. Thome, a former slaveholder himself, had liberated his own bondspersons. A native Maysville man that Thome helped escape told the Underground Railroad operatives north of the river that Thome "would get out of his bed in the middle of the night to help runaway slaves out of the reach of their masters, would give them clothes and money and sent them across the Ohio river." The fugitive added, by way of explanation, "He was very rich, he said, or he could not live there, meaning, it was understood, that his great wealth made his slave-holding neighbors afraid to injure him." Such relative safety was rare, however. Francis Fedric was helped to escape by a Mason County, Kentucky, "abolitionist planter," who transported him to the home of a white family in Maysville that "hazarded everything for me," only asking "me to remember them in my prayers."

Occasionally, white operatives were to be found even farther South, such as the one who helped a young enslaved boy named Cato escape from South Carolina, and a sympathizer of the oppressed who aided Charles Thompson in Mississippi. When traveling in North Carolina in 1875, William Robinson met the son of abolitionist Sam Fuller, who had attempted to help Robinson's father escape bondage in that state many years earlier. "When it was made known that his father had lost his life because he had tried to help my father secure his freedom . . . we both broke down and wept." His intentions divined, the elder Fuller had awakened one day to find a "crossbone and skull on a stick in front of his door." He disappeared a short time later, never to be seen again.[36]

Rescuing enslaved persons from the opposite side of the river did not always require special forces. A Jeffersonville, Indiana, woman, Mary Afflick, developed her own ingenious scheme, recorded by the *Louisville Courier*. "Tickets are bought at the Jeffersonville railroad office, then handed over to the negro [in Kentucky] that is ready to elope; the omni-bus calls for him about daybreak, and ensconced in that he rides to the ferry and across the river to the depot, whence he is rapidly whirled away by steam into the interior of Indiana. This is the latest and cutest abolition dodge, and appears to have worked successfully until the arrest of the woman in question."[37]

Far more often, the machinery was set in motion only by the arrival of fugitives at a point north of the Ohio River; occasionally, underground activity did not begin until the fugitives had crossed well beyond the Mason-Dixon Line. William Mallory, a runaway from North Carolina, went through Pittsburgh and wandered around Pennsylvania for a time "before I at last got into the hands of the Abolitionists, who conducted me, by means of the 'Underground Railway' to Canada." Or, as happened more often than the legend of the Underground Railroad would suggest, the fugitives never found their way to help. In the summer of 1844, a group of eight men landed near Gallipolis, Ohio, having made their way from Virginia. The forces they encountered were not those in the field to help them. An eyewitness testified, "One circumstance connected with this miserable affair is enough to make any man blush to be called an Ohioan. The Virginia slaveholders who had come over the river in pursuit seemed to think themselves too important personages to engage in such dirty work, so with the reward of $500 they procured plenty of our Buckeye gentry to go and do it for them." Though greatly outnumbered, the fugitives fought valiantly but could not overcome their armed opponents. Shot, stoned, and beaten, and in some cases critically injured, they were dragged back to the plantations from which they came, where further brutalization undoubtedly awaited.[38]

The risk of falling into the wrong hands was significant even at the busiest crossing points. Having made an improbable journey in which he eluded his pursuers, one fugitive reached the environs of Ripley, which must have seemed to him a safe haven, all the more so when the starving man received a warm welcome and a hearty meal. The result crushed the hopes that must have burned brightest at that moment, as newspaper accounts related: "[T]he treacherous landlord threw a rope over his head from behind, tied him fast, put him on board the first boat for Cincinnati, brought him to Covington [Kentucky], gave him up to his master, and of course was rewarded for his perfidy." John Hatfield barely succeeded in getting a group of thirteen fugitives away from a slave catcher disguised as an agent of the Underground Railroad in Cincinnati before their owners arrived to claim them. Four fugitives who made it to Madison, Indiana, were not so fortunate, being captured by eighteen bounty hunters from that city.[39]

Not all of the non-Underground Railroad traffic was stopped at the border. On October 15, 1842, thirteen African Americans showed up at Rundle Palmer's door in Huron County, Ohio, in the northernmost part of the state. He presumed them to be the "wayfaring people" they described themselves as, and his family accordingly offered them a meal. "[I]n a few minutes, to my surprise, my house was entered and surrounded, I should think, by ten or twelve men, armed with pistols, dirks, clubs, &c., with a Kentucky leader, backed up by a constable, holding a paper he called a warrant. The strangers manifested a disposition to defend themselves, but I advised them to use no violence, and we would procure for them a fair trial." Though some of his neighbors intervened, it was to no avail. Twelve were reclaimed; only one, who must have met with the others in their journey and was not named on the warrant, was allowed to proceed. Perhaps it might have been small consolation for the three women, five men, and four children returned to slavery to know that their brief presence in tiny Fitchville, Ohio, prompted the formation of an abolitionist society there to prevent further outrages of the kind and to lend its voice against "what are called up here Ohio Blood Hounds, or slave catchers" since such a man "forfeits the character of a worthy citizen, and may justly be called mean, servile, mercenary, and enemy to universal liberty, and merits the rebuke and indignation of every virtuous citizen."[40]

Though they were the exception, some fugitives made it through to Canada pursuing such an independent course. Israel Campbell and a friend successfully arrived on British soil on their own, helped only in southern Illinois by a few African American acquaintances and again in Detroit by George De Baptiste. Having escaped from Virginia slavery in the later 1830s, a fugitive known only as Aaron got as far as Lancaster, Ohio, where he decided to settle. So afraid of white people was he that he dared not ask even for food, preferring to steal what he needed. Only after his master turned up looking for him five years later was he assisted to safe refuge in New England by friends he had gradually come to trust in the interim. Andrew Jackson survived on his own in the hostile territory of southern Illinois, though not without once suffering capture and imprisonment as a runaway. John Little and his wife crossed the same territory alone en route to Canada.[41]

More often, runaways were directed to Underground Railroad facilities by African Americans who, as in Madison and Cincinnati, were still the most common first point of contact. This was true for James Williams of Maryland, as well as for Georgia native John Brown, who was assisted by a series of loosely connected black contacts from St. Louis, Missouri, through the state of Illinois before he was acquainted with the more formally organized institution. Jacob Green, having made it to Cincinnati in 1848, chose to put his trust in an African American girl, who put him in touch with the people best positioned to help him sing his "song of deliverance." Kentuckian Henry Parker, too, found the liberty line through the help of an African American living on the northern banks of the Ohio River.[42]

As such cases reveal, knowledge of the existence of the Underground Railroad was far from universal among the enslaved. Octavia Albert heard about it from her uncle in Louisiana, though she never had occasion to make use of its services. Henry Bibb was questioned closely about facilities for escape in the North after his recapture. But a significant number seemed to know little or nothing about it. When William Webb was sold from Mississippi to southern Kentucky he found that the enslaved persons in the vicinity knew about John Fremont's unsuccessful bid for the presidency but not about the Underground Railroad. William Singleton, living in North Carolina slavery, had heard the name by the late 1850s. "Of course we did not understand what the underground railroad was. We thought it was some sort of a road under the ground"—though they did know that "once you got into Canada they could not get you back again . . . you were free." Bibb, living just across the river from Ohio, had himself never heard of it before his escape in 1838. Neither had Andrew Jackson living a little farther south in that state, although he did manage to obtain information about the route he needed to take to make it through the North. Leonard Black, whose relatives had already escaped and communicated to him that he should do the same, had a vague sense of Northern geography but nothing about any facilities for traveling through it. Mattie Jackson said that her parents "knew no other resource than to depend upon their own chance in running away and secreting themselves." Still, her father successfully escaped, though her mother's attempts ended in failure.

Worse than being unaware of the Underground Railroad's existence, some misunderstood its intentions. Henry Clay Bruce's elders, including his mother, were frightened on being informed by a group of "poor white people" that when their steamboat landed at Cincinnati, abolitionists would attempt to rescue them. "Our people did not know what the word abolitionist meant; they evidently thought it meant some wild beast or Negro-trader, for they feared both and were greatly frightened." So much so, they actually informed their master, who had his contingent put ashore on the Kentucky side. Bruce remembered bitterly, "The ignorance of these women caused me to work as a slave for seventeen years afterwards."[43]

Knowledge of the geography of freedom was, however, substantially better. Georgia native John Brown had first "made for the high road, which I thought would lead me straight to England," his destination of choice. He had heard of Ohio—and adjusted his escape path to try to reach it instead. Andrew Jackson reported, "I am sometimes asked, how we learn the way to the free States? My answer is, that the slaves know much more about this matter than many persons are aware. They have means of communication with each other, altogether unknown to their masters, or to the people of the free states—even the route of some who have escaped is familiarly known to the more intelligent ones." Conversely, the Underground Railroad could serve as a source of information for those in the North or Canada about relatives living in the South. Fugitive James Pennington learned by such means of the imminent sale of his parents in time to initiate steps to secure their freedom.[44]

As historian Larry Gara first emphasized, fugitives were very far from being the passive participants implied by the notion of "passengers" conducted from station to station. They were, rather, the active locomotive that drove the entire railroad. Many fugitives did much more than ride the liberty line to Canada. Drawing on the same initiative they had used to reach the Ohio River when escaping, they became frontline operatives dedicated to liberating others. The transition from passenger to conductor—active agent in the war against slavery—was surprisingly frequent, and could be, as with James Williams of Pennsylvania, immediate. Those who returned to the South seeking loved ones included such fugitives as Henry Bibb and Josiah Henson. Some, like Bibb, also became regulars on the abolitionism speaking circuit and conductors on the Underground Railroad. A tour that took him through southern Ohio, "in sight of the State of Virginia," held special significance for him.[45]

The most famous conductor of all, Harriet Tubman, was a fugitive. So was the operative in the western theatre probably responsible for liberating more enslaved persons than any other, John Mason. William Wells Brown, who made his escape in Ohio, spent the next ten years helping fugitives from Cleveland and other ports across Lake Erie to Canada. Milton Clarke became similarly involved in that work in northern Ohio after his escape; his brother Lewis returned to the South to rescue their youngest sibling. Frederick Douglass, the leading African American abolitionist, was a runaway, as was the original of one of Harriet Beecher Stowe's most famous characters, Uncle Tom himself—who, despite the negative associations that have attached to his name, became an accomplished operative in the frontline struggle, making numerous trips into Kentucky to liberate the enslaved.[46]

For obvious reasons, however, most of those fugitives who became active in the antislavery underground would not achieve such fame. Successful participation required drawing as little attention to oneself as possible. Such was the case with one of Cincinnati's stalwarts, Kittie Doram. Cincinnati's most accomplished female operative escaped from slavery at the age of twelve. With the thirty-six cents she brought with her, Catherine Doram, known to friends as Kittie, established herself as a seamstress. By the time of the Civil War, she, like her fellow Cincinnatian Henry Boyd, was materially well off. An imposing woman, her friend Calvin Fairbank wrote of her, "She rose in her dignity like Sojourner Truth." She, too, was a longstanding member of Cincinnati's Underground Railroad, in which she had served since at least the early 1840s. Her home was used to shelter fugitives, and she was respected enough to be selected alongside "President" Levi Coffin to the committee formed to raise money for Fairbank on his release from prison in 1864. She was herself among the largest donors to his cause. Similarly, two of the leading forces in the Madison underground from the mid-1830s to the Civil War, William Anderson and Chapman Harris, were fugitives.[47]

John Curtis began work in the newly organized Stafford, Ohio, underground soon after his own escape in the autumn of 1846. A

John Curtis, fugitive from slavery and operative in the Stafford, Ohio, underground. From the collection of Henry Burke.

slave trader who posed as an abolitionist, offering to help the three Curtis boys to "freedom," had set the sixteen-year-old and his two brothers on a northward track. His real intention was to sell them into Cotton Belt slavery. Just before the party reached the Ohio River, the Curtises were alerted to their apparent benefactor's real intentions. Fleeing just in time, they crossed north over the Ohio rather than being shipped down it in shackles. With a slave posse on their heels, they moved into woods made treacherous by an early snowstorm. Unbeknownst to them, their pursuers turned back, while the terrified and weary fugitives hid in a cave for two weeks. At the end of that period, the youngest of the brothers, fourteen-year-old Benjamin, died of exposure. John and Harrison buried him in a makeshift grave, which was discovered soon thereafter. The Curtises suddenly found themselves confronted by unknown whites. Fortunately, the visitors proved to be friends. The young fugitives had happened upon the abolitionist stronghold of Stafford, Ohio. Rather than taking the Underground Railroad to Canada, the surviving brothers elected to remain there, first working in the mill owned by a local abolitionist, and later taking up farming. Harrison eventually left to head west, but John Curtis joined the ranks of the antislavery underground, guiding many a runaway like himself to points farther north—in particular, to an African American community in Guinea, Ohio. He would never leave the front line in the war against slavery—except to return to the South as a Union soldier to help deal the institution a deathblow.[48]

6

Prelude to Exodus

See those children dressed in red.
God's gonna trouble the water.
Must be the children who Moses led.
God's gonna trouble the water.
                    African American spiritual

The Polly family had realized its dream of freedom. In 1849 Douglass Polly, manumitted from Kentucky slavery by the terms of his owner's will, purchased his brother, Peyton, Peyton's wife, Violet, and their seven children, themselves enslaved in Kentucky. The reunited family settled on the north bank of the Ohio River, near the town of Ironton.[1]

The relatives of the deceased slaveholder, also named Polly, were not content to suffer the loss of persons they had come to regard as their human property. One of the slaveholder's Kentucky relatives, named Justice, paid another man three hundred dollars to hunt them down. Joined by an armed gang of accomplices hired for five dollars each, the slave hunter crossed the Ohio River on June 6, 1850. In the dead of night, the men invaded the Polly home. Peyton Polly barely escaped death, as the bullet fired at his head missed by less than an inch. But in the mad whirlwind of violence that had descended without warning, Peyton and Violet's seven children, and their infant grandchild born in Ohio, were stolen away. The youths, aged nine months to twenty-four years, were carried back to the bondage the family believed it had forever escaped.[2]

The only recourse for the stricken parents was the court system—of the slave state of Kentucky. Violet and Peyton soon exhausted their slender means. Aided by the Ohio legislature, the parents waited for three years as the case wended its way through the Kentucky courts. Three of the children and the grandchild were recovered.

Nelson, Harrison, Louisa, and Anna Polly were carried away into Virginia slavery. Ohio governor Reuben Wood wrote, "The sovereignty of Ohio has been thus wantonly violated[;] the constitutional and legal authority of the state government should not be permitted to sleep, until the aggression is redressed, and the dignity, honor and integrity of the state is fully vindicated."[3]

A decade passed. The case became bogged down in the Virginia courts, and Nelson Polly died in bondage, just fourteen years old. In circumstances of which the cruelty can only be guessed at, Louisa gave birth to her own child—at the age of thirteen. During that same time period, Lincoln was elected president; the nation lurched toward a war at least partly over the issue of slavery; and Southern states denounced the violation of their rights. Four members of the Polly family, abducted from their lawful residence in the free state of Ohio, languished in Virginia slavery.[4]

The Lawrence County, Ohio, prosecutor wrote to his governor, "The frequent visits from the mother of these children to make inquiries about them and her anguish are enough to move any person of correct feeling to energetic action." History contains no other record of Violet Polly's feelings as she gazed at the Ohio River that for ten long years had separated her from three of her children, and now a grandchild she had never laid eyes on. The Virginia plantation to which they had been taken lay just on the other side of the river from the Polly home.[5]

The Underground Railroad was, in part, a victim of its own success. The modus operandi that had developed in the Ohio Valley amounted to open defiance of the ability of the South or the North to stop the operations. Frederick Douglass pleaded with "some of our western friends" in the mid-1840s to say as little as possible about their activities, reminding them that continuing the underground operation required secrecy. "By openly avowing their participation in the escape of slaves," he averred, they had converted the Underground Railroad into the "*upperground railroad*," greatly to the detriment of those who would attempt escape in the future. Despite Douglass's warning that its activities attract as little publicity as possible, the underground's existence and workings were becoming better known to its opponents. Francis Fedric was told by conductors in Ohio that "one or two fugitive slaves, having described things too minutely, had put the slaveholders upon the right trace, and the Underground Railway [in the vicinity] had been torn up, to the injury of my brethren in bondage, who might otherwise have escaped." When Calvin Fairbank wanted to learn about the Ripley underground, he sought out the most notorious slave catcher in the region, who was able to tell him everything he needed to know.[6]

More than the growing fame of the Underground Railroad, the increased traffic on it, representing the accelerating flow of fugitives across the Mason-Dixon Line, engendered the desire of slaveholders to prosecute the frontline struggle with greater vigor. They did not need to be informed that they were losing their property at an alarming rate. Tens of thousands of formerly enslaved African Americans resided in Canada by 1850. The loss was particularly felt in the border states of Kentucky and Virginia—by this time largely converted into slave-breeding territories for sale to the expanding cotton frontier in the Deep South. Kentucky slaveholders had been particularly vocal in their insistence that Ohioans stop abetting the escape of their chattel. As early as 1817, the Kentucky legislature petitioned the state of Ohio to do something about the flow of runaways across its soil. A meeting held just across the river from Cincinnati in the aftermath of the 1841 riot assured Ohioans that the best way to keep the peace in the future was to clamp down on those who aided the disappearance of their property.[7]

The result of the growing uproar in the South was the Fugitive Slave Law of 1850—a component of the Compromise of 1850, the brainchild of Kentucky's Henry Clay. If the fugitive slave clause in the Constitution and the existing federal fugitive slave legislation were oppressive, the 1850 incarnation was nothing short of draconian from the standpoint of African Americans and white abolitionists. In the first place, the new act completely denied due process to African Americans lawfully resident in the North. A prospective claimant of a fugitive effectively only had to present an affidavit that a particular African American belonged to her or him and then establish the identity of the person—for which the slaveholder's word alone was deemed sufficient—to lawfully claim that person as his or her property. No other form of proof was required, and no right was given to the "fugitive" to present a defense—even to contest a case of mistaken identity or present freedom papers. African Americans claimed as "fugitives" were specifically forbidden from testifying on their own behalf. The law mandated the creation of a corps of commissioners who would have sole jurisdiction of all cases involving alleged fugitives. It provided that these officials be paid twice as much if they ruled in favor of the slaveholder's claim over that of the alleged runaway. At the same time the Fugitive Slave Law of 1850 deprived free African Americans of every vestige of civil rights, it effectively conscripted all Northern white people into the slave-catching business. The commissioners were given the power to appoint agents to issue warrants, and the agents had the authority to command the help of any and all citizens of the free states in capturing—and for all they knew, kidnapping—African Americans. Persons whose actions were construed as in any way obstructing the execution of the law were subjected to the enormous fine of one thousand dollars per "fugitive" and a six-month term of imprisonment. Salmon P. Chase, by this time a U.S. Senator, declared the measure "as thoroughly unconstitutional as any Congress could possibly pass."[8]

A greater miscarriage of justice in a free Republic was difficult for abolitionists to imagine. Opponents of slavery held meetings throughout the North to denounce the proslavery legislation. Three weeks after its passage a mass convention of Cleveland's citizenry declared that the law "repudiat[ed] the doctrines of the Declaration of Independence" and was "hostile to every principle of justice and humanity, and, if persevered in, fatal to Human Freedom." Madison, Indiana, abolitionists described it as "the most tyrannical and unjust enactment that ever disgraced the annals of any country, pagan or Christian."[9]

The threat it posed to every African American in the North was immediate and palpable. Boston abolitionist William Lloyd Garrison proclaimed, "In consequence of the passage of the Fugitive Slave Law, at the last session of Congress, a general flight from the country of all fugitive slaves in the Northern States has become necessary as a matter of personal safety." A mass emigration of African Americans to Canada followed—and revived interest in the colonizationist movement. In the autumn of 1850, Daniel Hise of Salem, Ohio, wrote in his diary, "Our fugitives have all gone to Canada, in consequence of the infamous slave bill." Well-known Boston abolitionists Ellen and William Craft were forced to flee to Canada when their master showed up with a warrant to claim them. The Rev. Thomas H. Jones was not far behind. The renowned abolitionist and Underground Railroad conductor Samuel Ringgold Ward, whose parents escaped from bondage with him in his early childhood, set out on a lecture tour of Ohio and neighboring states in 1851. Shortly after his return he and his wife "concluded that resistance was fruitless, that the country was hopelessly given to the execution of this barbarous enactment, and that it were vain to hope for the reformation of such a country." The battle-hardened James Williams—whose missions took him within a few miles of the plantation from which he had escaped—also abandoned the work he had devoted himself to since the age of sixteen and headed as far from danger as he could.[10]

Not everyone who left was a fugitive. Even such a stalwart of the Cincinnati underground as John Hatfield, who claimed to have had as many as fifteen fugitives in his house at once, opted to leave, citing the "oppressive laws of the United States." He had remained in Cincinnati through the hard times of the 1830s, the riot of 1841, but his patience finally wore out. The longtime activist lamented, "I have as good friends in the United States, colored and white, as ever a man had,—I never expect to have such good friends again—but the laws were against me." He was not alone. The list of refugees was extensive, including underground operatives William Mitchell and William Howard Day. Many who remained at home neverthe-less became—at least in the initial aftermath of the harsh legisla-tion—proponents of emigration. At an African American convention in Cincinnati in January 1852, the list of speakers endorsing the principle of seeking freedom in foreign parts included such aboli-tionist veterans as John Mercer Langston, his brother Charles, and Peter H. Clark. An opponent reminded them that such an action amounted to "giving up, in utter despondency, the cause of their enslaved brethren."[11]

Although the Fugitive Slave Law of 1850 dealt a short-term setback to the antislavery movement, in the longer run it possibly proved far more costly to the defenders of slavery. An Ohio aboli-tionist reported,

> That iniquitous measure of the last Congress has done more to drive Ohio men into our ranks, to open their eyes to see the working of the "peculiar institution" and their ears to hear what others know of it, than all the lectures that have been delivered, from the first dawn of the Liberty party movement to the present time. It is perfectly aston-ishing to witness the excitement, the enthusiasm, the unanimity, with which all parties meet together, all over the country, to give vent to their indignation and abhorrence of the outrageous law and the men that perpetrated it.

He added, presciently, "Every attempt at reclamation, under the law, will tend to keep up the excitement." The legislation may well have numbered among the factors that prompted Harriet Beecher Stowe to publish *Uncle Tom's Cabin*, the most successful political tract since Thomas Paine's *Common Sense*. It was certainly on her mind as she wrote it, as Stowe symbolically denounced Northern politicians for supporting the passage of the bill: her character of the Ohio Senator faces the chastisement of his wife for voting in the bill's favor, a crime for which she has him do penance by aiding in the escape of the novel's heroine, Eliza Harris. The frontal assault on the rights of the North began to stiffen the region's resolve to combat the arrogance of what abolitionists increasingly referred to as the "slave power"—the economic and political stranglehold of the South over the nation. A spirit of defiance began to manifest itself, as in the Cleveland mass meeting organized against the law. It resolved, "[W]e *deem it the duty of* EVERY GOOD CITIZEN *to denounce, oppose and* RESIST" the law. The Madison underground was more forthright in its declaration: "We will 'feed the hungry, clothe the naked, and shelter the stranger,' as God commands, to the best of our abilities."[12]

The most defiant were those with the most to lose—an earlier generation of fugitives who crossed the Ohio River and refused to be chased out of the nation of their birth or to desist from helping others escape their bondage. Underground operative (and escapee from enslavement) Charles Garlick's first response to the new conditions was to go to Canada. A few months later, however, he experienced a charge of heart, deciding to "return to the states and take my chances." James Smith was terror stricken—dreaming that his master had come for him in the night and imagining that he saw him by day—but he stayed. If anyone had reason to know how tenuous freedom was for African Americans in the best of circumstances, that person was J.W. Loguen, who was born into Southern slavery because his mother had been kidnapped out of Ohio when she was seven years old. As not only a fugitive but also a well-known Underground Railroad operative whose activities had already led to his arrest, trial, and fortunate acquittal, Loguen was in a situation that could hardly be more dangerous. The man who had realized a childhood dream by crossing the Ohio River to freedom refused to moderate his Underground Railroad activities, at which no one in his vicinity worked harder, and in conduct of which no one was more public, as evidenced by his public avowal of participation in the press. All the less would he heed the advice of his Syracuse, New York, friends to emigrate to Canada or negotiate with his former master to obtain his legal freedom. A coworker on the liberty line recalled: "If the old man wanted him [Loguen] hoped he would come himself. . . . He was not going to Canada or to Tennessee, nor would he ask the aid of his friends, but he gave notice to all concerned that he should trust in *Loguen* and in Providence for protection, and principally and first of all in Loguen." The fugitive-turned-minister predicted that if anyone tried "to enforce that law . . . *somebody will get hurt.*"[13]

Loguen was left unmolested, and so never had the chance to translate his words into deeds, but Louis Talbert of Cabin Creek, Indiana, did. Also a fugitive, he had made five trips back into his native Kentucky to liberate others, until finally being captured on his last attempt and sold to New Orleans; en route he escaped once again. He settled in the African American community near Newport, Indiana, where on Coffin's removal he assumed a leadership position. Mayberry Lacey, later a Civil War major, described him as "an odd genius . . . very quiet and slow to talk, but . . . keen, shrewd and desperate." He and Cal Thomas were the most prominent of a group of between fifteen and twenty fugitive underground operatives in that area. Not long after the passage of the Fugitive Slave Law, the legal owners of Talbert and Thomas assembled an armed, mounted posse, also of between fifteen and twenty men, to pursue them, "boast[ing] that they would capture these two runaways or kill every Abolitionist in Newport." Apprised of their imminent arrival, Talbert and Thomas disdained the idea of further flight. "The ex-slaves were fully prepared and were determined to give battle." A crowd gathered as the showdown loomed. Lacey recalled, "The Kentuckians rode boldly into the crowd and demanded that every Negro surrender or they would be killed, and if the people interfered the town would be burned to ashes." Thomas's erstwhile owner, the first to recognize his target, reached for his pistol. Thomas set himself, took aim with his rifle, and "told him if he made another move he would blow him into eternity." Into the breach calmly walked a few unarmed Quakers, who boldly requested that the slave hunters leave town. As the crowd pressed in around them, the proslavery forces complied. Regrouping at a distance, they held a heated discussion, overheard by a local resident. A few were in favor of going back and fighting it out, but their leader announced that "he had a wife and children at home that he thought more of than any Negroes." They slunk out of town, never to return.[14]

The Fugitive Slave Law undoubtedly emboldened slaveholders. Many in the antislavery underground were determined to meet them head on. Abram Brooke and the abolitionists with whom he was staying in Salem, Ohio, became aware that a regular flow of enslaved persons passed through their town on the railroad. They determined to do something to stop it. When word reached an Anti-Slavery Society meeting on August 28, 1854, that a train had pulled in with an enslaved child aboard, Brooke, Ben Brown, Doc Thomas, and visiting Cincinnatian Henry Blackwell rushed into action. The meeting had resolved on obtaining a writ of habeas corpus to obtain her release, but Brooke said he "knew from experience how little help was to be expected from the law, and without hesitation took hold of the child to bear her off." As the young girl was whisked away, Brooke obstructed the path of the irate slaveholder, preventing him from pursuit. Brooke defied anyone present to challenge the propriety of his act. "When it was over and a call had been made from the window of the car 'I would like to see the man who would do such an act' I announced my name and residence, inviting them to prosecute if they saw fit." Though he was overheard by all, and his words were printed in the paper, no one ever attempted legal proceedings against him. Fifty dollars was immediately subscribed to fund the education of the child, whom Blackwell named Abby Kelly Salem after the town that secured her liberty. Outraged Kentuckians did, however, make noises about bringing assault charges against Blackwell, who was closer to their reach. Supported by proslavery forces in the Queen City of the West, they also vowed to take retribution on his wholesale hardware business. The *Anti-Slavery Bugle* pointed out that they had targeted the wrong person. "Mr. Blackwell is not the man to be intimidated at that." When his adversaries threatened to have a full account of his part in the rescue published in an attempt to drive off his customers, Blackwell offered to pay a share of the printing costs of such a notice, prompting one paper to note, "He is of the class of merchants who have *goods, not principles in market.*"[15]

A former member of Cincinnati's underground took part in a more celebrated rescue on September 13, 1858, in Oberlin, Ohio. Charles Langston, John Mercer's older brother, was visiting his sibling at Oberlin when rumors surfaced of slave hunters in the vicinity poised to pounce on a fugitive living there. The unfortunate victim was John Price, who had made Oberlin his home for several years. After a U.S. marshall seized Price, a group of African Americans, including Charles Langston, took him back, leading to the arrest of a number of Price's rescuers. At the trial, Charles Langston gave a memorable speech. He said that he had heard of the misfortune of "a man, a brother, who had a right to his liberty under the law of God, under the laws of Nature, and under the Declaration of Independence. . . . Being identified with that man by color, by race, by manhood, by sympathies such as God has implanted in us all, I felt it my duty to go and do what I could toward liberating him." Making reference to his and John's father, a prominent Virginia planter who was a leader in the American forces in the War for Independence, he averred that he "had been taught by [his] Revolutionary father, and by his honored associates, that the fundamental law of this Government is, that all men have a right to life and liberty." There was one inescapable conclusion: "I know that the courts of this country, that the laws of this country, that the governmental machinery of the country are so constituted as to oppress and outrage the colored men: men of my complexion. I cannot, then, of course, expect, judging from the past history of the country, any mercy from the laws, from the Constitution, or from the courts of the country." In any case, he proclaimed, the Fugitive Slave Law "is an unjust one, one made to crush the colored man. . . . I have nothing to do with its constitutionality; and about it I care a great deal less." Langston created a "sensation" in the courtroom when he said he acted "as a citizen of Ohio" and then quickly added, "[E]xcuse me for saying that, sir—[I meant to say] as an outlaw of the United States." Charles Langston was given a twenty-day sentence. But John Price was saved from being transported back to Southern slavery.[16]

Closer to the front lines than Oberlin, violence had long been a feature of daily operations, and such small-scale clashes were probably more frequent and attracted far less notice. The *Cincinnati Commercial* recorded an instance in which a Kentucky posse caught up with two fugitives in the hands of the Underground Railroad, resulting in the capture of one. A crowd soon gathered and made possible the escape of the second runaway. "We understand that the conductors of the opposing trains drew sundry revolvers and made various hostile demonstrations, but no blood was shed." Nor did the matter end up in court. Though not unheard of, legal action was not the usual course in this region where two armed camps had long fought each other in the African American struggle for freedom.[17]

Signs of the growing intensity of the frontline struggle abounded. John Parker was reminded of that one night as he jumped onto the Ohio River bank, leaving his boat where he could find it at a moment's notice. He was in enemy territory, in the slave state of Kentucky, keeping a rendezvous with a group of soon-to-be fugitives. As he hurried along in the darkness, he could not help wondering about all the proclamations tacked to trees and posts. Striking a match and holding it up to one of them, he read: "Reward $1,000 for John Parker, dead or alive."[18]

Underground operatives were accustomed to danger—whichever side of the river they happened to be on. The deep connection of the port cities of the Ohio and their hinterlands to the economy of slavery resulted in a deeply divided region, with strong antislavery sentiment animating many, and others just as fervently supporting the institution. "Fierce passions swept this little town," Parker said of Ripley, Ohio, "dividing its people into bitter factions."[19]

Parker's house was kept under surveillance; his enemies lay in wait. Their chance at the one thousand dollar bounty on his head, the price of his participation in the work of aiding fugitives, came while he was aboard an Ohio River steamer. Returning from a business trip to Cincinnati, Parker fell asleep and missed the Ripley landing. The next stop was on the Kentucky side. He found his cabin surrounded by Kentucky slaveholders who wanted the reward for his capture. He peered outside his door to find armed guards. With an African American Ripley neighbor who represented his only ally, Parker decided to make a break for it. Two men flew at him with guns in hand. Parker shot one at point-blank range, and the other ducked into a cabin. Parker and his neighbor tried to untie a small lifeboat to make their escape. They became entangled in its roping; the boat suddenly broke loose, propelling the two into the water. While his friend disappeared, never to be seen again, Parker managed to grab hold of the boat. "If I stayed where I was, I was a helpless target for my enemies. In the twilight I saw a man. Then I knew my end had come." The man was not, as Parker feared, one of the Kentucky slaveholders, but a Kentucky doctor for whom Parker had once done a service. The doctor cut the rope, and John Parker floated free down the Ohio River.[20]

Madison, Indiana, operative William Anderson's scrape with death, like Parker's, stemmed from a chance encounter on a riverboat. Found with abolitionist literature on his person, Anderson was placed under arrest. "With a heavy heart and bewildered mind, and in care of a strong guard, I was taken on up the river." Incarcerated in a Louisville jail, he found himself on trial for "stealing" African Americans in the slave state of Kentucky, albeit the charges named a different man. "Some five or six witnesses were examined. They all testified that I had said that I had helped off one hundred slaves. One man swore that on one occasion I said I had just returned from Canada, to where I had taken a lot of slaves from Kentucky." The antislavery lectures and poems he had on him were read. The case against him looked grim. "It seemed that I was going to the State Prison for life." Fortunately for him, the judge ruled that despite the antislavery literature on his person the prosecution had failed to prove its case. He nevertheless threatened Anderson with prison if he could not post five hundred dollars bond. Finally he was released, and, though dispossessed of a considerable sum of money he had brought with him, left on the Indiana side of the Ohio River to walk the long journey back to Madison.[21]

Unfortunately for Anderson, the incident was to result in serious damage to his reputation in the underground. The same day he was released, fellow minister of the gospel and Madison operative Elijah Anderson (no relation) was picked up aboard a steamboat and imprisoned in the Kentucky state penitentiary. While William Anderson made no forays into Kentucky in pursuit of fugitives, Elijah Anderson did so frequently. His final trip was to cost him his life. Having crossed the Ohio River at the fervid entreaties of a freed father to help his enslaved wife and their four grown daughters to liberty, Elijah Anderson became more than ever a marked man. William seems to have been the unsuspecting victim of the desire for retribution; in any case, he did nothing—nor was in any position to do anything—to lure Elijah into a trap. Still, the unfortunate coincidence convinced many that the former had betrayed his fellow operative. It did not help matters that after his arrest William Anderson was denounced as a Democratic agent by a Republican Congressman from Indiana in an acrimonious Washington debate among the state's delegation. A Democratic allegation, stemming in part from the abolitionist literature found on Anderson, that black abolitionists were among the Republicans' supporters provoked the countercharge regarding Anderson, which evidently amounted to political one-upmanship.

To a principal in an underground movement, however, such a suspicion raised against him was as good as fatal. For simply being seen in the company of the most notorious slave catcher in Ripley, Ohio, Calvin Fairbank found himself regarded with extreme suspicion by activists in that locale—even though he was well known to Cincinnati agents of the Underground Railroad. John Parker endured the whispers that resulted from his neighbor's death in the ill-fated river voyage in which both sought to escape the Kentucky slaveholders. H.B. Northrup, a well-known New York abolitionist and Underground Railroad veteran, was suspected despite a complete lack of evidence. When he arrived at Pittsburgh's Monongahela House—an active center of underground work—the word somehow got out that he was a slave hunter in search of fugitives. The whole African American community was soon roused against him before he succeeded in correcting the mistake. After Elijah Anderson suffered great hardship in the settlement of the John Simmons lawsuit (see chapter 5), he very nearly lost his own reputation in the effort to recover. As he sought to reestablish himself, he found himself denounced as a "swindler" and "knave" by the ever-vigilant Ripley antislavery forces and eventually had to repair to Cleveland, where he again built a solid reputation as a tireless worker in the cause of the fugitive. The loose links that necessarily bind underground movements, coupled with the endemic dangers of betrayal the movements face, lend themselves to such misunderstandings. This was all the more true for the Underground Railroad since it was not uncommon for slave hunters to pose as friends of the fugitive—even contributing money to collections for their journey—in order to close in on them, as the captors of Henry Bibb did in Cincinnati.[22]

Given the previous history of treachery and the resulting suspicion in the Madison movement, it is not surprising that acrimony arose as to the timing of the arrests and subsequent fates of the two Andersons. On one hand, the reaction also showed that Elijah remained in good repute in Madison, despite the attack on his character launched from Ripley. Otherwise no hostility would have been directed toward William Anderson. On the other hand, the latter was evidently never able to fully rehabilitate his reputation, though nothing was ever proved against him, and feeling himself unjustly suspected he displayed considerable bitterness in his memoirs, which were published before the movement reached its successful conclusion. Even the best-organized underground movement was susceptible to these hazards, especially along the front lines where the enemy was so close at hand.[23]

The Fugitive Slave Law complicated operations of the Underground Railroad. A rescue could misfire in the blink of an eye, as when James Ditcher escorted three fugitives, a mother and her two children, to John J. Stewart's Poke Patch home in 1860. Of mixed African American, Native American, and European ancestry, Stewart was born into a family of free persons of color in Virginia. He later relocated to Ohio, where his uncle had served as a missionary to the Wyandot nation. The next day, Stewart and Ditcher took the fugitives to the nearest railroad junction. After 1850 many fugitives were put on Ohio's railroad lines and safely and quickly transported to waiting friends in Detroit or Cleveland, who secured their safe passage to Canada. This time, the slave owner was waiting on board. Not bothering with the mother, who had become too old to be useful to him, he took only her two children back to his Kentucky plantation. On the journey back to a location fifty miles farther to the south they passed the Virginia plantation on which lived their enslaved cousins, the kidnapped Polly children. James Ditcher was forced to disappear to avoid prosecution. These were the only charges under his care that he had ever lost in two decades of Underground Railroad work.[24]

Despite being continuously menaced by proslavery forces, underground operatives prosecuted their joint struggle with increasing vigor. Not everyone, however, was fortunate enough to survive the conflict that raged in the 1850s. The period took a heavy toll on the forces of the antislavery underground. Six years after the 1846 beating death of his younger brother, Thomas Woodson Jr., who refused to divulge the whereabouts of the fugitives in his charge, Jackson County's John Woodson endured similar treatment for similar reasons at the hands of Kentucky slaveholders in search of runaways. During the year he lay dying after his brutalization, he bore without complaint his intense suffering. Seth Conklin, a white operative from the East who frequently passed through the West on missions and was well known in the Cincinnati underground, lost his life in 1854 in a rescue attempt in Alabama.[25]

The same fate awaited Elijah Anderson, who died in Kentucky's state penitentiary in 1861, unlike Conklin his memory all but lost to history. The cause of Anderson's death, which occurred almost at the end of his term, is not known. A few years earlier, however, an African American operative based in Evansville, Indiana, also sentenced to that prison for aiding an enslaved person's escape, died "some time after receiving a severe blow, from one of the keepers," a fellow prisoner of conscience disclosed.[26]

The conditions in a Kentucky prison that led to Anderson's death can be understood from a consideration of the fate of Calvin Fairbank. In his memoirs, he tried to convey experiences for which words seemed inadequate:

> For aiding those slaves to escape from their bondage, I was twice imprisoned—in all seventeen years and four months; and received . . . thirty-five thousand, one hundred and five stripes from a leather strap fifteen to eighteen inches long, one and a half inches wide, and from one-quarter to three-eighths of an inch thick. It was half-tanned leather, and frequently well-soaked, so that it might burn the flesh more intensely. These floggings were not with a rawhide or cowhide, but with a strap of leather attached to a handle of convenient size and length to inflict as much pain as possible, with as little real damage as possible to the working capacity.[27]

Despite the setbacks, operations of the Underground Railroad in the Ohio Valley peaked in the 1850s, when, according to available evidence, more fugitives passed through its terrain than in any other period. One principal boasted, "The Underground Railroad was never in a more hopeful condition. The Fugitive law has raised the stock on some of our Western tracks, at least 50 to 75 per cent. Some new tracks have lately gone into successful operation, and the old tracks have undergone a thorough repair. No accidents have occurred." Cleveland abolitionists reported that between May and December of 1854 they received 275 fugitives from points along the river. Detroit operatives counted fifty-three within a fortnight during the same year. The *Pittsburgh Visiter* announced, "The business on this road has trebled since the passage of the Fugitive Act." Cincinnati papers were full of the news of fugitives in that city. In 1855, for example, the *Cincinnati Columbian* noted, "The travel over the under- ground railroad for the past few days has been, we are informed, unusually active, and no fewer than seven lots of runaway slaves have arrived at this terminus within a week." *Voice of the Fugitive*, a Canadian paper published by former Ohio Valley fugitive Henry Bibb, inserted a notice on the arrival of a contingent of thirteen fugitives from Covington, Kentucky (the city directly across from Cincinnati)— five of whom belonged to the mayor. Word followed a few months later of an additional sixteen runaways from the same city, provid- ing further testimony to the activity and continued efficiency of the Cincinnati underground. A Kentucky newspaper chimed in, com plaining, "There has been an immense stampede of the negroes in the upper part of the State"—one it attributed mainly to the machi- nations of forces to the north of the river. On traveling through Kentucky, a *New York Herald* correspondent who professed admi- ration for the South's labor system felt compelled to echo the senti- ments of slaveholders to whom he had spoken: "The negroes are getting very scarce in the northern part of the State, owing to the close proximity of the enemy across the Ohio. None but the most faithful of Slaves can be kept by farmers along the border, so well arranged is the Underground Railroad system, in the southern coun- ties of Ohio and Indiana." The results could be seen north of the U.S. border as well; by 1860 some thirty thousand fugitives were living in western Canada.[28]

The growing sense of impotence on the southern bank of the Ohio expressed itself, perhaps, most tangibly in the arrest (on trumped-up charges of abetting escapes) and conviction of South- ern whites who had nothing to do with the Underground Railroad. Following a series of escapes in his vicinity, Thomas Brown, a mer- chant in Henderson, Kentucky, was sent to join Elijah Anderson and Calvin Fairbank in the state penitentiary in Frankfurt. As he later wrote, "The slaveholders of Henderson and the adjoining coun- ties, supposed that their 'chattels' . . . could not escape without assistance, and they were on the alert to find who aided them." They settled on Brown as the likely suspect, based on his failure to express fondness for the system of slavery, the fact that his busi- ness necessitated travel and the ownership of a horse-drawn wagon, and his recent relocation from Cincinnati. The escapes did not cease with Brown's incarceration. Consequently, one year later, Presbyte- rian minister T.B. McCormick, who had had the temerity to introduce a resolution challenging the morality of slavery at an Indiana state meeting of his denomination, was indicted in absentia by a grand jury for running off the very same group of enslaved persons. The evidence for the latter case was simply reproduced from the earlier trial and McCormick's name substituted for Brown's. That the accused had not stepped foot in his native state of Kentucky for a number of years was not regarded as being material to the case, even by the Indiana governor, who ordered McCormick extradited to stand trial. The Kentucky slaveholders' search for those responsible for "running off" their enslaved women and men did not stop their bondspersons from disappearing, but it did end in the ruin of a prosperous nonslaveholding family, the flight of a woman and her two young daughters from the state under threat of violent reprisal, as well as the conversion of a respected clergyman into a fugitive from justice.[29]

The Underground Railroad became increasingly public in its operation in the 1850s—effectively answering the challenge to its operations provided by the Fugitive Slave Law. A Cincinnati convention of African Americans publicly associated itself with the illegal work of aiding fugitives to liberty. George De Baptiste, forced to leave Madison, Indiana, when his safety was threatened, openly acknowledged his underground work from Detroit. Frederick Douglass began running frequent testimonials to the success of Underground Railroad operations in his paper, despite having blamed his western comrades for that alleged sin only a few years earlier. He went as far as mentioning one operative, Rev. J.W. Loguen, by name. Loguen was not the only participant to proclaim his participation publicly. Numerous sets of memoirs and tracts detailing some of the inner functioning of the liberty line appeared, including those of Madison's William Anderson (which acknowledged his status as both an underground agent and a fugitive), Ohio's William Mitchell, and others.[30]

As well, more operatives who were active in the field ventured into the South and brought out runaways with increasing boldness. These included John Parker, John Mason, John Fairfield, Rial Cheadle, Elijah Anderson and his many coworkers in Madison, Indiana, William Casey, William Mitchell, Calvin Fairbank, and Alexander Milton Ross. Just as important were the African American communities all along the river that remained in place and intensified their activities. The *Pittsburgh Journal* was impressed by "how earnest our citizens are in their opposition to the Fugitive Slave law," as evidenced by their vigorous prosecution of Underground Railroad work and by their vigilant pursuit of those who tried to enforce its provisions. The paper declared, "[W]e are of opinion that a slave-catcher would stand but small chance in this city, as without doubt the colored persons here keep themselves posted up perfectly." As far north as Chicago, slave catchers were menaced by the "threat of 'tar and feathers' from the excited colored population, who are up in arms, and nightly, as well as daily, on the watch for white gentlemen with sallow complexions and broad rimmed hats."[31]

All of this combined, many in the underground believed, to render the Fugitive Slave Law virtually inoperative. The *National Era* estimated that recovery rates were no better than one in a hundred, and that the expenses of recovery even in those cases were greater than the value of the property lost. The Cincinnati correspondent of *Frederick Douglass' Paper* asked, only half jokingly, "What's the Fugitive Slave Bill? Is it a dead letter?" One of Ohio's U.S. Senators, Salmon P. Chase, certainly thought so: "The number of fugitives now escaping is greater than ever before. . . . There are but few captured under this law. . . . hundreds escape where one is taken back." In his estimation, the Fugitive Slave Law never was and never would be anything more than "a badge and symbol of northern servitude . . . a token of incapacity to resist aggression." If that was indeed the infamous act's purpose, the *National Era* saw in it a distinct failure. "In the present state of the public mind, every attempt to enforce this law is immediately heralded through the papers from one end of the country to the other, and all the facts tending to excite sympathy for the fugitive are carefully collected and sent upon the wings of the wind."[32]

The underground in the Ohio Valley, which had long been able to hold its own in the trenches, was now emerging as an important cog in a political struggle that was closer to victory in ending slavery than ever. The more abolitionism moved in a political direction, the more the western theatre—where a political approach to the issue had gained considerable acceptance—assumed prominence. It was no accident that first the Free Soil movement, which sought to prevent the spread of slavery from its current boundaries, and later the Republican Party, which adhered to largely the same position, had strong western roots. The Liberty Party held all but its founding convention in Ohio, where it garnered thousands of votes as a third party, even before its 1848 merger with the Free Soil Party. The latter, in its turn, gave rise to the Republican Party, formed in 1854 largely in the states that had been created from the Northwest Territory. The new party owed its genesis to the fallout from the Compromise of 1850, which included the Fugitive Slave Act. Salmon P. Chase, the old Cincinnati abolitionist lawyer, who came to prominence defending Underground Railroad conductors brought up on charges of assisting fugitives, was among its first important leaders elected to the Senate. Though he shunned the label "abolitionist" for political reasons, he continued to take a legal role in cases involving kidnapped African Americans and the Underground Railroad. The Republican victory in the 1860 presidential election, which would precipitate the nation into the crisis that ended slavery, featured a candidate who embodied something of the spirit of western abolitionism. Abraham Lincoln was a native Kentuckian whose family moved to Indiana partly out of hatred for the institution of slavery. He would become the first American leader to ask the nation to support a war to abolish it—one, however, that he never would have started had he been left with the choice.[33]

A young man strode out of the Rankin house at daybreak on a Sunday morning, headed straight down the hill to John Parker's residence on the edge of the water, and awakened him with a sharp knock. It was one of John Rankin's sons. His father had summoned an emergency council of the Ripley, Ohio, underground, and Parker was instructed to bring all the guns he owned. "I knew something serious was up, because this was the first time I had ever been called on to come armed with anything but small arms," Parker recalled.[34]

Across the river in Kentucky a group of fugitives was in peril. They had reached the Ohio River after daybreak and dared not cross. They sat helplessly near the riverbank. Looking back, Parker could not help but marvel, "How the word got across the river to Reverend John Rankin I never did know, but he did receive the message." And he was determined to do something about it. "Seeing the fugitives aroused Rev. Rankin to a fever pitch. . . ." Rankin's plan was as simple as it was audacious—others called it foolhardy. He, his six sons, John Parker, and whoever else would agree to join them would make an armed foray across the river and take the runaways by force if need be. Parker was all for it, even though Rankin's plan would have meant a pitched battle not only on the Kentucky side of the river, but on the Ohio shore, where slave catchers would be waiting for the chance at the enormous reward of one thousand dollars offered for the return of the fugitives. John Rankin and John Parker's counsel did not win the day. The decision was made to delay the rescue until nightfall.[35]

The fire that lit Rankin was evident to all that day in church as he preached his weekly sermon. Parker related, "When he came to that part of his service that called for prayer, the wrought-up preacher almost revealed the presence of the slaves and their serious situation in his appeal to the Almighty for their protection during the day." When night fell, seven operatives stole across the river "armed with muskets in a little flotilla of three boats, two occupied by the guard and one for the slaves." They brought the fugitives safely across. Their freedom assured, five of the many thousands of fugitives who crossed into Ripley passed onto the Underground Railroad. John Parker reflected, "That's how near the Ripley abolitionists came to anticipating John Brown and his Harpers Ferry adventure."[36]

To many, that most famous of all frontline clashes sounded the tocsin for an all-out assault on the institution of slavery. With a small force of twenty-two men, Brown made an attack on the federal armory at Harpers Ferry, Virginia, hoping to spur a rebellion of the enslaved. The attackers fought bravely but their venture was doomed from the start—and cost most of the participants their lives. Though the action occurred east of the Ohio Valley, many veterans of Ohio's underground, including Brown himself, played a central role in the frontal assault on slavery. John Brown had gotten his start as an antislavery activist in Ohio, where he grew up and became an early participant in its Underground Railroad. Brown had long sought, however, to combine its rescue operations with a more direct form of guerilla operations south of the Mason-Dixon Line. He once described his plan as Underground "Rail Road business on a *somewhat extended* scale."[37]

Brown found support from prominent Eastern abolitionists, who helped fund the raid. But the western underground supplied half of its combatants, including two Oberlin, Ohio, African Americans, the younger of whom simply desired "to liberate a few of my poor and oppressed people"; both were killed in the raid. A third African American was a fugitive, newly arrived via the Underground Railroad when he met and decided to join John Brown. Another participant who met his death with John Brown on the scaffold was a young Quaker, Edwin Coppoc, who hailed from the underground stronghold of Salem, Ohio. After his execution, his body was returned to Salem, where six thousand people attended his funeral, determined to build a monument in his honor. His brother and fellow raider, Barclay Coppoc, quietly resolved that "his death [would] be avenged." A year later, he was among the first volunteers from Salem to enlist in the Union army.[38]

John Brown was not the only veteran of the Ohio underground to give up his life in those years for African American liberty. John Fairfield had once told Levi Coffin, "When I undertake to conduct slaves out of bondage I feel that it is my duty to defend them, even to the last drop of my blood." His words proved prophetic. On the eve of the Civil War, he died side by side with a group of enslaved African Americans he had joined in a rebellion that ended in a valiant, though futile, attempt to hold off a mob of slavery's defenders. Fairfield went to his death among the people with whom he had chosen to spend his life.[39]

The climate had changed—acknowledgment of the need for a frontal assault on slavery was much greater. From Indiana, Quaker abolitionist and Underground Railroad operative Valentine Nicholson objected to a sermon against the looming battle. "It seemed to me as rather a selfish request to make, to ask that a war might be put off in order to let some of the present inhabitants leave this world without having to pass the crisis of the time when the war was in actual operation. The thought in my mind was that if such a war had got to come, the sooner it could be passed through the better, as one of its effects [would be] to give freedom to the multitudes held in bondage." On the day of John Brown's execution, another activist, Daniel Hise, wrote in his diary in Salem, Ohio, "[T]oday Poor Old John Brown, of Kansas notoriety, dies on the gallows at Charleston, Va.; his crime (as they call it) was trying to liberate the slaves. Generations to come will erect his monument." The same day Levi Coffin, who described himself as "a peace man and . . . always opposed [to] anything in the shape of war," confided to a friend,

> This is the day of execution of that brave, that noble, that good (though mistaken or unwise in his plans as we think) man John Brown. It may be that he was an instrument in the hands of the Almighty to commence the great work of the deliverance of the oppressed and of

the scourge of the land of the south. . . . I believe that every drop of John Brown's blood that they spill will raise up a man against them. This should be a solemn day with all the true friends of the oppressed. I feel deeply on this occasion, for I think this is only the beginning of the end. A terrible day is brewing, and more lives may yet be sacrificed in the cause of the oppressed. Slavery, I fear, will end in blood.[40]

Some argued that, far from undermining the institution of slavery in America, the Underground Railroad actually strengthened it. "The fugitives are generally the most intelligent, enterprising, and fearless of the slaves," wrote Cincinnati-based abolitionist Gamaliel Bailey. "Is it best to diminish the number of these in the slave states?" One theory held that doing so constituted a sort of "safety valve" to release the pent-up pressure created by the most potentially rebellious among the enslaved. That thesis assumed, first, that bondage in the United States was susceptible to overthrow by means of rebellion by the enslaved—a rather doubtful proposition when one considers the small proportion of the nation's populace that was caught up in slavery's yoke. It presupposed, too, that the phenomenon of fugitives from enslavement played no role in the abolition of the system. On the contrary, their perpetual presence in the South was a time bomb waiting to explode, capable of posing a genuine threat given the right conditions. Those circumstances manifested themselves during the Civil War. The tradition of resistance in the form of escape, nourished by the Underground Railroad, gave African Americans a powerful weapon with which to help forge the conditions of their own freedom. "I had heard so much about freedom, and of the colored people running off and going to Canada, that my mind was busy with this subject even in my young days," recalled Kentucky's Elijah Marrs. As a youth, he was inspired to learn to read and write; as an adult, to run off and join the Union army.[41]

With the South straining to maintain a war effort against an opponent with four times its population, it was crucial that production continue at full throttle. That capacity relied above all on its main labor force—enslaved African Americans. By the hundreds of thousands, they deserted their plantations, factories, and workshops, engaging in what W.E.B. Du Bois called a "Great Strike." The Underground Railroad continued to function throughout that conflict, as the network kept up and even increased its activity. Mattie Jackson was helped to freedom by Louisville African Americans who, even then, served as the initial contacts. Still, the surest bet for escaping slavery was right in the South in the form of the Union army. John Quincy Adams remembered a few years later, "On Saturday, June 27, 1862, we left old mistress, and young miss, and every other kind of miss." Having escaped their native Virginia with the aid of Union forces, the family settled in Pennsylvania, but the seventeen-year-old Adams could not forbear a trip of a few months in Cincinnati just to celebrate his freedom. Thousands more liberated themselves by dogging the Union army's every step through the heart of the Confederacy, just as at an earlier time some managed to snatch liberty by making use of networks of friends, relatives, and even strangers, who kept many a fugitive alive in the vicinity of the plantation they had walked away from.[42]

Henry B. Stanton, one of the Lane rebels who went on to abolitionist fame, had warned the South of the consequences of disunion. "Does the South imagine that that act will widen the Ohio river?" he queried. Given the eventuality, he foresaw "[a] black tide pour[ing] over the line and lo! the South is emptied of her slaves." If not quite in the form of the almost biblical prophesy of Stanton, the flow was certainly greater than at any time previous. Ohio was as much a natural destination during and after the war as before. During her years at Oberlin College from 1860 to 1865, Fanny Jackson-Coppin witnessed the "[f]reedmen [begin] to pour into Ohio from the South." Unfortunately, the refugees continued to encounter resistance north of the Ohio River. The beginnings of what would become a long exodus from slavery stirred the same feelings among much of Ohio's white population that it had since the state's inception. Mobs descended on members of the African American community in Cincinnati once again, as complaints about their role in the escape of enslaved persons across the river were revived. The *Cincinnati Enquirer* asked provocatively, "How do our white laborers relish the prospect that the emancipation of the blacks spreads among them?" The Democratic convention in Columbus, July 4, 1862, went on record against emancipation as a war aim because, its attendees said, they did not want to "fill Ohio with a degraded population." Petitions poured into the state legislature asking it to stem the tide of the new mass migration.[43]

But nothing did. Levi Coffin traveled five hundred miles down the Ohio River to its mouth, at Cairo, Illinois, to look into the conditions of several thousand African Americans who left slavery to run

127th Regiment, Ohio Volunteer Infantry, the first African American regiment recruited in Ohio. From the collection of the Ohio Historical Society.

to the Union lines during the Civil War. He found appalling conditions among the people the army called "contrabands": "The deepest emotions of pity and sympathy were called forth as we witnessed their extreme desperation and suffering. Many were sick from exposure and for want of sufficient clothing. A large part of the contrabands collected at this point were women, children, and old people." What struck Coffin more forcefully than their misery was the exuberance of their rejoicing. At a religious meeting he experienced singing like nothing he had ever heard before: "I thought of the day of the Pentecost, when the disciples being all of one accord in one place, there came a sound from heaven as of a rushing mighty wind that filled the house where they were sitting, and filling them with the Holy Ghost so that they spoke as the Spirit gave them utterance. Their hearts seemed filled to overflowing with praise to God for their deliverance from slavery."[44]

As the exodus continued unchecked, the effects of what amounted to perhaps the greatest wartime labor action in world history took a heavy toll on the Confederacy's ability to prosecute

the war. The longer the battle raged, the less chance the secession-
ists had of winning. Even so, the massive numbers of fugitives had
perhaps a more significant effect on the Union. Their presence created for President Lincoln, who for political reasons preferred to
keep the issue of slavery out of the conflict, a problem that could no
longer be ignored. Pressured by his general staff, to which he had
given the heartless task of returning runaways to bondage, Lincoln
finally acquiesced in making the abolition of slavery a war aim, is-
suing the Emancipation Proclamation. With a Union victory, the
bonds of slavery would be forever torn asunder.[45]

Having fought a clandestine war against slavery for decades,
underground operatives embraced the opportunity to fight in the
open conflict that would conclude their work. Ohio's governor first
rejected their petitions to join the war—turning away a whole company organized by Cincinnati African Americans. He told 150 black
volunteers from Wilberforce University: "[T]his is a white man's war
. . . the Negro [has] nothing to do with it." Force of circumstances
later changed that policy. John Parker secretly helped hundreds of
fugitives obtain positions in the Union ranks. John Mercer Langston's
war recruiting was more official, since he served as the chief agent
of the famed Massachusetts Fifty-fourth and Fifty-fifth. Six of John
Rankin's sons, and one of his grandsons, served in the Union cause.
Perhaps most symbolically, one of the many thousands of fugitives
from slavery, John Curtis—veteran of the underground on the front
lines—returned to the state of Virginia for the first time since his
escape almost two decades before. This time, however, he and his
seven African American neighbors from Stafford, Ohio, were armed
as soldiers in the U.S. Colored Infantry, and would do the chasing.[46]

In a nation that has always represented itself as a beacon of liberty,
it took a war to end slavery. The Civil War is often referred to as our
nation's battle of brother against brother. In truth, America had
been fighting a family war since its inception. Fugitive and Ohio
antislavery activist Milton Clarke remembered the dying words of
his father, a Scottish immigrant disabled in the American War for
Independence. The Revolutionary veteran was looking on helplessly
as his enslaved wife and children mounted the auction block at the
direction of her half-sisters, their masters. He lamented: "[I] had
never expected when fighting for the liberties of this country, to see
[my] own wife and children sold in it to the highest bidder." In the

John Curtis, in hat to left of smaller horse, with his family, on his Stafford, Ohio, farm. From the collection of Henry Burke.

preamble of the Constitution, the Founding Fathers wrote of their intention to "ensure the blessings of liberty to us and our posterity." These words were meant to apply only to certain of their children. Others they kept in slavery.[47]

Slavery is coerced labor based on force—violence. To view it as warfare on the enslaved, both on their persons and on their humanity, is no mere application of a metaphor. The enshrining of the institution of slavery in the Constitution of the United States ensured neither justice nor domestic tranquility, but rather a per petual war fought out among an interrelated American people until slavery was permanently removed from American soil.

The Civil War has always occupied a prominent place in the nation's memory, in certain respects more central to the national imagination than either the Revolutionary War or World War II. The preceding decades-long conflict, a main theatre of which took place along a river separating a land of bondage from one of freedom, has been more than simply forgotten. This simmering prelude to the final drama, an internecine war of a nation and a people, has been transformed in the national psyche into something quite different. As the legendary Underground Railroad, a part of the story has been substituted for the whole, one that emphasizes less belligerent themes. The guerilla tactics, the underground form, the occasional pitched battles, have been shunted into the background. In their place, the focus has been shifted to the conveying of fugitives from enslavement to safety and freedom along a network of stations throughout the North. Significantly, the group most closely associated with this movement, the Quakers, is well known for pacifist views. In successfully debunking the mythical liberty line, historian Larry Gara nevertheless considers one of its central characteristics to be "the important example of successful nonviolent action the underground railroad provided."[48]

Nations, like individuals, carry their past with them as a constant commentary on their present. Seemingly eager to at once put its slave past behind it, and yet at the same time recognize the positive heritage of resistance to the evil, America has recently embraced the Underground Railroad with renewed fervor. As might have been foretold, it has been far easier to catch hold of the legend of the Underground Railroad than the full context that it connoted north of the Ohio River: the Black Laws, the racial violence, and the necessity of an underground movement in a nation with no foreign power occupying its territory. To come to grips with the legacy of the Underground Railroad is to be reminded that in democratic America ending slavery required a war, an important portion of which raged for decades along the banks of the Ohio River under an unlikely and misleading name, the Underground Railroad.

Notes

Preface

1. Horton and Horton, *In Hope of Liberty*; Hodges, *Root and Branch*; Reed, *Platform for Change*; Gomez, *Exchanging Our Country Marks*; Rivers, *Slavery in Florida*; Shaw, *What a Woman Ought To Be and To Do*; Kelley, *Race Rebels*. Dillon's *Slavery Attacked* gives significant credit to the actions of the slaves themselves in giving the impetus to Northern abolitionism.

2. Quarles, *Black Abolitionists*, 143–67; Gara, *Liberty Line*, xiii; Horton, *Free People of Color*, 53–74; Horton and Horton, *In Hope of Liberty*, 229–34. Two other important studies centered in the Ohio Valley deserve mention: Weisenburger's *Modern Medea*, which focuses on the single case of Kentucky fugitive Margaret Garner, and Runyon's *Delia Webster and the Underground Railroad*. See also Lumpkin, "'The General Plan Was Freedom.'" In stressing the interracial nature of the struggle in the Ohio Valley region, this account supports the findings of Stanley Harrold, *Abolitionists and the South*, and also builds on the work of John Stauffer, *Black Hearts of Men*.

3. Siebert, *Underground Railroad*; Siebert, *Mysteries*; U.S., Department of the Interior, National Park Service, *Underground Railroad*, 3.

4. Gara, *Liberty Line*. On the 1829 riot, see Ware, "Negro in Cincinnati."

1. River of Slavery, River of Freedom

1. On the economy that developed along the Ohio River in the antebellum period, see Trotter, *River Jordan*; Taylor, introduction to *Race and the City*, 1–28; Bigham, "River of Opportunity," 130–81; Dillon, *Abolitionists*, 24–26.

2. Siebert, *Mysteries*, ix.

3. Ibid.; Siebert, *Underground Railroad*, viii.

4. For an authoritative volume taking precisely this perspective, see Franklin and Schweninger, *Runaway Slaves*. For the perspective of a single fugitive, the famous Margaret Garner, Weisenburger's *Modern Medea*, also deserves mention in this respect.

5. Siebert, *Mysteries*, xi.

6. For a discussion of the origin of the name, see Gara, *Liberty Line*, 173–74. One earlier study begins, "The Underground Railroad, contrary to misinformation, was neither under the ground, nor was it a railway" (McClure, "The Underground Railroad," 1). A recent History Channel documentary starts by reciting the same popular formula.

7. J.H. Tibbetts to Elizabeth Nicholson, [1884], box 2, folder 2, Steele Papers.

8. Quarles, in *Black Abolitionists*, employs the term. Horton and Horton's use in *In Hope of Liberty* corresponds quite closely to what is meant here.

9. On underground movements in occupied nations at war, see, for example, Michel, *The Shadow War*.

10. Executive Committee of the New York Anti-Slavery Society to the Executive Committee of the Ohio State Anti-Slavery Society, August 26, 1836, in *Collection of Valuable Documents*, 67–75, quoted, 74–75.

11. Levine, *Black Culture and Black Consciousness*; Trotter, *River Jordan*; Taylor, *Race and the City*.

12. Trotter, *River Jordan*; Litwack, *North of Slavery*. On race riots in antebellum urban America, see Curry, *Free Black in Urban America*, 96–111.

13. The first generation of scholarly works went as far as to question whether African Americans participated at all. After a cursory examination of the subject, Mary Harrison Games concluded, "In any event the negro worked more effectively when directed by a white man" (Games, *Underground Railroad in Ohio*, 43).

14. Gara, *Liberty Line*; Siebert, *Underground Railroad, Mysteries*.

15. Its participants also left a vast literature: William Anderson, *Life and Narrative*; Bearse, *Reminiscences of Fugitive-Slave Law Days*; Butler, *My Story of the Civil War*; Cockrum, *History of the Underground Railroad*; Addison Coffin, *Life and Travels*; Levi Coffin, *Reminiscences*; Fairbank, *Rev. Calvin Fairbank during Slavery Times*; Haviland, *Woman's Life-Work*; H.U. Johnson, *From Dixie to Canada*; Malvin, *North into Freedom*; William Mitchell, *Under-Ground Railroad*; John Parker, *His Promised Land*; Ross, *Memoirs of a Reformer*; Smedley, *History of the Underground Railroad*; Still, *Underground Railroad*; George Thompson, *Prison Life and Reflections*; Walker, *Branded Hand*.

16. Levi Coffin, *Reminiscences*, 107, 119; Gara, *Liberty Line*.

17. Levi Coffin, *Reminiscences*, 118; *Richmond Palladium-Item*, January 17, 1962 (reprint of Lacey manuscript as "Underground Railroad").

2. No Promised Land

This particular version of the epigraph appears in William Anderson, *Life and Narrative*, 77–78; Games, *Underground Railroad in Ohio*, 112, gives a slightly different version that she got from an African American informant born circa1860. Reference to the song is also found in Butler, *My Story of the Civil War*, 181.

1. Wilhelm, "Settlement . . . in the Ohio Valley," 67–75; Bigham, "River of Opportunity," 130–72; Abdy, *Tour in the United States*, 3:25–34, quoted, 3:32;

Torrey, *Portraiture of Domestic Slavery*; Royster, *Fabulous History of the Dismal Swamp Company*, 423–28; Franklin and Schweninger, *Runaway Slaves*, 278.

2. Williamson, *New People*; Trotter, *River Jordan*, 26–27; Litwack, *North of Slavery*, 3; Wesley, *Ohio Negroes in the Civil War*; J.C. Brown narrative in Drew, *North-Side View of Slavery*, 240–48. For detailed accounts of African Americans in the antebellum North, see Trotter, *River Jordan*; Curry, *Free Black in Urban America*; Horton, *Free People of Color*; Horton and Horton, *In Hope of Liberty*; Hodges, *Slavery and Freedom in the Rural North*; Reed, *Platform for Change*; Litwack, *North of Slavery*.

3. Abdy, *Tour in the United States*, 3:25–34; Ohio Anti-Slavery Society, *Proceedings, 1835*, 18–19; Ohio Anti-Slavery Society, *Memorial to the General Assembly of Ohio*, 10–13, quoted, 13; Torrey, *Portraiture of Domestic Slavery*; Royster, *Fabulous History of the Dismal Swamp Company*, 423–28.

4. Ohio Anti-Slavery Society, *Memorial to the General Assembly of Ohio*, 10–13, quoted, 12; Ohio Anti-Slavery Society, *Proceedings, 1835*, 18–19; Abdy, *Tour in the United States*, 3:25–34, quoted, 3:38, 36, 53. Rev. S.J. May of New York gives a good description of Abdy's zeal to communicate directly with African Americans in gathering all he could of the conditions of American slavery and freedom: "[H]e an accomplished English gentleman . . . riding on the driver's box of a stage-coach, side by side with an American slave-woman, that he might learn more of her history and character." Nor was Abdy merely a passive observer. He attempted to convince her to escape, with May's help, though he failed in this endeavor. *Frederick Douglass' Paper*, February 4, 1853.

5. Royster, *Fabulous History of the Dismal Swamp Company*, 49–61; Wilhelm, "Settlement . . . in the Ohio Valley," 67–75; on the history of Ohio, see Hutchinson, *Bounty Lands of the American Revolution*; Berquist and Bowers, *New Eden*; Hurt, *Ohio Frontier*.

6. Onuf, *Statehood and Union*; Middleton, *Ohio and the Anti-Slavery Activities of Salmon Portland Chase*; Chase, "Preliminary Sketch of the History of Ohio," in Chase, ed., *Statutes of Ohio*, 1:18; Chase, *Speech of Salmon Chase in the Case of the Colored Woman, Matilda*, 29–30.

7. Hutchinson, *Bounty Lands*; Berquist, *New Eden*; Hurt, *Ohio Frontier*.

8. Ohio Anti-Slavery Society, *Memorial to the General Assembly of Ohio*, 10–13; Chase, ed., *Statutes of Ohio*, 1:393–94; Middleton, *Black Laws in the Old Northwest*; Litwack, *North of Slavery*, 69–74, 93–95.

9. Chase, *Reclamation of Fugitives from Service*, 74; *Philanthropist*, February 8, March 1, May 3, 1843.

10. Cochran, *Western Reserve and the Fugitive Slave Law*, 9–53; Chase, ed., *Statutes of Ohio*, 1:89; Chase, *Reclamation of Fugitives from Service*, 95;

11. Chase, *Speech of Salmon Chase in the Case of the Colored Woman, Matilda*, 14, 19, 26, 32; Chase, ed., *Statutes of Ohio*, 2:1052.

12. Chase, ed., *Statutes of Ohio*, 1:555.

13. *Philanthropist*, November 12, December 7, December 21, 1842, March 8, April 12, 1843, May 7, 1845.

14. Ohio Anti-Slavery Society, *Report of the Fourth Anniversary*, 50; *Philanthropist*, February 26, 1845; William S. Edwards narrative in Drew, *North-Side View of Slavery*, 328–30; Ohio Anti-Slavery Society, *Proceedings, 1835*, 33; *Phi-*

lanthropist, February 20, March 13, 1838; *Colored American*, December 16, 1837; Adam Rankin, "Autobiography," 82–84; *Philanthropist*, November 12, 1842. Throughout the 1830s and 1840s, such kidnappings occurred with alarming regularity, as the pages of the *Philanthropist* attest. See, *e.g.,* May 3, 1843; see also *New York Evangelist*, May 3, 1834. For a full account of kidnapping in antebellum America, see Wilson, *Freedom at Risk.*

15. Chase, ed., *Statutes of Ohio*, 2:1052, 3:1878; Abdy, *Tour in the United States*, 2:379; Hawkins, *Lunsford Lane*, 1863; Delaney, *From the Darkness Cometh the Light*, 9–10; Conklin quoted in Pickard, *Kidnapped and the Ransomed*, 284–85; Wilson, *Freedom at Risk.*

16. Litwack, *North of Slavery*; Middleton, *Black Laws in the Old Northwest*; Trotter, *River Jordan*; Curry, *Free Black in Urban America*, 81–95; Ohio Anti-Slavery Society, *Memorial to the General Assembly of Ohio*, 5–6; Ohio Anti-Slavery Society, *Proceedings, 1835*, 31–32, 40; *Colored American*, October 12, 1839, December 26, 1840, January 23, 1841; Blair, *Book for the People*, 4; *Palladium of Liberty*, April 3, 1844.

17. *Philanthropist*, December 21, 1842. By early the following year, the *Philanthropist* reported that interest in the case had "almost died away" (March 8, 1843).

18. Abdy, *Tour in the United States*, 2:364–79; Ohio Anti-Slavery Society, *Proceedings, 1835*, 20–21.

19. Ohio Anti-Slavery Society, *Proceedings, 1835*, 20; Abdy, *Tour in the United States*, 3:38.

20. Litwack, *North of Slavery*, 64–112; Dillon, *Abolitionists*, 19–27; Staudenraus, *African Colonization Movement*, 1–3.

21. Trotter, *River Jordan*, 33; John Rankin, "Address to the Churches," 36; Dillon, *Abolitionists*, 19–20; Litwack, *North of Slavery*, 20–21.

22. Ohio State Colonization Society, *A Brief Exposition*, 7; Abdy, *Tour in the United States*, 2:394–400, 3:44–50.

23. Abdy, *Tour in the United States*, 2:398–400.

24. Ibid., 3:28; Isaac Beeson to [?], April 19, 1851, box 2, folder 1, Beeson Papers; Levi Coffin, *Reminiscences*, 157–60.

25. Levi Coffin, *Reminiscences*, 157–60. The law in Indiana was repealed a year later, as it inspired a fear in clergy about performing any marriage ceremony with such a heavy penalty hanging over their heads. A similar case occurred in Cleveland in 1841, also producing a violent response (*Colored American*, March 20, 1841).

26. Hervey Heth to Thomas Posey, March 10, 1814, English Collection; Abdy, *Tour in the United States*, 3:35; Randolph quoted in *Cincinnati Daily Gazette*, July 29, 1836; *Philanthropist*, July 29, August 5, 1846; *Madison Courier*, August 1, 1846; Hallie Q. Brown, *Homespun Heroines*, 30–32; Litwack, *North of Slavery*, 69–70; *Freedom's Journal*, December 14, 1827; Asher, *Incidents in the Life of Rev. Asher*, 70; Bagley, *Speech of Hon. Bagley*, 5 ("negroes coming in droves" quote). A few years earlier Shelby County whites had petitioned the state legislature to prevent mulattoes from voting and attending county schools (*Palladium of Liberty*, February 28, 1844).

27. John Rankin, "Address to the Churches," 37.

28. J.C. Brown narrative in Drew, *North-Side View of Slavery*, 233–48;

Malvin, *North into Freedom*, 11–16; Abdy, *Tour in the United States*, 3:10–11, 2:384; Ware, "The Negro in Cincinnati, 1800–1829," 43–57; *Cincinnati Daily Gazette*, July 4, September 14, 1829; Pease and Pease, *Black Utopia*, 46–49.

29. David Smith, *Biography of Rev. David Smith*, 71; Malvin, *North into Freedom*, 12; Eli Artis, Henry Johnson, and Ephraim Waterford narratives in Drew, *North-Side View of Slavery*, 306–7, 373–75; *Colored American*, March 7, 1840. On emigrationism in the antebellum, Northern African American community, see Reed, *Platform for Change*, 163–212.

30. *Freedom's Journal*, March 14, 1829.

31. Ibid., March 14, 1829; Boyko, *Last Steps to Freedom*; Bramble, *Black Fugitive Slaves in Early Canada*; Tulloch, *Black Canadians*; J.C. Brown narrative in Drew, *North-Side View of Slavery*, quoted, 244–45; *Cincinnati Daily Gazette*, July 30, 1829; Malvin, *North into Freedom*,, 11–16; Ohio Anti-Slavery Society, *Proceedings, 1835*, 20.

32. Ware, "The Negro in Cincinnati," 49–50; *Cincinnati Daily Gazette*, July 24, July 28, 1829; *Cincinnati Directory*, 1819, 32, 1825, 114; 1829, 155; *Cincinnati Daily Gazette*, July 27, 1829.

33. *Cincinnati Daily Gazette*, July 20, July 24, July 28, August 2, August 17, 1829.

34. Abdy, *Tour in the United States*, 3:10–11; *Cincinnati Daily Gazette*, July 27, 1829. Cincinnati was not the only Ohio township to take such steps. In 1838 Fairfield issued a similar proclamation (*Colored American*, March 7, 1840).

35. *Cincinnati Daily Gazette*, July 28, 1829; Malvin, *North into Freedom*, 5–14; Ohio Anti-Slavery Society, *Proceedings, 1835*, 19–20.

36. Malvin, *North into Freedom*, 12; J.C. Brown narrative in Drew, *North-Side View of Slavery*, 244–45; *Cincinnati Daily Gazette*, July 29, September 14, 1829; Pease and Pease, *Black Utopia*, 46–49; *Colored American*, August 28, 1841; Thomas Cressup is listed in the Cincinnati tax lists for 1818 (Dichore, *Census for Cincinnati, 1817*). Agents also visited other African American communities throughout the North, sparking follow-up movements the next year in New York. *Colored American* (October 7, 1837).

37. *Cincinnati Daily Gazette*, July 29, August 2, September 17, 1829.

3. Home Over Jordan

1. Hallie Q. Brown, *Homespun Heroines*, 30–32; Wilkerson, *History of His Travels*, 2–5, 33–34; John Parker, *His Promised Land*, 25–96; Langston, *From Virginia Plantation to the National Capitol*, 11–67; Cheek and Cheek, *John Mercer Langston*. Samuel Ringgold Ward listened to an imprisoned fugitive slave, "son of a wealthy planter in Tennessee," proclaim, "Gentlemen, is this a free country? Why did my fathers fight the British, if one of their poor sons is to be treated in this way?" (Ward, *Autobiography*, 119–20). For a biography of Ward, see Burke, *Samuel Ringgold Ward*.

2. *Cincinnati Sentinel* quoted in *Western Star*, August 29, 1829; Abdy, *Tour in the United States*, 2:381–84; David Smith, *Biography of Rev. David Smith*, 74–75; Steward, *Twenty-Two Years a Slave*, 173–74.

3. *Cincinnati Sentinel* quoted in *Western Star*, August 29, 1829; Abdy, *Tour in the United States*, 2:381–84. On the political geography of Cincinnati's

African American community, see Taylor and Dula, "The Black Residential Experience."

4. *Colored American*, October 31, 1840; Justus, *Down from the Mountain*; Woodson, *President in the Family*, quoted, 1; Rothman, "James Callendar and Social Knowledge of Interracial Sex."

5. *Colored American*, September 30, 1837, November 4, 1837; November 2, 1839, October 31, December 12, 1840; *Freedom's Journal*, January 31, 1829; Woodson, *President in the Family*, 87–104; Justus, *Down from the Mountain*; Ohio Anti-Slavery Society, *Memorial to General Assembly of Ohio*; Trotter, *River Jordan*; Wesley, *Ohio Negroes in the Civil War*, 6. On early black nationalism, see, Moses, *Golden Age of Black Nationalism*.

6. Woodson quoted in *Colored American*, May 3, June 2, July 28, 1838.

7. *Colored American*, October 31, 1840; Woodson, *President in the Family*, 87–104; David Smith, *Biography of Rev. David Smith*, 100–111.

8. Ohio Anti-Slavery Society, *Memorial to the General Assembly of Ohio*; *Palladium of Liberty*, October 16, 1844; Levi Coffin, *Reminiscences*, 143, 170–77; *Richmond Palladium-Item*, January 15, January 17, January 19, January 22, 1962 (reprint of Lacey manuscript as "Underground Railroad"); John Bond to Wilbur Siebert, January 30, 1895, J.A. Locke to Siebert, January 6, 1896, Charles Osborn to Siebert, March 4, 1896, box 80, Siebert Papers; "Interview with William or 'Bush' Johnson," and "Interview with Rev. Jacob Cummings, an Escaped Slave," box 80, Siebert Papers; *Colored American*, October 14, 1837, August 4, 1838, March 2, 1839; October 31, 1840, January 23, 1841. We know less about African Americans in the antebellum rural North than about their urban existence. For a pioneering account covering a county in New Jersey, see Hodges, *Slavery and Freedom in the Rural North*.

9. John Parker, *His Promised Land*, 31; *Philanthropist*, May 31, 1843; *Colored American*, December 26, 1840; *Address and Reply on the Presentation of a Testimonial to S.P. Chase*, 14; William Anderson, *Life and Narrative*, 50–51.

10. H.B. Stanton to Leavitt, March 10, 1834, in *Debate at the Lane Seminary*, 7 (italics in original). John Meachum, who purchased himself out of Kentucky slavery, had bought the freedom of twenty more people by 1846. Meachum, *Address to All the Colored Citizens*, 5; *Colored American*, October 14, December 23, 1837; Justus, *Down from the Mountain*.

11. Andrew Jackson, *Narrative and Writings*, 12; Brown, *Three Years in the Kentucky Prisons*, 12. The best account of the fugitive slave is Franklin and Schweninger, *Runaway Slaves*. For an account of runaways in colonial times, see Meaders, *Dead or Alive*.

12. Douglass, *My Bondage and My Freedom*, 334; Fedric, *Slave Life in Virginia and Kentucky*, 103; see also Franklin and Schweninger, *Runaway Slaves*; McDougall, *Fugitive Slaves*.

13. John Parker, *His Promised Land*, 72; Mary Reynolds WPA narrative in Rawick, ed., *American Slave*, vol. 5, pt. 3, 236–46; Jones, *Experience of Thomas H. Jones*, 37–38; Louis Hughes, *Thirty Years a Slave*, 87–90; Joseph, *Life and Sufferings*, 7.

14. John Parker, *His Promised Land*, 49; John Warren narrative in Drew, *North-Side View of Slavery*, 182–87; Bruner, *A Slave's Adventures*, 30.

15. Silverman, "American Fugitive Slave in Canada"; Siebert, *Underground Railroad*, 340–42; Hembree, "Question of 'Begging'"; Franklin and Schweninger, *Runaway Slaves*, 97–109; Martin Jackson narrative in Rawick, ed., *American Slave*, vol. 4, pt. 2, 187–92; Bibb, *Narrative of the Life*, 170; Thomas Cole WPA narrative in Rawick, ed., *American Slave*, vol. 4, pt. 1, 225–35; Campbell, *Bond and Free*, 163.

16. *Freedom's Journal*, January 9, 16, 24, 1829.

17. David Smith, *Biography of Rev. David Smith*, 75; Henson, *Life of Josiah Henson*, 23; Bibb, *Narrative of the Life*, 169; John Lindsey narrative in Drew, *North-Side View of Slavery*, 77–78; *Colored American*, June 20, 1840; Horton, *Free People of Color*, 63–67; Horton and Horton, *In Hope of Liberty*, 234. The life of an African American riverboat steward was perilous at best. Because the boats generally journeyed into the South, the threat of enslavement was significant. One of Isaac Johnson's friends on his Kentucky plantation—a Cincinnati riverboat man originally from Canada—became entrapped through these means. Isaac Johnson, *Slavery Days in Old Kentucky*, 26. See also *Colored American*, January 27, 1838.

18. Malvin, *North into Freedom*, 14–16.

19. J.C. Brown narrative in Drew, *North-Side View of Slavery*, 241–44.

20. John Parker, *His Promised Land*, 90–96

21. Ibid.; *Cincinnati Commercial Tribune*, February 18, 1900, copy in box 102, Siebert Papers.

22. William Brown, *Narrative of William W. Brown*, 94–95; John Little narrative in Drew, *North-Side View of Slavery*, 204; James G. Birney to Lewis Tappan, February 27, 1837, in *Letters of James Birney*, ed. Dwight Dumond, 1:376–77; Levi Coffin, *Reminiscences*, 107, 270–310; Abdy, *Tour in the United States*, 2:370–80, 3:23.

23. Bibb, *Narrative of the Life*, 55; Levi Coffin, *Reminiscences*, 171–78; *Richmond Palladium-Item*, January 15, January 17, January 19, January 22, 1962 (reprint of Lacey manuscript as "Underground Railroad"). The Cabin Creek community was linked to the settlement just across the state line in Ohio, and fugitives were sometimes transferred between the two in cases of danger. "Interview with Rev. Jacob Cummings, an Escaped Slave," box 80, Siebert Papers.

24. William Mitchell, *Under-Ground Railroad*, 17–20.

25. Works Progress Administration, Survey of State and Local Historical Records, 1936, Church Records Form, Macedonia Missionary Baptist, copy in vertical file, Ironton, Ohio Public Library; *North Star*, June 9, 16, 1848; Cheek and Cheek, *John Mercer Langston*, 48–83; *Colored American*, October 12, 1839, October 17, 1840. On the role of the black church in antebellum African American community formation, see Reed, *Platform for Change*, 17–56.

26. Fairbank, *Rev. Calvin Fairbank during Slavery Times*, 35, 60, 150; *Colored American*, August 17, 1839; Henry Boyd entry in Mott and Wood, eds., *Narratives of Colored Americans*, 252–56; Ohio Anti-Slavery Society, *Proceedings, 1835*, 35; Stowe, *Uncle Tom's Cabin*, 450; Abdy, *Tour in the United States*, 2:409–15; *Cincinnati Directory*, 1834, 1836, 1861, 1862; U.S., Census Office, *Sixth Census, 1840*, *Seventh Census, 1850*; H. Lyman to Wilbur Siebert, April 1, 1898, box 106, Siebert Papers; Hayden, *Narrative of William Hayden*, 34; *North*

Star, February 11, May 20, 1848. On Watson, see Cheek and Cheek, *John Mercer Langston*, 48–83; Stowe, *Uncle Tom's Cabin*, 450. See also Horton and Flaherty, "Black Leadership in Antebellum Cincinnati."

27. "Negroes in and around Jefferson County," Jefferson County Historical Society, Madison, Indiana; Levi Coffin, *Reminiscences*, 110–70; Abdy, *Tour in the United States*, 2:370–79; J.H. Tibbetts to Elizabeth Nicholson, [1884], box 2, folder 2, Steele Papers; "Minute Book of Neel's Creek Anti-Slavery Society, 1839–1845," Indiana State Library, Indianapolis; "Eleutherian Institute" and "The Fugitive Slaves in Jefferson County," box 80, Siebert Papers; F.M. Merrell to Wilbur Siebert, March 10, 1895, box 80, Siebert Papers.

28. William Anderson, *Life and Narrative*, 5–40; *Provincial Freeman*, January 3, 1857; "Register of Negroes and Mulattoes in Jefferson County," Jefferson County Historical Society, Madison, Indiana.

29. Richard Daly interview, *Louisville Journal*, August 12, 1894, copy in box 80, Siebert Papers; "Negroes in and around Jefferson County"; Levi Coffin, *Reminiscences*, 139–44; 160–70; Haviland, *Woman's Life-Work*, 109–20.

30. Bibb, *Narrative of the Life*, 48–51; Levi Coffin, *Reminiscences*, 206–16; *Richmond Palladium-Item*, January 15, January 17, January 19, January 22, 1962 (reprint of Lacey manuscript as "Underground Railroad").

31. Levi Coffin, *Reminiscences*, 206–16; Bibb's recapture on his return for his family is confirmed by his former master; Bibb, *Narrative of the Life*, vii; Clarke and Clarke, *Narratives*, 85–91.

32. *Colored American*, February 2, 1839; Roper, *Narrative of Adventures and Escape*, 55–56; James G. Birney to Lewis Tappan, February 27, 1837 in *Letters of James Birney*, ed. Dwight Dumond, 1:376–77; Edward Moxley to Wilbur Siebert, July 31, 1895, box 106, Siebert Papers; Adam Rankin, "Autobiography," Ohio Historical Society, Columbus, 59–61, 67–74; Birney letter in Bibb, *Narrative of the Life*, v–vi; Quarles, *Black Abolitionists*, 144; *North Star*, July 28, 1848.

33. Dillon, *Slavery Attacked*, 206–7; *Colored American*, February 16, September 28, 1839, March 21, October 17, 1840; Rial Cheadle manuscript [1856] in Humphries, *Underground Railroad*, 32–43; Clarke and Clarke, *Narratives*, 84; James G. Birney to Lewis Tappan, February 27, 1837, in *Letters of James Birney*, ed. Dwight Dumond, 1:376–77.

34. Hallie Q. Brown, "As the Mantle Falls," unpublished autobiography in the Hallie Q. Brown Collection, box 29; Hallie Q. Brown, *Homespun Heroines*, 30–2; Hallie Q. Brown, *Tales My Father Told*, 3–5; W.S. Scarborough, "The Late T.A. Brown's Slavery," typescript, box 2, Frances Hughes Collection; Wilkerson, *History of His Travels*, 2–5, 33–34.

35. Wilkerson, *History of His Travels*, 2–5, 33–4; David Smith, *Biography of Rev. David Smith*, 84; Langston, *From Virginia Plantation to the National Capitol*, 11–67.

36. Hallie Q. Brown, *Homespun Heroines*, 30–32; James G. Birney to Lewis Tappan, February 27, 1837, in *Letters of James Birney*, ed. Dwight Dumond, 1:376–77.

37. *Cincinnati Daily Gazette*, August 10, August 11, 1841.

38. *Cincinnati Enquirer*, September 9, 1841; *Western Christian Advocate* quoted in *Colored American*, June 19, 1841.

39. Langston, *From Virginia Plantation to the National Capitol*, 11–67; Cheek and Cheek, *John Mercer Langston*, 48–83.
40. *Cincinnati Daily Times*, June 26, 1841; *Cincinnati Daily Gazette*, June 26, 1841; Hayden, *Narrative of William Hayden*, 88–91.
41. Langston, *From Virginia Plantation to the National Capitol*, 63; *Cincinnati Enquirer*, September 9, 10, 1841.
42. Langston, *From Virginia Plantation to the National Capitol*, 63–66; *Cincinnati Daily Times*, September 4, 6, 8, 1841; *Cincinnati Enquirer*, September 4, 6, 8, 9, 10, 1841; *Philanthropist*, September 8, 1841; *Cincinnati Daily Republican*, September 6, 7, 8, 9, 1841; *Cincinnati Daily Gazette*, September 6, 7, 8, 9, 1841.
43. Langston, *From Virginia Plantation to the National Capitol*, 66; *Cincinnati Daily Times*, September 4, 1841.
44. *Cincinnati Daily Times*, September 6, 1841
45. *Cincinnati Daily Gazette*, September 7, 1841; *Philanthropist*, September 8, 1841; *Colored American*, September 18, 1841; *Cincinnati Daily Times*, September 4, 6, 7, 1841; *Cincinnati Daily Republican*, September 7, 1841.
46. *Cincinnati Daily Times*, September 8, 10, 1841; *Cincinnati Enquirer*, September 10, 1841.
47. *Cincinnati Enquirer*, September 21, 1841; *Cincinnati Daily Times*, September 25, 1841; *Colored American*, September 25, November 20, 1841.
48. *Colored American*, February 13, March 20, October 16, 1841; *Cincinnati Daily Times*, September 25, 1841. On racial riots in antebellum urban America, see Curry, *Free Black in Urban America*, 96–111.

4. Band of Angels

1. John Parker, *His Promised Land*, 74, 85; Gregg, "Original Introduction," in John Parker, *His Promised Land*, 19; Ripley abolitionist W.B. Campbell credited Parker with "plucking over 1,000 slaves from bondage," *Cincinnati Commercial Tribune*, February 18, 1900, copy in box 102, Siebert Papers; Eugene Settles, interview with author, August 1, 2001; Levi Coffin, *Reminiscences*, 304–12, 428–46.
2. John Parker, *His Promised Land*, 25; Levi Coffin, *Reminiscences*, 304–12, 428–46; Butler, *My Story of the Civil War*, 179–203; H.N. Wilson to Wilbur Siebert, April 14, 1892, box 106, Siebert Papers; Fitch Reed to Wilbur Siebert quoted in Siebert, *Underground Railroad*, 54; U.S., Census Office, *Census for 1820*; *Fifth Census, 1830*; *Sixth Census, 1840*; *Seventh Census, 1850*; *Western Citizen* quoted in *Palladium of Liberty*, February 21, 1844.
3. Levi Coffin, *Reminiscences*, 206–16; *Richmond Palladium-Item*, January 15, January 17, January 19, January 22, 1962 (reprint of Lacey manuscript as "Underground Railroad").
4. Levi Coffin, *Reminiscences*, 304–12, 428–46; Butler, *My Story of the Civil War*, 181–82
5. Butler, *My Story of the Civil War*, 181–82.
6. Harrold, *Abolitionists and the South*, quoted, 5; Levi Coffin, *Reminiscences*; Addison Coffin, *Life and Travels*; Isaac Beeson to Joshua Stanley, February 26, 1841, box 1, folder 6, Beeson Papers.

7. *Frederick Douglass' Paper*, May 13, 1852; *North Star*, June 16, 1848. Delany also revealed to the reading public that the real "depot" was not Rankin's house, "but situated in a cavern about two miles south, of the whereabouts of which none but abolitionists are aware. This accounts for the great mistake on the part of the soul-seekers, who frequently, or at least have at different times, by brute force, entered the house of this aged gentleman, when they knew him to be unprotected—his eldest son being absent, and none but children and females at home—in search of their victims, but without success." Delany's account of the cavern appears to be a misunderstanding on his part, though there are to be found occasional references to the use of other hiding places. John Parker, *His Promised Land*, 97, 118–21; John Rankin, "Autobiography, Written by Himself in His 80th Year," Ohio Historical Society, Columbus; Adam Rankin, "Autobiography"; Ritchie, *The Soldier*, Gragston narrative in Mellon, ed., *Bullwhip Days*, 263–69; *Cincinnati Daily Gazette*, September 24, 1841.

8. *Frederick Douglass' Paper*, May 20, 1853; John Rankin, "Autobiography"; Adam Rankin, "Autobiography," 2–3, 25–6; John Rankin, *Letters on American Slavery*; Ritchie, *The Soldier*, undated newspaper clipping, box 1, folder 1, Rankin Papers.

9. John Rankin, "Autobiography"; Adam Rankin, "Autobiography," 10–26.

10. John Rankin, "Autobiography"; Adam Rankin, "Autobiography," 59–61; *Colored American*, June 20, 1840; Stauffer, *Black Hearts of Men*, 1; John Rankin, "Address to the Churches," 30–38; *North Star*, June 16, 1848; Nicholson, "Reminiscences," box 1, folder 6, Nicholson Papers. John Parker's attitude toward religion was said to have been one of outright hostility. According to a colleague in the Ripley underground, Parker "kept aloof from the churches. He looked upon them, as a class, as the enemy of his people" (*Cincinnati Commercial Tribune*, February 18, 1900, copy in box 102, Siebert Papers).

11. Levi Coffin, *Reminiscences*, 304–12, 428–46; Butler, *My Story of the Civil War*, 179–203; H.N. Wilson to Wilbur Siebert, April 14, 1892, box 106, Siebert Papers; Fitch Reed to Wilbur Siebert quoted in Siebert, *Underground Railroad*, 54. Smallwood describes the circumstances surrounding the incident, without giving Fairfield's name and places the events in 1847 or 1848 (*Narrative of Thomas Smallwood*, 57–58).

12. Levi Coffin, *Reminiscences*; Haviland, *Woman's Life-Work*; Fairbank, *Rev. Calvin Fairbank during Slavery Times*, 150–55. Elisha Green, *Life of Rev. Elisha W. Green*, 8–9.

13. Bibb, *Narrative of the Life*, 54; Henson, *Life of Josiah Henson*, 52–57; Henson, *Truth is Stranger than Fiction*, 113–27; William Brown, *Narrative of William W. Brown*, 97–107; Clarke and Clarke, *Narratives*, 82–88; L. Clarke, *Narratives*, 32–43; James Adams narrative in Drew, *North-Side View of Slavery*, 19–28. Meaders's *Dead or Alive*, a study of fugitives through the year 1830, finds evidence of "harborers" but no organized network.

14. Levi Coffin, *Reminiscences*, 230–36; Haviland, *Woman's Life-Work*, 32–34; Addison Coffin, *Life and Travels*; Isaac Beeson to [?], December 19, 1844, December 8, 1845, box 1, folder 6, Beeson Papers; Isaac Beeson to "Respected Brother," February 4, 1845, box 1, folder 6, Beeson Papers; biographical sketch of Valentine Nicholson, box 1, folder 5, Nicholson Papers; Coffin, *Reminiscences*, quoted, 136.

15. *Indianapolis Journal* quoted in the *Provincial Freeman*, November 24, 1855; J.H. Tibbetts to Elizabeth Nicholson, [1884], box 2, folder 2, Steele Papers; biographical sketch of Valentine Nicholson, box 1, folder 5, Nicholson Papers.

16. For a detailed study of the Lane Seminary debate, see Lesick, *Lane Rebels*. For evidence of early connections between Coffin, while still in Indiana, and the Rankins, see Levi Coffin, *Reminiscences*; typescript by John Rankin Jr. and A.T. Rankin, box 1, folder 2, John Rankin Papers; and Adam Rankin, "Autobiography."

17. Bradley, "Brief Account of an Emancipated Slave," in *Oasis*, ed. Lydia Maria Child, 106–12; H.B. Stanton to Leavitt, March 10, 1834, in *Debate at the Lane Seminary*, 4; Abdy, *Tour in the United States*, 2:404–6; Lane Seminary, *Annual Report of the Trustees*.

18. Bradley, "Brief Account of an Emancipated Slave," in *Oasis*, ed. Lydia Maria Child, 106–112; Lesick, *Lane Rebels*, 75–76; "Review of the Statement of the Faculty of Lane Seminary in Relation to the Recent Difficulties in that Institution," box 1, folder 1, John Rankin Papers; *A Statement of the Reasons Which Induced the Students of Lane Seminary*; *Frederick Douglass' Paper*, December 17, 1852; Abdy, *Tour in the United States*, 2:404–6. On Weld, see Abzug, "Theodore Weld: A Biography."

19. H.B. Stanton to Leavitt, March 10, 1834, in *Debate at the Lane Seminary*, 4; Lesick, *Lane Rebels*, 80, 167–228; Harrold, *Gamaliel Bailey*, 14–16.

20. *A Statement of the Reasons Which Induced the Students*, 4; H.B. Stanton to Leavitt, March 10, 1834, in *Debate at the Lane Seminary*, 5; *Colored American*, November 4, 1837; January 27, 1838, June 1, 1839. A correspondent of the *Colored American* who met Wattles concurred that he was a "devoted friend of our people" (February 17, 1838); Abdy, *Tour in the United States*, 2:386–412, 3:1–20; Lesick, *Lane Rebels*, 1–2, 90, 167–228, Weld quoted, 92; "Interview with Rev. Jacob Cummings, an Escaped Slave," box 80, Siebert Papers; H. Lyman to Wilbur Siebert, April 1, 1898, box 106, Siebert Papers; John Rankin Jr., typescript, box 1, folders 2, 3, John Rankin Papers; Adam Rankin, "Autobiography," 59–73.

21. *A Statement of the Reasons Which Induced the Students*; Abdy, *Tour in the United States*, 2:387–88; Lesick, *Lane Rebels*, 92–94, 116–46; see also Levi Coffin, *Reminiscences*; Addison Coffin, *Life and Travels*.

22. John Rankin, "Review of the Statement of the Faculty of Lane Seminary in Relation to the Recent Difficulties in that Institution," box 1, folder 1, John Rankin Papers; John Rankin, "Autobiography"; Adam Rankin, "Autobiography," 30–46.

23. *Colored American*, April 29, 1837; Birney to Lewis Tappan, April 18, 1837, in *Letters of James Birney*, ed. Dwight Dumond, 1:379–81; on Birney, see also Dumond's introduction to *Letters of James Birney*, ed. Dwight Dumond, 1:v–xxvi; *Address and Reply on the Presentation of a Testimonial to S.P. Chase*, Gordon quoted, 12. For a biography of Chase, see Blue, *Salmon Chase*.

24. Ohio Anti-Slavery Society, *Proceedings, 1835*; *Philanthropist*, January 1, 1836; Adam Rankin, "Autobiography," 49–55; Ohio Anti-Slavery Society, *Narrative of the Late Riotous Proceedings against the Liberty of the Press*; *Cincinnati Advertiser*, July 27, 1836; *Cincinnati Daily Gazette*, August 1, 2, 1836.

25. Indiana Anti-Slavery Society, *Proceedings,* 1838; "Minute Book of Neel's Creek Anti-Slavery Society"; biographical sketch of Valentine Nicholson, box 1, folder 5, Nicholson Papers; Addison Coffin, *Life and Travels,* 19–20, 41, 59–60; Levi Coffin, *Reminiscences,* 223–31; Job Hadley to Elizabeth Nicholson, 1883, box 2, folder 4, Steele Papers; Isaac Beeson to Joshua Stanley, February 26, 1841, and Beeson to Benjamin Cox, May 18, 1845, box 1, folder 4, Beeson Papers. Magdol notes that many questions remain to be answered about western abolitionists: "Who were the petitioners, antislavery society members, and voters of Liberty, Free Soil, and Republican parties of Ohio, eastern Tennessee, Indiana, Illinois, and other Northwest Ordinance states and territories? Who was in the antislavery ranks in frontier or recently settled communities? How did they differ from Northeasterners?" (*Antislavery Rank and File,* 139–40).

26. Levi Coffin, *Reminiscences,* 108.

27. This account draws on recent works that have opened new windows into abolitionism, including Stauffer, *Black Hearts of Men;* Dillon, *Slavery Attacked;* Harrold, *Abolitionists and the South;* and the essays in Jacobs, ed., *Courage and Conscience.* Dillon, in particular, has begun the process of reexamining the importance of the actions of the enslaved in creating an effective antislavery resistance movement. Other recent works on abolitionism include McKivigan and Snay, eds., *Religion and the Antebellum Debate over Slavery;* Yee, *Black Women Abolitionists;* Jeffrey, *Great Silent Army of Abolitionism;* Ericson, *Debate over Slavery;* Yellin and Van Horne, eds., *Abolitionist Sisterhood;* Yellin, *Women and Sisters,* Magdol, *Antislavery Rank and File;* Strong, *Perfectionist Politics;* Stewart, *Holy Warriors;* Howard, *Conscience and Slavery;* Friedman, *Gregarious Saints.*

28. *Freedom's Journal,* December 14, 1827; Malvin, *North into Freedom,* 13; *Colored American,* July 22, 1837, July 21, 1838, March 14, July 11, 1840; *Palladium of Liberty,* December 27, 1843, April 17, October 10, November 13, 1844.

29. *Colored American,* July 28, 1838, November 2, 1839; Nicholson, "Reminiscences," box 1, folder 6, Nicholson Papers; *Palladium of Liberty,* March 20 and 27, 1844; Beeson to [?], April 19, 1851, box 2, folder 1, Beeson Papers. For information about Ray's political activism, see Hodges, *Root and Branch,* 248. Dillon notes that the desire to keep African Americans out of the North represented the majority outlook and accounted for the support for the institution of slavery (*Abolitionists,* 26). Beeson's case demonstrates that western abolitionism was far from immune to the pressures of public opinion.

30. Ohio Anti-Slavery Society, *Proceedings, 1835,* 10, 11. Though western white abolitionists probably lagged behind their Eastern colleagues, the formulation by the Ohio State Anti-Slavery Society was remarkably similar to what William Lloyd Garrison had written only a few years earlier: "Immediate abolition does not mean that the slaves shall immediately exercise the right of suffrage, or be eligible to any office, or be emancipated from law, or be free from the benevolent restraints of gradualism" (quoted in Dillon, *Abolitionists,* 38).

31. Ohio Anti-Slavery Society, *Proceedings, 1835,* 6, 7, 10.

32. Ohio Anti-Slavery Society, *Report of the Second Anniversary,* 13; Ohio Anti-Slavery Society, *Report of the Third Anniversary,* 13.

33. Ohio Anti-Slavery Society, *Proceedings, 1835,* 53–54.

34. Ohio Anti-Slavery Society, *Report of the First Anniversary*, 37.

35. *Philanthropist*, December 28, 1842. For a biography of Bailey, including his own inconsistent racial attitudes, see Harrold, *Gamaliel Bailey*.

36. *Philanthropist*, November 2, 1842.

37. Ohio Anti-Slavery Society, *Report of the Third Anniversary*, 13.

38. Typical of this trend is Levi Coffin's *Reminiscences*. Virtually the lone exception to this rule was Calvin Fairbank, whose memoir (*Rev. Calvin Fairbank during Slavery Times*) is very careful to credit African American operatives in Cincinnati and to record the interracial nature of the movement.

39. See, for example, *Address and Reply on the Presentation of a Testimonial to S.P. Chase*; Gaines and Perkins, *Orations Delivered upon the First of August 1849*. On the tactics of abolitionism, see Kraditor, *Means and Ends in American Abolitionism*; Kraut, ed., *Crusaders and Compromisers*.

5. Egypt's Border

1. William Mitchell, *Under-Ground Railroad*, 20–25; A.T. Rankin, typescript, box 1, folder 2, John Rankin Papers.

2. Ibid.

3. Ibid. Although Rankin's account of Mason's final mission differs in certain respects from Mitchell's, the similarities of these independent accounts are striking. Rankin, who gives the number of fugitives as six, was also under the impression that the fugitives escaped. In other respects, the two versions are nearly identical, as Mason is injured in the struggle—the two differing only in the exact nature of the injuries—gives his master's name, is taken to New Orleans, and escapes bondage there. Rankin lost track of Mason after his return to Cincinnati. Mitchell relates that his ultimate destination was Canada (*Under-Ground Railroad*, 20–25).

4. *Philanthropist*, February 15, 1843; July 23, 1845; reminiscence of Richard C. Rankin quoted in "Ripley, Brown Co., as an U.G.R.R. Station," box 102, Siebert Papers.

5. *Cincinnati Daily Gazette*, September 24, 1841; John Rankin, "Autobiography"; Adam Rankin, "Autobiography," 119–22.

6. William Parker, "The Freedman's Story," 155–63; Amanda Smith, *Autobiography*, 31–35; *Bucyrus Democratic* quoted in *Colored American*, September 28, 1839.

7. William Parker, "*Freedman's Story*," 162–63; Jacob Green, *Narrative of the Life*, 33; *Philanthropist*, May 7, 1845.

8. Beaver, *Fugitive Slaves in Ohio*, 1; *Madison Courier*, July 28, September 25, 1856; J.H. Tibbetts to Elizabeth Nicholson, [1884], box 2, folder 2, Steele Papers; Haviland, *Woman's Life-Work*, 101, 109; Levi Coffin, *Reminiscences*, 219; "Negroes in and around Jefferson County," 7; Andrew Jackson, *Narrative and Writings*, 13.

9. Fedric, *Slave Life*, 104–5; see also, for example, *Mansfield Shield and Manor* quoted in the *Colored American*, April 25, 1840; Henry Parker, *Autobiography*, 3; Campbell, *Bond and Free*, 113, 160, 174, 195; Garlick, *Life Including His Escape*, 9.

10. *National Era*, July 15, 1855; *Frederick Douglass' Paper*, July 27, 1855;

Madison Weekly Courier, February 18, 1860, quoted in "Negroes in and around Jefferson County," 26; Haviland, *Woman's Life-Work.*

11. *Madison Courier,* July 5, 1889; *Madison Courier* and *Madison Herald* quoted in "Negroes in and around Jefferson County," 30–32, 39; J.R Carr to Wilbur Siebert, January 19, February 20, 1896, box 80, Siebert Papers; *Provincial Freeman,* February 9, 1856; see also chapter 6, note 22.

12. *Philanthropist,* April 12, 1843.

13. *Mansfield Shield and Manor* quoted in the *Colored American,* April 25, 1840.

14. Rial Cheadle manuscript [1856] in Humphries, *Underground Railroad,* 32–43.

15. J.H. Tibbetts to Elizabeth Nicholson, [1884], box 2, folder 2, Steele Papers.

16. Levi Coffin, *Reminiscences,* 433; Fairbank, *Rev. Calvin Fairbank during Slavery Times,* 150–55.

17. Haviland, *Woman's Life-Work,* 110–79. W.B. Campbell reported a similar modus operandi for John Parker in Ripley, recalling that Ripley's leading African American underground operative "preferred to carry on his work independently even of Dr. Rankin, whom he always revered" (*Cincinnati Commercial Tribune,* February 18, 1900, copy in box 102, Siebert Papers).

18. Haviland, *Woman's Life-Work,* 167–68; Gara, *Liberty Line;* U.S., Census Office, *Seventh Census, 1850.*

19. Haviland, *Woman's Life-Work,* 170–76. Oberlin African Americans enacted precisely the same ruse in 1841 (Clarke and Clarke, *Narratives,* 86).

20. There are many examples of children of conductors who knew of or chose only to relate the names of white participants (see the voluminous correspondence in the Siebert Papers); *Cincinnati Commercial Tribune,* February 18, 1900, copy in box 102, Siebert Papers; Fairbank, *Rev. Calvin Fairbank during Slavery Times,* 15, 35, 60; Haviland, *Woman's Life-Work.*

21. Levi Coffin, *Reminiscences,* 304–12, 428–46; Fairbank, *Rev. Calvin Fairbank during Slavery Times;* Rial Cheadle manuscript [1856] in Humphries, *Underground Railroad,* 32–43; John Rankin, "Autobiography"; A.T. Rankin, typescript in John Rankin Papers; Adam L. Rankin, "Autobiography"; Haviland, *Woman's Life-Work,* 166–76. At least occasionally white Northerners traveling in the South may have agreed to help enslaved persons escape, as the Ohioan who offered to take Bethany Veney back with him. In this case, timely intervention from Veney's master prevented the Northerner from enacting any plan (Veney, *Narrative,* 13). A visiting Bostonian actually succeeded in helping off Henry Watson from Kentucky (Watson, *Narrative,* 33–38). See also Harrold, *Abolitionists and the South,* 64–83.

22. *Frederick Douglass' Paper,* July 27, 1855; Hallie Q. Brown, "As the Mantle Falls" (unpublished autobiography), box 29, Hallie Q. Brown Papers; Hallie Q. Brown, *Homespun Heroines,* 30–2; Hallie Q. Brown, *Tales My Father Told,* 3–5; W.S. Scarborough, "The Late T.A. Brown's Slavery," typescript, box 2, Frances Hughes Collection.

23. Hallie Q. Brown, *Tales My Father Told,* 3–5; W.S. Scarborough, "The Late T.A. Brown's Slavery," typescript, box 2, Frances Hughes Collection.

24. Hallie Q. Brown, "As the Mantle Falls" (unpublished autobiography),

box 29, Hallie Q. Brown Collection; Hallie Q. Brown, *Tales My Father Told*, 11–12; Hallie Q. Brown, "The Late T.A. Brown's Slavery," typescript, box 2, Frances Hughes Collection.

25. *North Star*, March 3, 1848; Garlick, *Life Including His Escape*, 6.

26. *Ironton Register*, December 16, 1860, October 31, 1878; "Interview with Gabe Johnson" and "Interview with Hiram Campbell," box 108, Siebert Papers; Catharine Cummings to Wilbur Siebert, December 23, 1893, Siebert Papers.

27. *Ironton Register*, October 31, 1878.

28. William Mitchell, *Under-Ground Railroad*.

29. Levi Coffin, *Reminiscences*; *Cincinnati Directory*, 1836; Union Association of Colored Men of New Richmond Records, Ohio Collection, Ohio Historical Society, Columbus; John Bond to Wilbur Siebert, January 30, 1895, J.A. Locke to Siebert, January 6, 1896, Charles Osborn to Siebert, March 4, 1896, box 80, Siebert Papers; "Interview with William or 'Bush' Johnson," and "Interview with Rev. Jacob Cummings, an Escaped Slave," box 80, Siebert Papers; *Richmond Palladium-Item*, January 15, January 17, January 19, January 22, 1962 (reprint of Lacey manuscript as "Underground Railroad").

30. William Mitchell, *Under-Ground Railroad*, 20–25; A.T. Rankin, typescript, box 1, folder 2, John Rankin Papers; Levi Coffin, *Reminiscences*, 304–12, 428–46; Butler, *My Story of the Civil War*, 179–203; John Parker, *His Promised Land*; "Register of Negroes and Mulattoes in Jefferson County"; "Negroes in and around Jefferson County."

31. Smallwood, *Narrative of Thomas Smallwood*, 57–58. According to Coffin, Fairfield spent a month in jail and then escaped, leading to the daring rescue narrated in chapter 4. Levi Coffin, *Reminiscences*, 435–37; Fairbank, *Rev. Calvin Fairbank during Slavery Times*; Haviland, *Woman's Life-Work*. For an account of the remarkable Webster, see Runyon, *Delia Webster and the Underground Railroad*; see also Eisan, *Saint or Demon?*

32. H. Lyman to Wilbur Siebert, April 1, 1898, box 106, Siebert Papers; Jeffrey devotes a section to women in the Underground Railroad (*Great Silent Army of Abolitionism*, 180–90). She comments that "Although many of the stories about conductors on the underground railroad highlight the role of men, black women, like their white counterparts, did much of the routine work upon which the smooth operation of the underground railroad depended" (181). Hodges has also given an account of women in the Underground Railroad in New York (*Root and Branch*, 249–51). See also Yee, *Black Women Abolitionists*, especially 98–100; Young, *Antebellum Black Activists*; Yellin and Van Horne, *Abolitionist Sisterhood*.

33. Siebert, *Mysteries*, 121; Henry Burke, interview with author, August 2000; Richard Daly interview, *Louisville Journal*, August 12, 1894; Harry Smith, *Fifty Years of Slavery*, 95, 127; see also "Negroes in and around Jefferson County."

34. Gragston narrative in Mellon, ed., *Bullwhip Days* 263–69; *Philanthropist*, August 5, 1846; *Frederick Douglass' Paper*, May 13, 1852.

35. Gragston narrative in Mellon, ed., *Bullwhip Days* 263–9; Siebert, *Mysteries*, 121; Henry Burke, interview with author, August 2000.

36. *Colored American*, June 1, 1839; Fedric, *Slave Life*, 101–4; Albert, *House of Bondage*, 120–22; Charles Thompson, *Biography of a Slave*, 76–78; Robinson, *From Log Cabin to Pulpit*, 14–15. On white operatives in the South, see Harrold,

Abolitionists and the South, 64–83. For autobiographical accounts, see Walker, *Branded Hand,* and George Thompson, *Prison Life and Reflections;* see also Hensel, *Christiana Riot.*

37. *Louisville Courier* quoted in *Provincial Freeman,* May 20, 1854.

38. Mallory, *Old Plantation Days,* 6–12; Bibb, *Narrative of the Life,* 51; Black, *Life and Sufferings,* 22–33; *Philanthropist,* July 26, 1844.

39. *Philanthropist,* December 7, 1842; Joseph Sanford and John Hatfield narratives in Drew, *North-Side View of Slavery,* 358–66; *Madison Courier,* September 27, 1854.

40. *Philanthropist,* February 8, 1843.

41. Campbell, *Bond and Free,* 169–201; Aaron, *Light and Truth of Slavery,* 18, 26–29, 36–37; Andrew Jackson, *Narrative and Writings,* 7–22; John Little and Mrs. John Little narratives in Drew, *North-Side View of Slavery,* 187–232.

42. James Williams, *Life and Adventures,* 9–15; Brown, *Slave Life in Georgia,* 150–60; Jacob Green, *Narrative of the Life,* 35; Henry Parker, *Autobiography,* 1–2.

43. Albert, *House of Bondage,* 120–22; Bibb, *Narrative of the Life,* 88–89; Webb, *History of William Webb,* 26; Singleton, *Recollections of My Slavery Days,* 6; Andrew Jackson, *Narrative and Writings,* 7–10; Leonard Black, *The Life and Sufferings of Leonard Black,* 22–27; Mattie Jackson, *Story of Mattie J. Jackson,* 6; Bruce, *New Man,* 23.

44. John Brown, *Slave Life in Georgia,* 70–75; Andrew Jackson, *Narrative and Writings,* 15; Pennington, *Fugitive Blacksmith,* 61.

45. Gara, *Liberty Line,* 3; James Williams, *Life and Adventures,* 13–15; Bibb, *Narrative of the Life,* 178–79; *Palladium of Liberty,* August 14, 1844.

46. William Brown, *Narrative of William W. Brown,* 100–106; William Brown, *American Fugitive in Europe,* 28–9; L. Clarke, *Narratives,* 45–61; Clarke and Clarke, *Narratives,* 83–7; Henson, *Truth is Stranger than Fiction,* 144–64; Henson, "Uncle Tom's Story of His Life," 107–20. For a biography of William Wells Brown, see Whelchel, *My Chains Fell Off.*

47. Fairbank, *Rev. Calvin Fairbank during Slavery Times;* Siebert, summary of letter from unidentified correspondent in Angelica, NY, April 3, 1896, Siebert Papers; *Williams' Cincinnati Directory for 1862,* 121; *Williams' Cincinnati Directory for 1863,* 148; William Anderson, *Life and Narrative;* "Negroes in and around Jefferson County," 20.

48. Henry Burke, interview with author, August 2000; U.S., Census Office, *Seventh Census, 1850.*

6. Prelude to Exodus

1. Jno. S. George to Reuben Wood, Feb. 22, 1851, Charles W. Blair to Wood, February 27, 1851, box 1, folder 3, Wood Papers; bill of sale and depositions, box 1, folder 2, Medill Papers, box 1, folder 10, Wood Papers, and Peyton Polly, Case Transcripts; freedom papers of Douglass Polly, box 1, folder 10, Wood Papers.

2. *Frederick Douglass' Paper,* March 4, 1852; *Ohio State Journal,* June 28, 1850; Jno. S. George to Reuben Wood, Feb. 22, 1851, Ralph Leete to Reuben

Wood, February 22, 1851, box 1, folder 3, Wood Papers; Wilson, *Freedom at Risk*, 76–81.

3. J. Harlan to William Medill, September 17, 1853, box 1, folder 4, J.W. Wilson to Ralph Leete, March, 1854, box 2, folder 1, John Saidley to J.W. Wilson, April 16, 1854, box 2, folder 4, Medill Papers; copy of resolution, signed Charles W. Blair, Clk. House of Representatives, N.A. Swift, Clk. Senate, box 1, folder 3, Wood Papers; Ralph Leete to H.W. King, March 1, 1851, Leete to [Wood], March 3, 1851, Wood to Joel Wilson, June 6, 1850, James Harlan to Wood, March 8, 1851, Jos. McCormick to Wood, March 4, 1851, Wilson to Wood, March 14, 1851, box 1, folder 4, Wood Papers; Lughborough Ballard to Wood, October 16, 1851, box 2, folder 2, Wood Papers; Wilson, *Freedom at Risk*, 76–81.

4. *Ironton Register*, December 16, 1860; "Case of the Polly Negroes Memorandum," May 15, 1856, Chase Papers; Ralph Leete to A.M. Gangener, November 25, 1859, Polly Papers.

5. S.S. Rice to John Saidley, April 3, 1857, Rice to Chase, February 16, 1859, Chase Papers. A few years later, the county in which the Polly children were enslaved would join its neighbors in forming the state of West Virginia.

6. Douglass, *Narrative of the Life*, 101; Fedric, *Slave Life*, 106–7; Fairbank, *Rev. Calvin Fairbank during Slavery Times*, 46.

7. Hembree, "Question of 'Begging'"; Drew, *North-Side View of Slavery*; Cochran, *Fugitive Slave Law*, 72.

8. Cochran, *Fugitive Slave Law*; *Frederick Douglass' Paper*, September 16, 1853.

9. Cochran, *Fugitive Slave Law*, 9; *Madison Courier*, November 27, 1850.

10. Hise, Diary, October 5, 1850; Craft, *Running a Thousand Miles*, 87–108; Jones, *Experience of Thomas H. Jones*, Garrison quoted, 3; see also Mason, *Life of Isaac Mason*, 49–57; Ward, *Autobiography*, 3, 115–39; James Williams, *Life and Adventures*, 24. For a discussion of the aftermath of the passage of the Fugitive Slave Law of 1850, see Horton and Horton, "Federal Assault"; Pease and Pease, *They Who Would Be Free*, 206–32; Curry, *Free Black in Urban America*, 230–33.

11. John Hatfield narrative in Drew, *North-Side View of Slavery*, 363–66; William Mitchell, *Under-Ground Railroad*; *Frederick Douglass' Paper*, February 5, 1852, November 17, 1854.

12. *National Era*, January 16, 1851; Stowe, *Uncle Tom's Cabin*. Stowe described her motivations in a letter to Lord Denison: "I wrote what I did because as a woman, as a mother, I was oppressed & broken hearted, with the sorrows & injustice I saw, because as a Christian I felt the dishonor to Christianity—because as a lover of my country, I trembled at the coming day of wrath" (Stowe Papers). Cochran, *Fugitive Slave Law*, 97; *Madison Courier*, November 27, 1850. On the personal liberty laws that Northern states passed in response to the Fugitive Slave Law, see Rosenberg, "Personal Liberty Laws and Sectional Crisis."

13. Garlick, *Life Including His Escape*, 10; James Smith, *Autobiography*, 90–92; Pettit, *Sketches*, 143–44, italics in original; Loguen, *The Rev. J.W. Loguen*, 12–14, 70–75, 250ff.; *Frederick Douglass' Paper*, June 8, 1855; *National Era*, July 23, 1857. For a biography of Loguen, see Hunter, *To Set the Captive Free*; an account of his Underground Railroad activities are found on pages 151–76.

14. Levi Coffin, *Reminiscences,* 206–16; *Richmond Palladium-Item,* January 15, January 17, January 19, January 22, 1962 (reprint of Lacey manuscript as "Underground Railroad").

15. *Anti-Slavery Bugle,* September 2, 16, 23, 1854; Hise, Diary, August 28, 1854; Abram Brooke to [Valentine Nicholas], September 23, 1854, Nicholas Papers. Abolitionists in Madison, Indiana, were outraged to discover that a local railway there was aiding in slave-catching activities (*Madison Courier,* September 3, 1855).

16. Langston, *Freedom and Citizenship,* 14–27; Cheek and Cheek, *John Mercer Langston,* 316–41; Shipherd, *History of the Oberlin-Wellington Rescue.*

17. *Cincinnati Commercial* quoted in *Frederick Douglass' Paper,* September 22, 1854. Perhaps the single most famous fugitive slave case did take place in Cincinnati—the trial of Margaret Garner, chronicled in Weisenburger, *Modern Medea.*

18. John Parker, *His Promised Land,* 127–28.

19. Ibid., 74.

20. Ibid., 127–36.

21. *Madison Courier,* May 31, 1855; *National Era,* December 25, 1856; *Provincial Freeman,* January 3, 1857; William Anderson, *Life and Narrative,* 53–56.

22. *Provincial Freeman,* July 11, 1857; William Anderson, *Life and Narrative,* 56; *National Era,* December 25, 1856; Fairbank, *Rev. Calvin Fairbank during Slavery Times,* 46; John Parker, *His Promised Land,* 136; J.H. Tibbetts to Elizabeth Nicholson, [1884], box 2, folder 2, Steele Papers; *Frederick Douglass' Paper,* April 20, July 27, 1855; *National Era,* July 15, 1855; *Christian Recorder,* March 30, 1861; Bibb, *Narrative of the Life,* 60–65.

23. William Anderson, *Life and Narrative,* 56; *National Era,* July 15, 1855; *Frederick Douglass' Paper,* April 20, 1855.

24. *Ironton Register,* December 16, 1860, October 31, 1878; Joseph Mitchell, *Missionary Pioneer.*

25. Justus, *Down from the Mountain;* Pickard, *The Kidnapped and the Ransomed. Being the Personal Recollections of Peter Still,* 297–409.

26. *Christian Recorder,* March 30, 1861; Thomas Brown, *Brown's Three Years in the Kentucky Prisons,* 20.

27. Fairbank, *Rev. Calvin Fairbank during Slavery Times,* 10; Fairbank's description of his brutalization is confirmed by the account of a fellow prisoner, Thomas Brown, published long before Fairbank's release (Thomas Brown, *Three Years in the Kentucky Prisons,* 20–21).

28. *Ohio Columbian* quoted in *Frederick Douglass' Paper,* June 10, 1853; *Anti-Slavery Bugle,* September 16, 1854; *Frederick Douglass' Paper,* November 17, 1854, January 26, 1855; *Pittsburgh Visiter* quoted in *Frederick Douglass' Paper,* February 25, 1853; *Cincinnati Gazette* quoted in *Provincial Freeman,* April 7, March 15, 1856, February 23, 1856, and in *Frederick Douglass' Paper,* May 4, 1855; "Cincinnatus" in *Frederick Douglass' Paper,* August 3, 1855; *Cincinnati Columbian* quoted in *Frederick Douglass' Paper,* February 9, April 6, 1855; *Voice of the Fugitive* quoted in *Frederick Douglass' Paper,* January 27, 1854; *Detroit Tribune* quoted in the *Provincial Freeman,* December 16, 1854; Kentucky newspaper quoted in *Provincial Freeman,* March 8, 1856; *New York Herald* quoted in

American Anti-Slavery Society, *Anti-Slavery History of the John-Brown Year*, 51; Hembree, "Question of 'Begging.'"

29. Brown, *Three Years in the Kentucky Prisons*, 1–13; *Frederick Douglass' Paper*, November 9, 1855. Another white Kentuckian, Rev. Norris Day, was arrested on similar charges, but his trial produced a hung jury. He left the state before further action could be taken (*Madison Courier*, February 2, 1854).

30. *Frederick Douglass' Paper*, February 5, July 23, 1852, November 17, 1854, August 3, 24, October 12, December 7, 14, 1855; William Anderson, *Life and Narrative*; William Mitchell, *Under-Ground Railroad*; Drew, *North-Side View of Slavery*.

31. John Parker, *His Promised Land*; William Mitchell, *Under-Ground Railroad*, 20–25; A.T. Rankin, typescript, box 1, folder 2, John Rankin Papers; Levi Coffin, *Reminiscences*, 304–12, 428–46; Butler, *My Story of the Civil War*, 179–203; H.N. Wilson to Wilbur Siebert, April 14, 1892, box 106, Siebert Papers; Fitch Reed to Wilbur Siebert quoted in Siebert, *Underground Railroad*, 54; Rial Cheadle manuscript [1856] in Humphries, *Underground Railroad*, 32–43; Ross, *Memoirs of a Reformer* quoted in *Frederick Douglass' Paper*, July 27, 1855; *Chicago Democrat* quoted in the *North Star*, October 31, 1850.

32. *National Era*, March 20, 1851; *Frederick Douglass' Paper*, October 26, 1855; September 16, 1853. See also Gara, "Fugitive Slave Law."

33. Chase, *Speech of Hon. Salmon Chase*; Chase and Cleveland, *Anti-Slavery Addresses of 1844 and 1845*; Northup, *Twelve Years a Slave*, 312–13; Pickard, *The Kidnapped and the Ransomed. Being the Personal Recollections of Peter Still*, 312–13. On the development of antislavery partisanship, see Blue, *Free Soilers*; Kraut, ed., *Crusaders and Compromisers*. See also Eric Foner, *Free Soil, Free Labor, Free Men*; Blue, *Salmon Chase*; Eric Foner, *Reconstruction*; McPherson, *Struggle for Equality*.

34. John Parker, *His Promised Land*, 118–19.

35. Ibid., 119–20.

36. Ibid., 120–21.

37. Oates, *To Purge This Land with Blood*, Brown quoted p. 227; Finkelman, ed., *His Soul Goes Marching On*; Quarles, *Allies for Freedom*; Rossbach, *Ambivalent Conspirators*.

38. Oates, *To Purge This Land with Blood*, quoted, 179; Rossbach, *Ambivalent Conspirators*; Douglass, *Life and Times*, 322–26; Hise, Diary, December 16, 30, 1859, February 6, 1861.

39. Levi Coffin, *Reminiscences*, 304–12, 428–46.

40. Nicholson, "Reminiscences," box 1, folder 6, Nicholson Papers; Hise, Diary, December 2, 1859; Coffin, "Letter to Daniel Huff from the Famous Underground Railroad Agent, Written on the Day John Brown Was Executed," Indiana State Library, Indianapolis. Interpretations of the importance of the slavery conflict to the coming of the Civil War differ considerably. For summary accounts, see Eric Foner, "The Causes of the Civil War: Recent Interpretations," and Ericson, *Debate over Slavery*, 157–65.

41. *Philanthropist*, August 2, 1843; George Williams, *History of the Negro Race in America*; Marrs, *Life and History*, 12–21.

42. Du Bois, *Black Reconstruction*, 145–47; Mattie Jackson, *Story of Mattie*

Jackson, 20–23; Adams, *Narrative of the Life,* 35–40. See also Franklin and Schweninger, *Runaway Slaves.* For an account of the longstanding tradition of North American marronage, see Leaming, *Hidden Americans.*

43. Stanton, *Remarks of Henry B. Stanton,* 69; Jackson-Coppin, *Reminiscences of School Life,* 16–19; Wesley, *Ohio Negroes in the Civil War,* 16; *Cincinnati Enquirer,* July 15, 1862.

44. Levi Coffin, *Reminiscences,* 620–23.

45. Eric Foner, *Reconstruction;* McPherson, *Struggle for Equality.*

46. Wesley, *Ohio Negroes in the Civil War,* 15; James Smith, *Autobiography,* 83. Stewart Seely Sprague, preface to John Parker, *His Promised Land,* 9; Cheek and Cheek, *John Mercer Langston,* 383–418; Henry Burke, interview with author, August 2000. For a broad overview of African Americans in the Civil War, see McPherson, *Struggle for Equality.* On the wartime actions of Cincinnati's African American community, see Peter H. Clark, *Black Brigade of Cincinnati.*

47. Clarke and Clarke, *Narrative of Milton Clark,* 70.

48. As David Blight has shown in *Race and Reunion,* American memory of the Civil War provides a parallel case of how "romance triumphed over reality" (4) in writing African Americans out of that history. Gara, *Liberty Line,* xii.

Bibliography

Manuscript Collections and Unpublished Primary Sources

Beeson, Isaac W. Papers. Indiana State Library, Indianapolis.

Brown, Hallie Q. Papers. Central State University, Wilberforce, Ohio.

Chase, Samuel P. Papers. Ohio Historical Society, Columbus.

Coffin, Levi. "Letter to Daniel Huff from the Famous Underground Railroad Agent, Written on the Day John Brown Was Executed." Indiana State Library, Indianapolis.

Frances E. Hughes Collection. National Afro-American Museum and Cultural Center, Wilberforce, Ohio.

Hise, Daniel. Diaries. Ohio Historical Society, Columbus.

Lane Seminary Papers. Ohio Historical Society, Columbus.

Medill, William. Papers. Ohio Historical Society, Columbus.

"Minute Book of Neel's Creek Anti-Slavery Society, 1839–1845." Indiana State Library, Indianapolis.

"Negroes in and around Jefferson County." Jefferson County Historical Society, Madison, Indiana.

Nicholson, Valentine. Papers. Indiana Historical Society, Indianapolis.

Polly, Peyton. Case Transcripts. Ohio Historical Society, Columbus.

———. Papers. Ohio Historical Society, Columbus.

Rankin, Adam. "Autobiography." Ohio Historical Society, Columbus.

Rankin, John. "Autobiography, Written by Himself in His 80th Year." Ohio Historical Society, Columbus.

———. Papers. Ohio Historical Society, Columbus.

"Register of Negroes and Mulattoes in Jefferson County." Jefferson County Historical Society, Madison, Indiana.

Siebert, Wilbur. Papers. Ohio Historical Society, Columbus.

Steele, Theodore L. Papers. Indiana Historical Society, Indianapolis.

Stowe, Harriet Beecher. Papers. Huntington Library, San Marino, California.

Underground Railroad Vertical File. Wilberforce University Library, Wilberforce, Ohio.

Underground Railroad Vertical File. Indiana Historical Society Library, Indianapolis.

Underground Railroad Vertical File. Ironton Public Library, Ironton, Ohio.

Union Association of Colored Men of New Richmond Records, Ohio Collection, Ohio Historical Society, Columbus.

Wayne County Vertical File. Indiana Historical Society Library, Indianapolis.

William H. English Collection. Special Collections Research Center, University of Chicago Library.

Wood, Reuben. Papers. Ohio Historical Society, Columbus.

Newspapers and Periodicals

Anti-Slavery Bugle
Christian Recorder
Cincinnati Advertiser
Cincinnati Daily Gazette
Cincinnati Daily Chronicle
Cincinnati Daily Republican
Cincinnati Daily Times
Cincinnati Enquirer
Cincinnati Journal
Colored American
Frederick Douglass' Paper
Freedom's Journal
Ironton Register
Louisville Journal
Madison Courier
New Era
New York Evangelist
North Star
Ohio State Journal
Palladium of Liberty (Columbus)
Philanthropist
Provincial Freeman
Richmond Palladium-Item
Western Star

Memoirs, Reminiscences, and Autobiographies

Aaron. *The Light and Truth of Slavery. Aaron's History.* Worcester, Mass.: The Author, 1845

Adams, John Quincy. *Narrative of the Life of John Quincy Adams, When in Slavery, and Now as a Free Man.* Harrisburg, Penn.: Sieg, 1872.

Albert, Octavia V. Rogers. *The House of Bondage, or, Charlotte Brooks and Other Slaves.* N.Y.: Hunt and Eaton, 1890.

Anderson, William. "Life and Narrative of William J. Anderson." Chicago: *Daily Tribune,* 1857.

Asher, J. *Incidents in the Life of Rev. Asher.* London: Charles Gilpin, 1850

Bearse, Austin. *Reminiscences of Fugitive-Slave Law Days in Boston.* Boston: Richardson, 1880.

Bibb, Henry. *Narrative of the Life and Adventures of Henry Bibb, an American Slave.* N.Y.: The Author, 1849.

Black, Leonard. *The Life and Sufferings of Leonard Black, a Fugitive from Slavery.* New Bedford: Benjamin Lindsey, 1847.

Blair, Norvel. *Book for the People.* Joliet, Ill.: Joliet Daily Record, 1880.

Bradley, James. "Brief Account of an Emancipated Slave." In *The Oasis,* edited by Lydia Maria Child, 106–12. Boston: Benjamin F. Bacon, 1834.

Brown, John. *Slave Life in Georgia: A Narrative of the Life, Sufferings, and Escape of John Brown, a Fugitive Slave.* Edited by Louis Alexis Chamerovzow. London: W.M. Watts, 1855.

Brown, Thomas. *Brown's Three Years in the Kentucky Prisons.* Indianapolis: Indianapolis Journal Co., 1858.

Brown, William Wells. *The American Fugitive in Europe.* Boston: J.P. Jewett, 1855.

———. *Narrative of William W. Brown, a Fugitive Slave.* Boston: American Anti-Slavery Society, 1847.

———. *Three Years in Europe.* London: C. Gilpin, 1852.

Bruce, Henry Clay. *The New Man. Twenty-Nine Years a Slave. Twenty-Nine years a Free Man. Recollections of H. C. Bruce.* York, Penn.: P. Anstadt, 1895.

Bruner, Peter. *A Slave's Adventures toward Freedom.* Edited by Carrie Bruner. Oxford, Ohio: n.p., 1918.

Butler, Marvin Benjamin. *My Story of the Civil War and the Under-Ground Railroad.* Huntington, Ind.: United Brethren Publishing, 1914.

Campbell, Israel. *Bond and Free: or, Yearnings for Freedom.* Philadelphia: The Author, 1861.

Clarke, Lewis Garrard, and Milton Clarke. *Narratives of the Sufferings of Lewis and Milton Clarke.* Edited by Joseph Cammet Lovejoy. Boston: Bela Marsh, 1846.

Cockrum, William M. *History of the Underground Railroad, As It Was Conducted by the Anti-Slavery League.* Indiana: J.W. Cockrum Printing, 1915.

Coffin, Addison. *The Life and Travels of Addison Coffin.* Cleveland: William Hubbard, 1897.

Coffin, Levi. *The Reminiscences of Levi Coffin, the Reputed President of the Underground Railroad.* Cincinnati: Western Tract Society, 1876.

Craft, William. *Running a Thousand Miles for Freedom; or, the Escape of William and Ellen Craft from Slavery.* London: William Tweedie, 1860.

Delaney, Lucy Ann Berry. *From the Darkness Cometh the Light; or, Struggles for Freedom.* St. Louis: J.T. Smith, 1891.

Douglass, Frederick. *Life and Times of Frederick Douglass.* Hartford, Conn.: Park, 1881.

———. *My Bondage and My Freedom.* N.Y.: Miller, Orton and Mulligan, 1855.

———. *Narrative of the Life of Frederick Douglass, An American Slave.* Boston: American Anti-Slavery Society, 1845.

Drew, Benjamin, ed. *A North-Side View of Slavery. The Refugee: or, Narratives of Fugitive Slaves in Canada.* Boston: J.P. Jewett, 1856.

Fairbank, Calvin. *Rev. Calvin Fairbank during Slavery Times: How He "Fought the Good Fight" to Prepare "The Way."* Chicago: R.R. McCabe, 1890.

Fairchild, James. *The Underground Railroad.* Cleveland, Ohio: Western Reserve Historical Society, 1895.

Fedric, Francis. *Slave Life in Virginia and Kentucky; or, Fifty Years of Slavery in the Southern States of America.* Edited by Rev. Charles Lee. London: Wertheim, Macintosh, and Hunt, 1863.

Garlick, Charles A. *Life Including His Escape and Struggles for Liberty.* Jefferson, Ohio: J.A. Howells, 1902.

Green, Elisha Winfield. *Life of the Rev. Elisha W. Green.* Maysville, Kentucky: Republican, 1888.

Green, Jacob D. *Narrative of the Life of J.D. Green.* Huddersfield, England: Henry Fielding, 1864.

Haviland, Laura. *A Woman's Life-Work: Labors and Experiences of Laura S. Haviland.* Chicago: Publishing Association of Friends, 1889.

Hawkins, William G. *Lunsford Lane; or, Another Helper from North Carolina.* Boston: Crosby and Nichols, 1863.

Hayden, William. *Narrative of William Hayden.* Cincinnati: The Author, 1846.

Henson, Josiah. *The Life of Josiah Henson.* Edited by Samuel A. Eliot. Boston: A.D. Phelps, 1849.

———. *Truth is Stranger than Fiction. Father Henson's Story of His Own Life.* Edited by Samuel A. Eliot. Boston: J.P. Jewett, 1858.

———. *"Uncle Tom's Story of His Life." An Autobiography of the Rev. Josiah Henson.* Edited by John Lobb. London: "Christian Age" Office, 1876.

Hughes, Louis. *Thirty years a Slave. From Bondage to Freedom.* Milwaukee: South Side, 1897.

Jackson, Andrew. *Narrative and Writings of Andrew Jackson, of Kentucky.* Syracuse, N.Y.: Daily and Weekly Star, 1847.

Jackson, Mattie Jane. *The Story of Mattie J. Jackson.* Lawrence, Mass.: Sentinel, 1866.

Jackson-Coppin, Fanny. *Reminiscences of School Life; and Hints on Teaching.* Philadelphia: A.M.E. Book Concern, 1913.

Johnson, H.U. *From Dixie to Canada: Romances and Realities of the Underground Railroad.* Orwell, Ohio: Johnson, 1896.

Johnson, Isaac. *Slavery Days in Old Kentucky.* Ogdensburg, N.Y.: Republican and Journal, 1901.

Jones, Thomas H. *The Experience of Thomas H. Jones.* Boston: Bazin and Chandler, 1862.

Joseph, John. *The Life and Sufferings of John Joseph.* Wellington, New Zealand: The Author, 1848.

Langston, John Mercer. *From the Virginia Plantation to the National Capitol.* Hartford: American Publishing Co., 1894.

Loguen, Jermain Wesley. *The Rev. J.W. Loguen, As a Slave and As a Freeman.* Syracuse, N.Y.: J. G. K. Truair, 1859.

Mallory, William. *Old Plantation Days.* Hamilton, Ont.: The Author, 1901.

Malvin, John. *North into Freedom: The Autobiography of John Malvin, Free Ne-*

gro, 1795–1880. Edited and with an introduction by Allan Peskin. Cleveland: The Press of Western Reserve University, 1966.

Marrs, Elijah Preston. *Life and History of the Rev. Elijah P. Marrs*. Louisville: Bradley and Gilbert, 1885.

Mason, Isaac. *Life of Isaac Mason as a Slave*. Worcester, Mass.: The Author, 1893.

Meachum, John B. *An Address to All the Colored Citizens of the United States*. Philadelphia: The Author, 1846.

Mitchell, William M. *The Under-Ground Railroad*. London: William Tweedie, 1860.

Mott, Abigail, and Mary S. Wood, eds. *Narratives of Colored Americans*. N.Y.: W. Woods, 1875.

Northup, Solomon. *Twelve Years a Slave. Narrative of Solomon Northrup*. Edited by David Wilson. Auburn, N.Y.: Derby and Miller, 1853.

Parker, Henry. *Autobiography of Henry Parker*. N.p.: The Author, 186[?].

Parker, John P. *His Promised Land: The Autobiography of John P. Parker*. Edited and with an introduction by Stuart Seely Sprague. N.Y.: Norton, 1996.

Parker, William. "The Freedman's Story." Parts 1 and 2. *Atlantic Monthly* (Feb. 1866): 152–66; (March 1866): 276–95.

Pennington, James W.C. *The Fugitive Blacksmith*. London: Charles Gilpin, 1849.

Pettit, Eber M. *Sketches in the History of the Underground Railroad*. Fredonia, N.Y.: W. McKinstry and Son, 1879.

Pickard, Kate E.R. *The Kidnapped and the Ransomed. Being the Personal Recollections of Peter Still and His Wife 'Vina,' after Forty Years of Slavery*. Syracuse, N.Y.: William T. Hamilton; N.Y.: Miller, Orton and Mulligan, 1856

Robinson, William H. *From Log Cabin to the Pulpit: Or Fifteen Years in Slavery*. Eau Claire, Wisc.: The Author, 1913

Roper, Moses. *A Narrative of the Adventures and Escape of Moses Roper*. Philadelphia: Merrihew and Gunn; London: Darton, Harvey and Darton, 1838.

Ross, Alexander Milton. *Memoirs of a Reformer, 1832–1892*. Toronto: Hunter, Burk & Co., 1893.

Singleton, William Henry. *Recollections of My Slavery Days*. Peekskill, N.Y.: Highland Democrat, 1922.

Smallwood, Thomas. *A Narrative of Thomas Smallwood*. Toronto: The Author, 1851.

Smedley, R.C. *History of the Underground Railroad in Chester and Neighboring Counties of Pennsylvania*. Lancaster, Penn: Lancaster Journal, 1883.

Smith, Amanda. *An Autobiography: The Story of the Lord's Dealings with Mrs. Amanda Smith, the Colored Evangelist*. Chicago: Meyer, 1893.

Smith, David. *Biography of Rev. David Smith of the A.M.E. Church*. Xenia, Ohio: Xenia Gazette Office, 1881.

Smith, Harry. *Fifty Years of Slavery in the United States of America*. Grand Rapids, MI: West Michigan, 1891.

Smith, James Lindsay. *Autobiography of James L. Smith*. Norwich, Conn.: The Bulletin, 1881.

Steward, Austin. *Twenty-Two Years a Slave and Forty Years a Freeman*. Rochester, N.Y.: W. Alling, 1857.

Still, William. *The Underground Railroad. A Record of Facts, Authentic Narratives, Letters & C*. Philadelphia: Porter & Coates, 1822.

Thompson, Charles. *Biography of a Slave*. Dayton, Ohio: United Brethren, 1875.

Thompson, George. *Prison Life and Reflections; or, A Narrative of the Arrest, Trial, Conviction, Imprisonment, Treatment, Observations, Reflections, and Deliverance of Work, Burr, and Thompson, Who Suffered an Unjust and Cruel Imprisonment in Missouri Pentientiary, for Attempting to Aid Some Slaves to Liberty*. Hartford, Conn.: A. Work, 1850.

Veney, Bethany. *The Narrative of Bethany Veney, a Slave Woman*. Edited by M.W.G. Worcester, Mass.: George H. Ellis, 1889.

Walker, Jonathon. *The Branded Hand: The Trial and Imprisonment of Jonathon Walker*. Boston: Anti-Slavery Office, 1845.

Ward, Samuel Ringgold. *Autobiography of a Fugitive Negro*. London: John Snow, 1855.

Watson, Henry. *Narrative of Henry Watson, a Fugitive Slave*. Boston: Bela Marsh, 1848.

Webb, William. *The History of William Webb*. Detroit: Egbert Hoekstra, 1873.

Wilkerson, Major James. *Wilkerson's History of His Travels & Labors, in the United States, as a Missionary, In Particular, That of the Union Seminary, Located in Franklin Co., Ohio, Since He Purchased His Liberty in New Orleans, La*. Columbus, Ohio, 1861.

Williams, James. *Life and Adventures of James Williams, a Fugitive Slave, with a Full Description of the Underground Railroad*. San Francisco: Women's Union, 1873.

Contemporary Publications and Historic Document Compilations

Abdy, E.S. *Journal of A Residence and Tour in the United States of North America, from April, 1833, to October, 1834*. 3 vols. London: John Murray, 1835.

The Address and Reply on the Presentation of a Testimonial to S.P. Chase, by the Colored People of Cincinnati. Cincinnati: Henry W. Derby & Co. 1845.

American Anti-Slavery Society. *The Anti-Slavery History of the John-Brown Year; Being the Twenty-Seventh Annual Report of the American Anti-Slavery Society*. 1861. Reprint, N.Y.: Negro Universities Press, 1969.

Bagley, A.C. *Speech of Hon. A.C. Bagley, of Hamilton County, on the Bill to Preserve the Purity of Elections, and to Prevent Negroes and Persons of African Descent from Voting. Delivered in the House of Representatives, March 29, 1859*. Columbus, Ohio, 1859.

Beaver, John. *Fugitive Slaves in Ohio. Report to the Senate, February 12, 1849*. Columbus, Ohio, 1849.

Brown, Hallie Q. *Homespun Heroines and Other Women of Distinction*. Xenia, Ohio: Aldine, 1926.

———. *Tales My Father Told*. Wilberforce, Ohio: Eckerle, 1925.

Chase, Salmon P. *Reclamation of Fugitives from Service. An Argument for the Defendant, Submitted to the Supreme Court of the United States, at the December Term, 1846, in the case of Wharton Jones vs. John Vanzandt*. Cincinnati: R.P. Donough & Co., 1847.

———. *Speech of Hon. Salmon P. Chase, Delivered at the Republican Mass Meet-*

ing, in Cincinnati, August 21, 1855. Columbus: Ohio State Journal Company, 1855.

———. *Speech of Salmon P. Chase, in the Case of the Colored Woman, Matilda, Who was Brought before the Court of Common Pleas of Hamilton County, Ohio, by Writ of Habeas Corpus; March 11, 1837*. Cincinnati: Pugh & Dodd, 1837.

———, ed. *Statutes of Ohio and of the Northwestern Territory, Adopted or Enacted from 1788 to 1833*. 3 vols. Cincinnati: Corey & Fairbank, 1833.

———, and Charles Dexter Cleveland. *Anti-Slavery Addresses of 1844 and 1845*. Philadelphia: J.A. Bancroft and Co., 1867.

The Cincinnati Directory. By a Citizen. Cincinnati: Oliver Farnsworth, 1819.

Cincinnati Directory for 1825. Cincinnati: Samuel J. Brown, 1825.

Cincinnati Directory for 1829. Cincinnati: Robinson & Fairbank, 1829.

Cincinnati Directory for 1831. Cincinnati: Robinson & Fairbank, 1831.

Cincinnati Directory for 1834. Cincinnati: E. Deming, 1834.

Cincinnati Directory for 1835. Cincinnati: E. Deming, 1835.

Cincinnati Directory for 1836–37. Cincinnati: J.H. Woodruff, 1836.

Cincinnati Directory for 1861. Cincinnati: Williams, 1861.

Cincinnati Directory for 1862. Cincinnati: Williams, 1862.

Clark, Peter H. *The Black Brigade of Cincinnati: Being a Report of its Labors and a Muster-roll of its Members*. Cincinnati: Joseph Boyd, 1864.

Debate at the Lane Seminary, Cincinnati. Speech of James A. Thome, of Kentucky, Delivered at the Annual Meeting of the American Anti-Slavery Society, May 6, 1834. Letter of the Rev. Dr. Samuel H. Cox, against the American Colonization Society. Boston: Garrison & Knapp, 1834.

Dichore, Marie. *Census for Cincinnati, Ohio, 1817 and Hamilton County, Ohio, Voters' Lists 1798 and 1799*. Cincinnati: Historical and Philosophical Society of Ohio, 1960.

Dumond, Dwight, ed. *Letters of James Gillespie Birney, 1831–1857*. 2 vols. N.Y.: D. Appleton Century, 1938.

Executive Committee of the New York Anti-Slavery Society to the Executive Committee of the Ohio State Anti-Slavery Society, August 26, 1836. In *A Collection of Valuable Documents, Being Birney's Vindication of Abolitionists—Protest of the American A.S. Society—to the People of the United States, or to Such Americans as Value their Rights*, 67–75. Boston: Isaac Knapp, 1836.

Gaines, John Isom, and J.H. Perkins. *Orations Delivered on the First of August 1849 before the Colored Citizens of Columbus and Cincinnati*. Cincinnati, 1849.

Indiana Anti-Slavery Society. *Proceedings of the Indiana Convention Assembled to Organize a State Anti-Slavery Society, Held in Milton, Wayne Co., September 12th, 1838*. Cincinnati: Alley, 1838

Lane Seminary. *Annual Report of the Trustees of Lane Seminary and a Catalogue of the Officers and Students*. Cincinnati: Corey and Webster, 1834.

Langston, John Mercer. *Freedom and Citizenship. Selected Lectures and Addresses of Hon. John Mercer Langston*. Washington, D.C.: R.H. Darby, 1883.

Mellon, James, ed. *Bullwhip Days: The Slaves Remember*. N.Y.: Weidenfield & Nicholson, 1988.

Middleton, Stephen. *The Black Laws in the Old Northwest: A Documentary History.* Westport, Conn.: Greenwood Press, 1993.

Mitchell, Joseph. *The Missionary Pioneer, or, A Brief Memoir of the Life, Labours, and Death of John Stewart (Man of Colour) Founder, Under God, of the Mission among the Wyandotts at Upper Sandusky, Ohio.* N.Y.: The Author, 1827.

Ohio Anti-Slavery Society. *Memorial of the Ohio Anti-Slavery Society to the General Assembly of the State of Ohio.* Cincinnati: Pugh & Dodd, 1838.

——. *Narrative of the Late Riotous Proceedings against the Liberty of the Press, in Cincinnati. with Remarks and Historical Notices, Relating to Emancipation.* Cincinnati: Ohio Anti-Slavery Society, 1836.

——. *Proceedings of the Ohio Anti-Slavery Convention. Held at Putnam, on the Twenty-Second, Twenty-Third, and Twenty-Fourth of April, 1835.* N.Y.: American Anti-Slavery Society, 1835.

——. *Report of the First Anniversary of the Ohio Anti-Slavery Society, Held near Granville, on the Twenty-Seventh and Twenty-Eighth of April, 1836.* Cincinnati: Ohio Anti-Slavery Society, 1836.

——. *Report of the Second Anniversary of the Ohio Anti-Slavery Society, Held in Mount Pleasant, Jefferson County, Ohio, on the Twenty-Seventh of April, 1837.* Cincinnati: Ohio Anti-Slavery Society, 1837.

——. *Report of the Third Anniversary of the Ohio Anti-Slavery Society, Held in Granville, Licking County, Ohio, on the 30th of May, 1838.* Cincinnati: Ohio Anti-Slavery Society, 1838.

——. *Report of the Fourth Anniversary of the Ohio Anti-Slavery Society, Held in Putnam, Muskingham County, Ohio, on the 29th of May, 1839.* Cincinnati: Ohio Anti-Slavery Society, 1839

Ohio State Colonization Society. *A Brief Exposition of the Views for the Society for the Colonization of Free Persons of Color in Africa.* Columbus: David Smith, 1827.

Rankin, John. "Address to the Churches on Prejudice against People of Color." In *Report of the Third Anniversary of the Ohio Anti-Slavery Society, Held in Granville, Licking County, Ohio, on the 30th of May, 1838,* by Ohio Anti-Slavery Society, 30–38. Cincinnati: Ohio Anti-Slavery Society, 1838.

——. *Letters on American Slavery, Addressed to Mr. Thomas Rankin, Merchant at Middlebrook, Augusta Co., Virginia.* Boston: Knapp, 1838.

Rawick, George P, ed. *The American Slave: A Composite Autobiography.* 5 vols. Westport, Conn.: Greenwood, 1972.

Ritchie, Andrew. *The Soldier, the Battle, and the Victory. Being a Brief Account of the Work of Rev. John Rankin in the Anti-slavery Cause.* Cincinnati: Western Tract and Book Society, 1873.

Shipherd, Jacob R. *History of the Oberlin-Wellington Rescue.* Cleveland: Henry P. B. Jewett, 1859.

Stanton, Henry B. *Remarks of Henry B. Stanton in the Representatives' Hall on the 23rd and 24th of February, 1837, before the Committee of the House of Representatives of Massachusetts.* Boston: Knapp, 1837.

A Statement of the Reasons Which Induced the Students of Lane Seminary, to Dissolve Their Connection with That Institution. Cincinnati, 1834.

Stowe, Harriet Beecher. *The Key to Uncle Tom's Cabin.* Cleveland: Jewitt, Proctor and Worthington, 1854.

——. *Uncle Tom's Cabin: Or, Life among the Lowly.* Boston: J.P. Jewett, 1851.
Torrey, Jesse. *A Portraiture of Domestic Slavery in the United States.* Ballston Spa, N.Y.: Torrey, 1818.
U.S., Census Office. *Census for 1820.* Washington: Gales and Seaton, 1821.
——. *Fifth Census; or, Enumeration of the Inhabitants of the United States, 1830.* Washington: Duff Green, 1832.
——. *The Sixth Census of the United States, 1840.* Washington.
——. *The Seventh Census of the United States, 1850.* Washington: Robert Armstrong, 1853.
Wattles, John O. *Annual Report of Educational Condition of the Colored People of Cincinnati, Including the Settlement in Mercer County, Ohio, Presented at the Exhibition of the Cincinnati High School, April 1847.* Cincinnati: John White, 1847.
Williams' Cincinnati Directory for 1862. Cincinnati: Williams, 1862.
Williams' Cincinnati Directory for 1863. Cincinnati: Williams, 1863.

Secondary Sources

Abzug, Robert H. "Theodore Weld: A Biography." Ph. D. diss., University of California, Berkeley, 1977.
Berquist, Goodwin F., and Paul Bowers. *The New Eden: James Kilbourne and the Development of Ohio.* Washington Island, Wisc.: Jackson Harbor Press, 2001.
Bigham, Darrel E. "River of Opportunity." In *Always a River: The Ohio River and the American Experience,* edited by Robert L. Reid, 130–81, Bloomington: Indiana University Press, 1991.
Blight, David. *Race and Reunion: The Civil War in American Memory.* Cambridge, Mass.: Harvard University Press, 2001.
Blue, Frederick. *The Free Soilers: Third Party Politics, 1848–54.* Champaign: University of Illinois Press, 1973.
——. *Salmon P. Chase: A Life in Politics.* Kent, Ohio: Kent State University Press, 1987.
Boyko, John. *Last Steps to Freedom: The Evolution of Canadian Racism.* Winnipeg: Watson and Dwyer, 1995.
Bramble, Linda. *Black Fugitive Slaves in Early Canada.* St. Catharines, Ont.: Vanwell, 1988.
Burke, Ronald K. *Samuel Ringgold Ward: Christian Abolitionist.* N.Y.: Garland, 1995.
Cheek, William, and Aimee Lee Cheek. *John Mercer Langston and the Fight for Black freedom, 1829–65.* Urbana: University of Illinois Press, 1989.
Cochran, William. *The Western Reserve and the Fugitive Slave Law: A Prelude to the Civil War.* Cleveland: Western Reserve Historical Society, 1920.
Curry, Leonard P. *The Free Black in Urban America, 1800–1850: The Shadow of a Dream.* Chicago: University of Chicago Press, 1981.
Dillon, Merton. *The Abolitionists: The Growth of a Dissenting Minority.* N.Y.: Norton, 1974.
——. *Slavery Attacked: Southern Slaves and their Allies, 1619–1865.* Baton Rouge: Louisiana State University Press, 1990.
Du Bois, W.E.B. *Black Reconstruction.* Millwood, N.Y.: Kraus Thomson, 1963.

Eisan, Frances K. *Saint or Demon? The Legendary Delia Webster Opposing Slavery*. N.Y.: Pace University Press, 1998.

Ericson, David F. *The Debate over Slavery: Antislavery and Proslavery Liberalism in Antebellum America*. N.Y.: New York University Press, 2000.

Finkelman, Paul, ed. *His Soul Goes Marching On: Responses to John Brown and the Harpers Ferry Raid*. Charlottesville: University of Virginia Press, 1995.

Foner, Eric. "The Causes of the American Civil War: Recent Interpretations and New Direction." In *Politics and Ideology in the Age of the Civil War*. N.Y.: Oxford University Press, 1980.

———. *Free Soil, Free Labor, Free Men: The Ideology of the Republican Party before the Civil War*. N.Y.: Oxford University Press, 1970.

———. *Reconstruction: America's Unfinished Revolution, 1863–1877*. N.Y.: Harper and Row, 1988.

Franklin, John Hope, and Loren Schweninger. *Runaway Slaves: Rebels on the Plantation*. N.Y.: Oxford University Press, 1999.

Friedman, Lawrence J. *Gregarious Saints: Self and Community in American Abolitionism, 1830–1870*. N.Y.: Cambridge University Press, 1982.

Games, Mary Harrison. *The Underground Railroad in Ohio*. 1937.

Gara, Larry. "The Fugitive Slave Law: A Double Paradox." *Civil War History* 10 (September 1964): 229–40.

———. *The Liberty Line: The Legend of the Underground Railroad*. Lexington: University Press of Kentucky, 1996.

Gomez, Michael A. *Exchanging Our Country Marks: The Transformation of African Identities in the Colonial and Antebellum South*. Chapel Hill: University of North Carolina Press, 1998.

Harrold, Stanley. *The Abolitionists and the South, 1831–1861*. Lexington: University Press of Kentucky, 1995.

———. *Gamaliel Bailey and Antislavery Union*. Kent, Ohio: Kent State University Press, 1986.

Hembree, Michael F. "The Question of 'Begging': Fugitive Slave Relief in Canada, 1830–1865." *Civil War History* 37 (December 1991): 314–27.

Hensel, W.U. *The Christiana Riot and the Treason Trials of 1851: An Historical Sketch*. N.Y.: Negro Universities Press, 1969.

Hodges, Graham Russell. *Root and Branch: African Americans in New York and East Jersey, 1613–1863*. Chapel Hill: University of North Carolina Press, 1999.

———. *Slavery and Freedom in the Rural North: African Americans in Monmouth County, New Jersey, 1665–1865*. Madison, Wisc.: Madison House, 1995.

Horton, James Oliver. *Free People of Color: Inside the African-American Community*. Washington, D.C.: Smithsonian Institution Press, 1993.

———, and Lois E. Horton. "A Federal Assault: African Americans and the Impact of the Fugitive Slave Law of 1850." In *Slavery and the Law*, edited by Paul Finkelman, 143–60. Madison, Wisc.: Madison House, 1977.

———. *In Hope of Liberty: Culture, Community, and Protest among Northern Free Blacks, 1700–1860*. N.Y.: Oxford University Press, 1997.

Horton, James Oliver, and Stacey Flaherty. "Black Leadership in Cincinnati." In *Race and the City: Work, Community, and Protest in Cincinnati, 1820–1970*, edited by Henry Louis Taylor Jr., 70–95. Urbana: University of Illinois Press, 1993.

Howard, Victor B. *Conscience and Slavery: The Evangelist Calvinist Domestic Missions, 1837–1861*. Kent, Ohio: Kent State University Press, 1996.

Humphries, Eck. *The Underground Railroad*. McConnelsville, Ohio: Herald Publishing Co., 1931.

Hunter, Carol M. *To Set the Captive Free: Reverend Jermain Wesley Loguen and the Struggle for Freedom in Central New York, 1835–1872*. N.Y.: Garland, 1993.

Hurt, R. Douglas. *The Ohio Frontier: Crucible of the Old Northwest, 1720–1830*. Bloomington: Indiana University Press, 1996.

Hutchinson, William Thomas. *The Bounty Lands of the American Revolution in Ohio*. N.Y.: Arno, 1979.

Jacobs, Donald J., ed. *Courage and Conscience: Black and White Abolitionists in Boston*. Bloomington: Indiana University Press, 1993.

Jeffrey, Julie Roy. *The Great Silent Army of Abolitionism: Ordinary Women in the Antislavery Movement*. Chapel Hill: University of North Carolina Press, 1998.

Justus, Judith. *Down from the Mountain: The Oral History of the Hemings Family*. Perrysburg, Ohio: Juskurtara, 1990.

Kelley, Robin D.G. *Race Rebels: Culture, Politics, and the Black Working Class*. N.Y.: Free Press, 1994.

Kraditor, Aileen. *Means and Ends in American Abolitionism: Garrison and His Critics on Strategy and Tactics*. N.Y.: Random House, 1967.

Kraut, Alan M., ed., *Crusaders and Compromisers: Essays in the Relationship of the Antislavery Struggle to the Antebellum Party System*. Westport, Conn.: Greenwood, 1983.

Leaming, Hugo Prosper. *Hidden Americans: Maroons of Virginia and the Carolinas*. N.Y.: Garland, 1995.

Lesick, Lawrence Thomas. *The Lane Rebels: Evangelicalism and Antislavery in Antebellum America*. Metuchen, N.J.: The Scarecrow Press, Inc., 1980.

Levine, Lawrence. *Black Culture and Black Consciousness: Afro-American Folk Thought from Slavery to Freedom*. N.Y.: Oxford University Press, 1977.

Litwack, Leon. *North of Slavery: The Negro in the Free States, 1790–1860*. Chicago: University of Chicago Press, 1961.

Lumpkin, Katherine DuPress. "The General Plan Was Freedom: A Negro Secret Order on the Underground Railroad." *Phylon* 28, no. 1: 63–77.

Magdol, Edward. *The Antislavery Rank and File: A Social Profile of the Abolitionists' Constituency*. N.Y.: Greenwood, 1986.

McClure, Stanley. "The Underground Railroad in South Central Ohio." Master's thesis, The Ohio State University, 1932.

McDougall, Marion Gleason. *Fugitive Slaves, 1619–1865*. Boston: Ginn, 1891.

McKivigan, John R., and Mitchell Snay, eds. *Religion and the Antebellum Debate over Slavery*. Athens: University of Georgia Press, 1998.

McPherson, James M. *The Struggle for Equality: Abolitionists and the Negro in the Civil War and Reconstruction*. Princeton, N.J.: Princeton University Press, 1964.

Meaders, Daniel. *Dead or Alive: Fugitive Slaves and White Indentured Servants Before 1830*. N.Y.: Garland, 1993.

Michel, Henri. *The Shadow War: Resistance in Europe, 1939–1945*. London: Deutsch, 1972.

Middleton, Stephen. *Ohio and the Anti-Slavery Activities of Attorney Salmon P. Chase, 1830–1849.* N.Y.: Garland, 1990.

Moses, Wilson. *The Golden Age of Black Nationalism, 1850–1925.* Hamden, Conn.: Archon Books, 1978.

Oates, Stephen B. *To Purge This Land with Blood: A Biography of John Brown.* 2d ed. Amherst: University of Massachusetts Press, 1984.

Onuf, Peter S. *Statehood and Union: A History of the Northwest Ordinance.* Bloomington: University of Indiana Press, 1987.

Pease, Jane H., and William H. Pease. *Black Utopia: Negro Communal Experiments in America.* Madison: State Historical Society of Wisconsin, 1963.

———. *They Who Would Be Free: Blacks' Search for Freedom, 1830–1861.* N.Y.: Athenaeum, 1974.

Quarles, Benjamin. *Allies for Freedom: Blacks and John Brown.* N.Y.: Oxford University Press, 1974.

———. *Black Abolitionists.* N.Y.: Oxford University Press, 1969.

Reed, Harry. *Platform for Change: The Foundations of the Northern Free Black Community, 1776–1865.* East Lansing: Michigan State University Press, 1994.

Reid, Robert L., ed. *Always A River: The Ohio River and the American Experience.* Bloomington: Indiana University Press, 1991.

Rivers, Larry. *Slavery in Florida: Territorial Days to Emancipation.* Gainesville: University of Florida Press, 2000.

Rosenberg, Norman L. "Personal Liberty Laws and Sectional Crisis: 1850–1861." *Civil War History* 17 (March 1971): 25–45.

Rossbach, Jeffery. *Ambivalent Conspirators: John Brown, the Secret Six, and a Theory of Slave Violence.* Philadelphia: University of Pennsylvania Press, 1982.

Rothman, Joshua. "James Callendar and Social Knowledge of Interracial Sex in Antebellum Virginia." In *Sally Hemings and Thomas Jefferson: History, Memory, and Civic Culture,* edited by Jan Ellen Lewis and Peter S. Onuf, 87–113. Charlottesville: University of Virginia Press, 1999.

Royster, Charles. *The Fabulous History of the Dismal Swamp Company: A Story of George Washington's Times.* New York: Borzoi Books, 1999.

Runyon, Randolph Paul. *Delia Webster and The Underground Railroad.* Lexington: University Press of Kentucky, 1996.

Shaw, Stephanie. *What a Woman Ought To Be and To Do: Black Professional Women Workers during the Jim Crow Era.* Chicago: University of Chicago Press, 1996.

Sherwood, Henry N. "The Settlement of the John Randolph's Slaves in Ohio." *Mississippi Valley Historical Association Proceedings* 5 (1948): 35–39.

Siebert, Wilbur H. *The Underground Railroad: From Slavery to Freedom.* With an introduction by Albert Bushnell Hart. N.Y.: Arno Press, 1968.

———. *The Mysteries of Ohio's Underground Railroads.* Columbus: Long's College Book Co., 1951.

Silverman, Jason H. "The American Fugitive Slave in Canada: Myths and Realities." *Southern Studies* (fall 1980): 214–27.

Staudenraus, Philip J. *African Colonization Movement, 1816–1865.* N.Y.: Columbia University Press, 1961.

Stauffer, John. *The Black Hearts of Men: Radical Abolitionists and the Transformation of Race.* Cambridge, Mass.: Harvard University Press, 2002.

Stewart, James Brewer. *Holy Warriors: The Abolitionists and American Slavery.* N.Y.: Hill and Wang, 1997.

Strong, Douglas. *Perfectionist Politics: Abolitionism and the Religious Tensions of American Democracy.* Syracuse, N.Y.: Syracuse University Press, 1999.

Taylor, Henry Louis, Jr. *Race and the City: Work, Community, and Protest in Cincinnati, 1820–1970.* Chicago: University of Illinois Press, 1993.

———, and Vicky Dula. "The Black Residential Experience and Community Formation in Antebellum Cincinnati" In *Race and the City: Work, Community, and Protest in Cincinnati, 1820–1970,* edited by Henry Louis Taylor Jr., 96–125. Urbana: University of Illinois Press, 1993.

Trotter, Joe William, Jr. *River Jordan: African American Urban Life in the Ohio Valley.* Lexington: University Press of Kentucky, 1998.

Tulloch, Headley. *Black Canadians: A Long Line of Fighters.* Toronto: NC Press, 1975.

United States Department of the Interior, National Parks Service. *Underground Railroad: Special Resource Study Management Concepts/Environmental Assessment.* Washington, D.C.: US Department of the Interior, 1995.

Ware, Richard C. "The Negro in Cincinnati, 1800–1830." *Journal of Negro History* 39, no. 1 (Jan. 1954): 43–57.

Weisenburger, Steven. *Modern Medea: A Family Story of Slavery and Child-Murder from the Old South.* N.Y.: Hill and Wang, 1998.

Wesley, Charles H. *Ohio Negroes in the Civil War.* Columbus: Ohio State University Press, 1962.

Whelchel, L.H. *My Chains Fell Off: William Wells Brown, Fugitive Abolitionist.* N.Y.: University Press of America, 1985.

Wilhelm, Hubert. "Settlement and Selected Landscape Imprints in the Ohio Valley." In *Always A River: the Ohio River and the American Experience,* edited by Robert L. Reid, 67–75. Bloomington: Indiana University Press, 1991.

Williams, George. *History of the Negro Race in America from 1619 to 1880.* 1883. N.Y.: Arno Press, 1968.

Williamson, Joel. *New People: Miscegenation and Mulattoes in the United States.* N.Y.: Free Press, 1980.

Wilson, Carol. *Freedom at Risk: The Kidnapping of Free Blacks in America, 1780–1865.* Lexington: University Press of Kentucky, 1994.

Woodson, Byron. *A President in the Family: Thomas Jefferson, Sally Hemings, and Thomas Woodson.* Westport, Conn.: Praeger, 2001.

Yee, Shirley. *Black Women Abolitionists: A Study of Activism.* Knoxville: University of Tennessee Press, 1992.

Yellin, Jean Fagan. *Women and Sisters: Antislavery Feminists in American Culture.* New Haven: Yale University Press, 1990.

———, and Van Horne, eds. *The Abolitionist Sisterhood: Women's Political Culture in Antebellum America.* Ithaca, N.Y.: Cornell University Press, 1994.

Young, R.J. *Antebellum Black Activists: Race, Gender, Self.* N.Y.: Garland, 1996.

Index

Abdy, Edward, 14, 21, 31–32, 38, 46, 133n4

abolitionism, 58–80; and African Americans, 69–70, 75–80, 82, 101–2, 115, 120; as political wing of antislavery underground, 72–80, 121, 123; connection to Underground Railroad, 10, 70–74, 118, 123, 140n7; formation in West, 67–74, 142n25; in Cincinnati, 51–54; in England, 26, 29, 66; political form of, 72, 80, 121–22; racial prejudice within, 75–79, 142 nn 29, 30; reaction to Fugitive Slave Law of 1850, 108–10, 121; role of whites from South in formation of, 60–65, 73, 68, 71–73; unpopularity of in North, 65–67, 71, 114; violence directed at proponents of, 7, 54–55, 57, 72, 115. *See also* antislavery movements

Africa, 20–21

African Americans, xiv; attempts to expel, 24–29, 31–34, 56, 126, 142n29; communities in Ohio Valley, xiii, 6–7, 10–11, 13–14, 30–57, (*see also* Berlin Crossroads, Cabin Creek, Poke Patch); historiography of, xi; hostility toward, among Ohio Valley whites, 13, 15–16, 20–29, 126, 128, 134nn25, 26 (*see also* riots); kidnapping of, 16–20, 43, 83–84, 105–6, 134n14, 137n17; migration to Ohio Valley, 12–16, 24–25, 27, 126; political activism of, 74–75, 115, 120, 128; settlement movement in Ohio Valley, 33–35. *See also* Black Laws; slaves, fugitive; Underground Railroad

American Anti-Slavery Society, 82

American Colonization Society, 21, 49. *See also* Colonization movement, Cincinnati Colonization Society

American Revolution: and settlement of Ohio, 14; and slavery, 1–2, 14–17, 30, 113, 128–29

Anderson, Elijah, xiv, 86, 88, 115–20

Anderson, William, 46–47, 102, 115–17, 120

antislavery movements, xi, xiii, 10, 30–31, 35, 121; religious denominations and, 3, 61, 64–74, 119–20. *See also* abolitionism

Bailey, Gamaliel, 55, 78, 90, 125

Beecher, Lyman, 22, 68

Beeson, Isaac, 66, 75, 142n29

Berlin Crossroads, Ohio, 32–34